In the series
American Subjects,
edited by
Robert Dawidoff

WRITING

FOREWORD BY JOHN LAHR

WRONGS

The Work of Wallace Shawn

W. D. King

Temple University Press : Philadelphia

Temple University Press, Philadelphia 19122.
Copyright © 1997 by Temple University. All rights
reserved. Published 1997. Printed in the United
States of America

♾ The paper used in this publication meets the
requirements of American National Standard for
Information Sciences—Permanence of Paper for
Printed Library Materials, ANSI Z39.48-1984

Library of Congress Cataloging-in-Publication-Data
King, W. D. (W. Davies)
Writing wrongs : the work of Wallace Shawn /
W. D. King ; foreword by John Lahr.
p.   cm. — (American subjects)
Includes bibliographical references and index.
ISBN 1-56639-517-8 (cloth : alk. paper)
1. Shawn, Wallace—Criticism and interpretation.
2. Politics and literature—United States—History—
20th century.   3. Political plays, American—History
and criticism.   4. United States—In literature.
I. Shawn, Wallace.   II. Title.   III. Series.
PS3569.H387Z74   1997   812'.54—dc20   96-27503

For our sisters, Mary Rosamond Shawn and Cynthia McKown King

Contents

Series Foreword

by Robert Dawidoff, Series Editor

It is hard to imagine a book better suited to launch the American
Subjects series than W. Davies King's illuminating and entertaining
study of Wallace Shawn. The series was conceived to tell unfamiliar
stories about American culture, by which we mean both how Americans have lived and what they have made or thought. *Writing
Wrongs* introduces the work of a stimulating contemporary playwright in the context of the cultural, theatrical, and political history
of his times, our times. That this playwright has remained largely unknown to American audiences is part of what makes *Writing Wrongs*
so good to have. What makes King's study invaluable, however, is
his compelling presentation of the plays and their fascinating playwright. He has written a wonderfully engaging book about an extraordinary contemporary artist. The better we come to know
Shawn, the more we will be able to appreciate the subtlety and sophistication with which this talented scholar has prepared us for the
work of this gifted artist. But you don't have to have seen or read
Shawn's plays to respond to the clarity, feeling, and wit of this book
about them. *Writing Wrongs* is complete in itself, a brilliant account
of a playwright's fate in the contemporary theatre and an innovative
example of how a scholar can enhance and serve the art he studies,
and in King's case the art he knows and loves.

Wallace Shawn's plays may be unfamiliar. Wallace Shawn is not.
His distinctive presence in such films as *My Dinner with André, Clueless,* and *Scenes from the Class Struggle in Beverly Hills,* and in television
shows like *Taxi* and *Murphy Brown* have made him one of the most
familiar of character actors. Audiences have taken to him, feeling
that they know this odd, endearing, prickly, and curious late-century

everyman Shawn plays. Part of the accomplishment and fun of *Writing Wrongs* is how King weaves the story of this character we think we know with that of the provocative and surprising playwright who has taken contemporary theater to exciting, uncomfortable, and anything but familiar places. King does this in part by telling Wallace Shawn's own story, the son of the great *New Yorker* editor, denizen of America's proudest liberal milieu. King has a keen eye for the historical detail that anchors Shawn and a committed interest in what Shawn has made of his life and work.

It is specially good to have John Lahr's introduction to *Writing Wrongs.* Lahr is not only a distinguished theater critic and essayist, but he was one of the first to recognize Shawn's distinctive contribution to contemporary theater.

King sees in Shawn's plays "by some measures, a history of failures, of wrong writings that either don't get seen or read or that make some portion of their audiences angry or anxious." He is convinced by their moral gravity and moved by their author's determination to "refit the theater" to express that "wound of conscience" that King, like Shawn, sees at the core of contemporary liberal culture. For King, Shawn's contribution is "something big and obtrusive and not easily comprehended." Just as he takes a character actor's humble and humbling shape, so his plays depart from ideal dramatic form and expectation. "In both capacities, he becomes the focal point for a subversive imagination." Shawn's persona gives shape and voice to the fantasies and anxieties the ordinary cannot conceal, and his plays exert "perhaps the most disruptive style in American drama." In *Writing Wrongs,* W. D. King has written a book about Wallace Shawn that will show that this disruptive and eccentric writer is important to read as an American subject.

Foreword

by John Lahr

Wallace Shawn has a big following. As a character actor, Shawn has appeared, at last count, in forty-one movies. He has co-written one cult film, *My Dinner with André,* and starred as the eponymous hero in another, *Vanya on 42nd Street.* But Shawn's charming, clownish public persona, which has made him popular on the screen, has obscured his larger talent as one of American theater's finest prose stylists and most subversive playwrights. Even the *International Who's Who, 1995–96,* lists as Shawn's "stage appearances"—*Aunt Dan and Lemon, Marie and Bruce,* and *The Fever*—without noting that Shawn in fact *wrote* those excellent plays. His plays have been staged at the most distinguished theaters in England and throughout Europe; but Shawn admits, "My plays are not actually performed in my own land." He adds, "It's very, very hard for your arrow to hit the target here. I'm not that discussed."

W. D. King's *Writing Wrongs* is the welcome first critical discussion of Shawn's provocative oeuvre; it arrives at a crucial moment in the fifty-four year old playwright's career, just after the staging of his masterpiece, *The Designated Mourner,* which made its debut on 24 May 1996, to sold out audiences at the Royal National Theatre in London and which has recently been filmed.

"Uh, Dave, are you there? It's . . . Wally Shawn . . . a character you've created": Shawn's phone message to King is the epigraph to King's final epilogue, on *The Designated Mourner,* and winks at Shawn's often parodied voice, which is at once halting and high-pitched, tentative and shrewd. As *Writing Wrongs* bears witness, Shawn is definitely a character, and his own greatest ironic invention. Although he claims not to understand stage sets, Shawn's droopy, comic silhouette provides a distracting backdrop to his contradictory nature. He is at once arrogant and modest, inept and cunning, dithering and bold, selfless and ambitious, well-mannered and radical, materialistic and spiritual. He is small, about five-feet-four. He is bald, with distinctive patches of side hair, which in the early seventies gave him the air of a mad professor. He has a lisp, which slightly deflates his seriousness, and when he's intellectually treading water, he punctuates a conversation with declarations ("Well, uh, gee, that's . . . just . . . incredible") that in his mouth, onscreen and off, become a fetching comic decoy for his acid thoughts. Shawn's round, pug-nosed, sweet face, which screws itself into various noncommittal moods of bafflement is his final risible ambiguous touch. He presents himself as the opposite of predatory. He disguises himself as a fumbling, somewhat timid, schlub: not someone streamlined for the brightness of day but, rather, an almost invisible night creature, like a slow loris, which survives by playing dead.

Writing Wrongs links Shawn's moral passion to his theatrical radicalism and sly story telling. In Shawn's work, the stage is stripped of most of its comforting dramaturgical devices—no plot, no set, no action—so the audience has nothing but the actor, the words, and its own moral compass to steer by. "My plays are really about the audience," he says. "The main character is you." His plays are a trap for consciousness. "I'm just too ambitious, really, to feel that it's enough to provide a little distraction for the few people who see my plays," says Shawn, who left Harvard with "every intention of becoming a diplomat," who would "make some difference in the world." Shawn, himself the son of great privilege and of great liberal pedigree, which King explores at length—Shawn's father was the late William Shawn, the renowned editor of the *New Yorker* from 1952 to 1987— is hard on his privileged audience. "I mean, the American upper class doesn't primarily need to be soothed and comforted," he explains, "although, like everybody else in the world, that's what they would like. That's not what *I* provide for because I feel that they're soothed and comforted already."

Although Shawn claims to feel sometimes like "an aristocrat in the seventeenth century," he lives more like a peasant. He has no television. He has no computer. He has no fax machine or microwave. One of his frequent retreats is at an undisclosed address above a laundry somewhere outside the chic boundaries of Manhattan. "I don't believe in habits or routines. I try not to have them," he says, and what he does for most of his day is also his secret. "You can say," Shawn told me, "that even the people who know him best honestly don't know what the fuck he does do all day long." This seems to be true. André Gregory, who has directed three of Shawn's plays and considers him "one of my closest friends in the world," isn't quite sure where Shawn works. "I think he has an office down in the Village somewhere," Gregory says. (Some of the actors from Gregory's *Vanya* company once followed Shawn in the subway to try and see where he worked.) "The truth is I move around a lot," Shawn, who is almost always lugging a large satchel, says. "There's a kind of wandering-minstrel thing going on."

Shawn won't discuss his writing routine ("I think it's bad luck"), and he characterizes much of his day-to-day activity as sort of mole-like, "doing little things." He also spends as much time as possible traveling in poor countries, which he sees as corrective behavior. "In the face of enormous suffering," he told me, "humorous detachment is too grotesque even for me." He went on: "The *New Yorker* was not really like Eustace Tilley looking at the butterfly through a monocle. But in some ways, the son of the *New Yorker* is like that. I have a certain coolness, which maybe someone who didn't like me would call coldness. A certain detachment. I'm not always totally in the moment. There's usually a certain amount of observing going on on my part. It's a habit I formed early. A teacher in high school said to me, 'You know, Wally, people were not actually put on the earth just to amuse you.'" Shawn, who bears a physical resemblance to his father, also acquired his father's Byzantine quality of containment; from the beginning, theater offered release from his self-consciousness.

Here, in W. D. King's sparky discussion, the shape of Shawn's self-consciousness and the shape of his daring theater are dissected. "Wally is a very rare species. A dangerous writer," the late producer Joseph Papp said around the time his Public Theatre mounted Wally's first produced play, *Our Late Night*. That play, like all

Shawn's work, managed to upset a lot of people. *Writing Wrongs* begins with the critic Martin Esslin pounding his desk after reading Shawn's *The Hospital Play*. "I will stake my career on the failure of this play!" Esslin screamed at the page; others—like some of the first night audiences at *Our Late Night, Aunt Dan and Lemon,* and *A Thought in Three Parts*—have screamed directly at the stage. Shawn persists in thinking against society, and King rightly places Shawn's cunning in its political context. As Shawn says in the interview that ends King's study, "The world needs writers. Not necessarily me, of course, but . . . we are a confused, terrible culture, which probably can be changed only because there are writers." He adds, "No one is going to give you a certificate for future writing, like a gift certificate that you can cash in . . . that will guarantee that you'll keep on writing or keep on writing well."

In his fierce, idiosyncratic, brave way, Shawn has engineered his own kind of theater and his own growth in a theatrical environment hostile to thought. He gets better and better. *Writing Wrongs* is ravished as much by the subtlety of Shawn's metaphors as it is by the complexity of his personality; this makes it a good guide to both.

Writing Wrongs

Introduction

"On the Way to Balducci's"

→ *E. H. Carr says that there are certain facts that are facts of history, and there are other facts that are just facts and they're not facts of history. And the fact that someone walked out of his house one day and on the way to Balducci's he slipped in the street, and then he picked himself up and continued his walk to Balducci's, that is not a fact of history. And that's what my plays have been really, except for* Aunt Dan and Lemon. *You know, they just sort of happened.*

—Wallace Shawn, interviewed by Mark Strand

→ *Forgive me. I know you forgive me. I'm still falling.*

—final words of *The Fever*

Wallace Shawn's fifth play, *The Hospital Play,* written in 1971, barely even happened. Critics never ignored it, because it never got beyond a reading at the Public Theatre. Some wonderful actors had participated in the reading, and some of the right people were there to listen. They heard a play fall and a playwright fail, once again, to get his play produced. The critic Martin Esslin was said to have pounded his desk and exclaimed, "I will stake my career on the failure of this play!"[1] And just like that the unfortunate man picked himself up and continued his walk to Balducci's, and that is the story of the nothing that was heard of this event in theater history.

But there is perhaps something more to be said of the nothing that was not heard of this event. There had at first been signs of glimmering interest. Shawn recalls that Joe Papp and Bernie Gersten expressed wild enthusiasm, recognizing in it some of his best writing.[2]

Better than what? At that time, Shawn had not yet had a single play produced, so rejection was nothing new. Just a few years later, when Wallace Shawn first became an entry in *Contemporary Dramatists,* he recollected the play in one line: it "has a lot of weeping and vomiting."[3] In a later edition of *Contemporary Dramatists,* the play is ignored, not even listed.[4] But then in 1993, Shawn tells me over the telephone it is his only play that shows "compassion." He might be wrong about that. Or he might be exaggerating for effect, specifically to correct my own initial Esslinesque opinion of the play. I don't know. Compassion is not what I had really noticed the first couple of times through the script. But the word reminded me of a line toward the end of *Aunt Dan and Lemon,* Shawn's very important play from 1985, a play that did make some history and a play from which compassion has been almost entirely scoured away. His character Lemon has just expressed her conviction that there is something in human nature that likes to kill, and this brings her to an evidently traumatic memory from her childhood, a time when she went badly wrong:

➼ *I remember my mother screaming all the time, "Compassion! Compassion! You have to have compassion for other human beings!" And I must admit, there's something I find refreshing about the Nazis, which is partly why I enjoy reading about them every night, because they sort of had the nerve to say, "Well, what is this compassion? Because I don't really know what it is. So I want to know, really, what is it?" . . . And I find it sort of relaxing to read about those people, because I have to admit that I don't know either. I mean, I think I've felt it reading a novel, and I think I've felt it watching a film — "Oh how sad, that child is sick! That mother is crying!" — but I can't ever remember feeling it in life.*[5]

I had always thought that I, unlike Lemon, knew what this thing called compassion was or should be. And I was struck because I had just read *The Hospital Play* and had not, in fact, particularly registered the compassion of it, even though this, among the works of an author I admired, was said by that author to be the only work that exhibited this quality. Just then, I became aware that I was in the midst of experiencing one of the stranger attacks of liberal guilt in recent memory. I felt a sudden connectedness to a victim of cruel neglect, a play that had tried and failed to communicate pity. *The Hospital Play* was the poster child of liberal guilt, and in this mirror held up to nature, I recognized my own.

Wallace Shawn was born at the epicenter of American liberalism, literary sophistication, and prosperity in New York City on 14 November 1943. His father was William Shawn, editor-in-chief of the *New Yorker* for fully a third of the twentieth century, a man universally respected and loved, and by all accounts a devoted husband and father, revered by his son. Young Wally was given the distilled essence of a liberal education at Dalton, Putney, Harvard, and Oxford. Shawn recalls: "I am virtually an experiment in receiving the most encouraging upbringing possible."[6] In a sense, all that was troubled about his childhood was the spectacle of the rest of the world. He describes an experience at summer camp: "The counselors were very tough and occasionally sadistic. Once, when they were annoyed with a boy, they actually suggested that we beat him up! The whole world turned out to be like that camp. I still can't get over it, and writing, for me, is a way of trying to make sense of this world I'm surprised to find myself in."[7]

In general, the world treats him quite well now. Complete strangers often greet him warmly, having recognized him from one of his many performances as a comic character actor in Hollywood movies and television shows. Meanwhile, though, the attempt to make sense of the world in all its brutality has led him to write some fourteen dramatic works, including *My Dinner with André, Marie and Bruce, Aunt Dan and Lemon,* and *The Fever.* In this struggle, he has not escaped the brutality. Critics and audiences have often been harsh in their rejection, beating him up for his rejection of the pleasure principle as the only instinct worth heeding in the theater. But many, too, have seen that the passionate provocation in his writing comes from his elevation of the dialectical art of theater to an unprecedented height.

Shawn had been writing seriously for two or three years by the time he wrote *The Hospital Play,* and had not yet begun or even contemplated the career as an actor that would sustain him through the

1980s and beyond. He was living by his day labors at the time, probably running a Xerox machine in a copy shop or some other form of underpaid, alienated labor. But some critical point had been passed with this play, because never again would a Shawn play pass entirely unnoticed. The next one, *Our Late Night,* was picked up for production by André Gregory and his Manhattan Project. And, like all the rest to come, it would antagonize or bore some, enlighten or thrill others, but it would make a mark, leave a scar, create its own bit of history. The *New York Times* critic would call it "one of the most unpleasant plays I have seen in years. Nevertheless, honesty is to admit that . . . its nastiness is given with a kind of defiant stylishness. Not, definitely not, a play to take your aunt to."[8] Yes, the production won an Obie. But the run was not long, and it does not register in most accounts of the period. Shawn himself would rate its impact as near zero, but I saw a production of this play not long ago in Los Angeles, directed by a member of its original cast, and there was, in and around this production, a perceptible disruption in time, a quick intake of historical breath. Moments of the past and present were in noisy contact in this repetition of a man falling on the way to Balducci's. History might attend to such an event.

The Hospital Play is the play that could have marked the death of Shawn's career (or Martin Esslin's, I suppose), but it might also be seen as the play that marked his career's onset. It is simultaneously a quintessentially negative play and, to be sure, a play of compassion—a play torn, and striving so willfully in opposite directions that it could not be resolved. Indeed, *The Hospital Play* is about a doctor, who should be saving lives, who instead lets creatures die or even causes their deaths. This particularly nightmarish incarnation of the Chekhovian doctor/playwright—a life-artist run amok—is perhaps an expression of the utmost cynical self-consciousness in Shawn. The vehement rejection that this vehemently rejecting play received was, in a way, a calling of Shawn's bluff. And after reaching that sheer limit of the impossible, Shawn somehow thereafter made his impulses possible, at least marginally more so.

Shawn tells me: "*The Hospital Play* is about how it's written. The difference between my writing and others' is a matter of how I write, not what it's about."[9] By the inherited rules of a certain dramaturgy, a dramaturgy aimed at engaging an audience, *The Hospital Play* is written wrong. It does not entertain, entice, allure, court, coax, or dandle. It writes wrongness. It writes wrongs. It's not black comedy, or the smile that freezes, or even satire. It is the inscription of what should not be a play, a story in which nearly everyone dies for no good reason, with weeping, vomiting, no hero, a little sex but no hope, and it is no wonder that it survives now only as a hundred yards of photocopy. The suffering of neglect and rejection, and a sabotage of the system: these are, indeed, both themes of the play and facts about it. It was the fifth and final of Shawn's plays to accomplish only wrongness.

The play is a manifestation of an upbringing in the arts that had relatively little to do with the struggle for acceptance: "I came to believe, like many other people from my class, that a person could do anything he wanted to do in life. . . . I thought, when I was a child, that you could do anything in theatre."[10] Life proved far less tractable for the adult Shawn. In fact, the world turned out to be a morass for the intrepid traveler, and the disabuse of his illusions left Shawn increasingly skeptical of notions of freedom, but the theater, which was in a moment of eager exploration around 1970, seemed to preserve the possibility of . . . possibility. Although he had shown early interest in writing for the theater, he took his degrees in history, economics, and philosophy (specializing in Chinese philosophy): "When I went off to college, I felt the world was in such a bad way that everyone should devote themselves to ending the arms race and preventing nuclear war and solving the problems of global poverty." He saw himself as a civil servant or politician. The nightmare of the Vietnam War led him to evolve "a somewhat more complex analysis," which ultimately came to rest on the belief "that artistic works may have their place in saving the world."[11]

For a man who never had anyone's version of "the rules of playwriting" impressed upon him by a teacher of playwriting, who had the example of his father to show that good can be done with neatly printed language, and who had doubts about just how he should use his power for practical good, a play as unusual and uncompromising as *The Hospital Play* (not even the most challenging or repulsive of his plays) might seem a natural outgrowth. What Shawn was learning at just the time of that play was that playwriting, as traditionally conceived and practiced, was not a natural outgrowth of his talents and abilities. Instead, in the spirit of that childhood belief in the infinite possibilities of life and theater, Shawn defied the intractable quality of the former by rejecting or rewriting the rules of the latter. Eventually this sort of manipulation of the form came to seem a standard operating procedure: "I've always had to invent some kind of form for my plays that will take the place of the form that plays usually have."[12] In being simultaneously someone who seems utterly wrong for the job and also someone who leaps tall buildings at a single bound, there is a Clark Kent/Superman quality to Shawn, though it is perhaps the Nietzschean *Übermensch,* the willful self-creator, not the do-good Marvel Comics man, who figures in this dialectic.

There is danger in the fall, as any clown or hero can attest, and the spectacle of the fall can be horrifying, but there are also delightful and grotesque, wild and uproarious, sublime and even beautiful, aspects of falling, as can be seen in Jack Ziegler's 1976 *New Yorker* drawing. These aspects are elemental to Shawn's plays, and they are why many audiences have found his plays unusually exhilarating and fresh. By some measures, Wallace Shawn is an unusual success in the theater, having developed the fall to such a fine art. A fall is the putting in motion of a body by removing a foundation (a standpoint) and releasing the inertia of that body (in question). Shawn's repeated gesture in the theater is to remove the theater itself—as a context of customary response, as a framework—and throw into question all the usual decorous and accepted relations between audience and play.

The Hospital Play is the longest of Shawn's plays. I have it here on my desk, and I don't like to read it even now. It was my stumbling block in this project, but I value it for what it made me see as I fell down. It is a "failure," as Esslin observed, just as Shawn's career as a writer is, by some measures, a history of failures, of wrong writings that either don't get seen or read or that make some portion of their audiences angry or anxious. Wallace Shawn's plays are plays of the fall, and one of the projects of this book is to understand that falling (and to feel the falling), and to say that there is history to be told even in that overlooked moment on the way to Balducci's, if only we read that slippage in terms of such moral gravity as Shawn has given to each of his plays.

I do not say that *The Hospital Play* typifies Shawn's writing. It is a play that was written at a cynical moment in American political self-consciousness by a writer who was, I think, desperately attempting to overcome a contemptuous self-consciousness of himself as an artist, and making adept use of an exaggerated, elite self-confidence to do so. That was, I speculate, what was going on with Shawn in 1972. I do believe that each of his plays, before and since, responds to some sharp agenbite of inwit, and each finds some way to refit the theater so that it will not mask or repress that wound of conscience, but instead show it plain. Shawn's career traces the history of a certain artistic impulse through a time that was not, generally speaking, amenable to it, and one of the projects of this book is to tell something of that unfolding narrative of the artist as a young and aging man. Empirical history, though, much less biography, are not the aim here. Shawn's plays ferociously draw attention to themselves, but even the most obviously reflexive of them raises innumerable challenges to anyone who hopes to emerge with a coherent narrative. History of another sort, the sort of history that gets made and told in incidental, suddenly revelatory flashes, and the sort of history that momentarily illuminates a complex textual and political structure of a moment, can be glimpsed in Shawn's writings. By some negotiation of the differences between what he knew and what he knows and what I know and what I knew, I hope to address that sort of historical nexus.

PERSON A

•◦ *Konstantin: New forms! New forms are what is needed, and if there are to be no new forms, then better there were nothing at all.*
—Chekhov, *Seagull*

If we are to judge by Konstantin Treplev's example, the quest for new forms (as in "I've always had to invent some kind of form for my plays that will take the place of the form that plays usually have") can be a suicidal course. Indeed, difficult, young Konstantin cannot even count on his mother to pay attention to him, and it is all—life, art, love—a big disappointment to him. "The life of a playwright is tough," says Wally at the beginning of *My Dinner with André*; "It's not easy, as some people think. You work hard writing plays, and nobody puts them on."[13] But then, in a world of "so much love" (as Dr. Dorn remarks), Treplev has proved unlovable. Wallace Shawn, by contrast, has made a living as a lovable figure. He's kind of adorable (*The Moderns*), even when he's out of temper (*The Princess Bride*), and is his own best critic (*Prick Up Your Ears*). He's whimsically not what you would expect (*Simon; Radio Days*). He essentializes a cute version of negated manliness (*Scenes from the Class Struggle in Beverly Hills; Clueless; Toy Story*).

My friends who have known I was working on this project have called me many times to say they had just spotted Shawn on television in this or that role. By the time I tune in (to *Taxi, The Cosby Show*, or *Murphy Brown*, or some *Star Trek* spinoff), it's almost always too late. Once, I fast forwarded through a week's videotaped episodes of some soap opera—*Days of Our Lives*, I think it was—because I heard he was playing a continuing character, but he did not show up. At the speed of prime time, I've almost always missed the fractional minutes or seconds when he is the face of network television. At the speed of general release, I've done better; in his movies, Shawn is glimpsed as a series of phantoms of self-love/self-hatred. Are there elements of the real Shawn in these characters? No doubt there are, but I suspect those elements have less to do with what makes him tick as a human being and an artist than with what makes him suitable (or unsuitable) for still other roles. That is, what one learns about him is mostly what makes him laughable and oddly compelling as a screen image—his squint, his squeal of frustration, his odd laugh. The camera loves these surface details, but not for long. The mass media hurry through the sudden, infinitesimal need for someone of his size and shape and hair, which are small and round and bald. They are usually more eager to focus upon some other, more perfect form.

The key thing is that he and his agent have done a good job of promoting him as one of the "short, bald character actors" of choice, and this, in an important way, has helped sustain his career as a writer of . . . anything.[14] He says, "Before becoming an actor, the previous job that I had was as a Xerox machine operator. I lived for ten years by borrowing money from friends, which is the sort of life that people traditionally find it very hard to return to. To give up acting would mean to give up the only way I've ever had of making a living."[15] Shawn has made very little money from his writing, even including his "cult" film, *My Dinner with André* ("Oh, I haven't made two cents from it. I haven't made one farthing!"[16]). But he has made a decent living acting (for two days of shooting in a film about a giant insect he recalled making more than he made in a year as a Latin teacher), and along the way he has worked with some very good directors and stars.

Konstantin Treplev's vexation with the world and his humiliation over the fact that his demanding art is ignored are compounded by the fact that his mother, Mme. Arkadina, is among those who mock him, and she is an actress in the bourgeois theater. Shawn has had to adjust himself to the fact that the art he might otherwise have scorned, or at least chosen to ignore along the way in his quest for self-expression, is the art that actually sustains him. He is thus both Konstantin and Mme. Arkadina in one. Yet the intensity with which he approaches his writing is still more fierce than Konstantin's, and he is also less at odds with the actor who has done his share of B-movies and sitcoms. He takes his acting work very seriously, applying himself fully to the challenges of playing anything from a space alien to a horny psychiatrist to a half-pint medieval heavy. He seems to enjoy being recognized on the street and other aspects of celebrity. He guards against taking roles that are too demeaning or retrograde, but in general the whole irony of his taking a small part in mass culture is one that gives him pleasure. Still, there are limits to how far he can unify this schizoid aspect of his career: "When I'm acting in a movie, I throw myself 100 percent into it, I enjoy it totally, and I tend not to talk too much about the things that are preoccupying me during the other weeks of my life when I become Person B. . . . Person B has done all my writing. I've often been asked, 'Why don't you write a movie for yourself! A movie that you could star in?' And the reason that I don't do it is because the only one of the two of us who can write is Person B, and he doesn't want Person A in his movie!"[17]

And so he is an actor only by trade. And, in fact, he is a sort of icon, a face and form that can be slotted into a variety of roles, always with a certain quirky, adorable (but also contemptible), nebbish quality. As a Person A, he is Reduced Man, the bare remnant of power, a weirdly oblivious, to-the-manner-born runt—someone who should by birthright be devastating, someone who should have acute vision, but who cannot even see his own impotence. The joke of the Shawn "mask" was pinpointed by Woody Allen in *Manhattan* (1979), in which Shawn had his first screen role. Shawn played Diane Keaton's character's former husband, a genius whom she had described as a lady-killer, the man who had "opened her up" sexually, turned her to jelly.[18] When Woody (short and skinny) chances to meet his predecessor (short and plump) in a clothing store, he is shocked to find that the man she was referring to was "this little homunculus." The camera increases the appearance of fleshiness in a person, but even on camera Allen comes across thin, sort of pinched, with exaggerated eyes and hair on top. Wally is thick, doughy, a little like a pig (a recurrent image in his plays). The head is round, with hair mainly on the brim of the good-sized dome, and the visual emphasis is somehow on the lips. They are anamorphic versions of each other, and both are comic variations on the lower limit of what American culture has defined as masculinity. They are (ordinary) non-men dealing with the non-fulfillment of their desires. The dif-

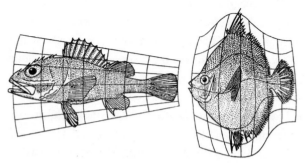

From D'Arcy Wentworth Thompson, On Growth and Form

ference is Woody writes his films and Mariel Hemingway (or some version of her youthfulness) winds up very happy in his bed, if only briefly, and a paying audience has a good laugh, whereas Wally waits for a telephone call and a script.

They are also different, of course, in the social roles they project. Woody plays on underclass, Coney Island, American Jewish stereotypes translated through the *haute bourgeois* cultural vocabulary of Manhattan, the heaven of entrepreneurial success, while Wally, whose ancestry is also Jewish, is a Manhattanite who comes off as well-born and well-educated but also somehow fumbling, *déclassé,* destined for Manhattan hell. His characterizations often play on the folklore type known as The Boss's Son, the comic stereotype that helped make a laughing stock of Dan Quayle. Neither Woody nor Wally gets the American dream. Both fall short, literally, of the ideal, but Wally has no Diane Keaton to lift him up. Two or five or ten days of shooting, being his dense screen self, and then he's out of there. He is somehow captivated by the image of falling, and, by the final reel, he has usually fallen by the wayside, but there are a few nice moments when he is the feature.

PERSON B

What I have described up to this point is a writer whose plays are ignored and an actor of peripheral significance. A marginal artist. To be sure, Wallace Shawn's mature plays have gotten some fine productions, some good reviews, some audience. They have had some impact, and some are considered worth remembering or reviving. And his performances in a few dozen feature films, with several well-respected directors, are indelibly there on celluloid, or on videocassette. They get seen and shown and occasionally reshown, and his performances are sometimes singled out for discussion. On these levels, he is, twice, a small topic, writer and actor. Homunculus.

But he is also something big and obtrusive and not easily comprehended. The degree to which his physical form differs from the platonic or Hollywood ideal mirrors the degree to which his plays deviate from the usual dramatic form. In both capacities, he becomes the focal point for a subversive imagination. Whereas his acting persona is notable for its appealing quality, with an underside of terrorism, his dramas are notable for their assaultive qualities—and their idiosyncratic vividness, humor, charm. As an actor, he is a body onto which American culture locates many of the fantasies and anxieties men feel about the limits of the individual. As a writer, he exerts perhaps the most disruptive style in American drama, and his plays embody catastrophe in the making, the endgame of art.

Shawn is certainly not the "best" writer of his generation, because his writings do not aim for the standard markers of achievement in the form: masterful plotting, appealing characters, scintillating dialogue, and so on. He has said, "It's laughable, in a way, that someone who has no sense of character or plot would become a playwright."[19] Along the way he has won three Obies for distinguished playwriting, but he seems to care little about occupying the winner's circle, either as a cultural icon or as an artist hero. He tends to trade on the baroque, backwater, eddying energy of the second thrust, the more swirled complexity and grandeur that comes of not getting through the aperture the first time or the easy way. All of his writings can be interpreted according to the belief, quoted earlier, that "artistic works may have their place in changing the world," but this belief seems to flow with difficulty past an equally strong skepticism of the power of art, particularly the theater, and this is what gives to each of his writings its unstable, ambivalent, eddying quality. One critic, in attempting to define just what nauseated him about the typical Shawn play, used the same metaphor to describe what he saw as a grave fault: "Everything seems caught in some eternal, hellish eddy, whirling nowhere to no purpose, and the energy of the plays comes not from action but from the seething frustrations of the trapped characters."[20] Quite right.

It would be possible to analyze this indrawn, turbid energy in terms of modernist trends—Strindberg, Chekhov, Kafka, Sartre, Pinter—and indeed it is likely that Shawn feels kinship with these trends. As a child, he saw a good deal of theater, at places like the Cherry Lane Theatre and the Circle in the Square, and he especially recalls productions of Beckett and Ionesco plays and José Quintero's productions of O'Neill. But Shawn's plays differ radically from the likes of *The Iceman Cometh* or *Endgame* because he goes beyond the modernist challenge of traditional structures to an art that approaches a negation of the theater itself. The modernist tradition undermines usual patterns, especially Aristotelian form, but uses the theater to make an even bolder, purer statement. Thus, O'Neill and the others can still use affective mechanisms and write masterpieces, whereas Shawn continually defuses the affect and concentrates instead on an antithetical approach that begins with minority—the minor effect. Thus, his plays (and his career) seem small, oddly shaped, repressed, subversive, much like his screen persona. This was true of his writing from the very first play. When, in 1971, he wrote an exceptional play that was big and encompassing and gloomy, filled with compassionate drama, a world historical statement in the face of war, a modernist play not unlike *The Iceman Cometh,* he had indeed created something exceptional and impossible (for him). *The Hospital Play* was a play that could not be, and consequently it *was* not. With his next play, he returned to the minor, the little peculiar non-play, and that was the practical beginning of his postmodern career.

Erik MacDonald, in his recent study of *Theatre at the Margins: Text and the Post-Structured Stage,* has posed the question, "What might arise if the textual assumptions of a mode of writing that radically questions its world were themselves interrogated from the perspective of the slippage within that world's own defining terms?"[21] This is a puzzle MacDonald poses to critics, but Shawn, among a few other writers whom MacDonald analyzes in this book, has already absorbed this line of inquiry into his own ultramarginal writing, a kind of playwriting that shifts the marginal to the center, only ironically to see it marginalized again because (*contra* Yeats) the center often holds all too well (and that's what worries him). What MacDonald wants to say is that there is, within this line of poststructuralist theatricality, a return to text or textuality, because there and only there are to be found the more subtle deconstructions of the power mechanism called theater. The writings I examine in this book might be read as examples of those deconstructions.

Shawn's screenplay *My Dinner with André* (1980), cowritten with André Gregory, self-consciously explores the question of how (or if) theater can take a role in saving the world, or at least awakening stupefied audiences. Shawn and Gregory played versions of themselves in this film, which critics called unique, audacious, exasperating, maddening, torturous, brilliant, bizarre, and surprisingly entertaining. At one point during this dinner, André says to Wally: "Plays are great. But what kind of plays are appropriate today? It's very confusing. Because, for instance—for instance, I think that if you put on serious contemporary plays by writers like yourself, you may only be helping to deaden the audience in a different way. I mean, there was a time when contemporary plays of a certain kind would have had a prophetic function and would have been *warnings* to people, but now I think there has been *such* a degeneration, and the world is *so* dark and cold, that even those works which once were outcries *against* the darkness can now only contribute to the deadening process."[22] The character "Wally" is appalled by this suggestion, but the writer Shawn, Person B, has taken special measures to insure that his plays (and this very same screenplay) come across in a way that is neither a simple confirmation of expected beliefs nor a cynical negativism that might undermine the need to look at the world anew. And by including just such a passage as I have quoted, Shawn enables the "actor" Gregory to "write" just such an interrogation of the textual assumptions of a mode of writing, as MacDonald calls it, "from the perspective of the slippage within that world's own defining terms." This is the characteristic that associates Shawn's writing with "post-structured" theatricality, although that terminology is hardly required to define an effect that has considerably more history than MacDonald or other postmodern critics of the theater ordinarily allow. Still, the transition that André is describing from the play seen as a prophetic warning to the play seen as "part of the deadening process" might be interpreted as the transition from the modern to the postmodern. The move from a crisis of conscience to a retraction of conscience, from outcry to muteness, is just what conservatives have decried about postmodernism, but Shawn alternately ironizes and amplifies this critique by internalizing it within his filmscript (which was, in fact, initially performed as a play).

Anyone familiar with the apparatus of deconstructive criticism should see in this configuration of dichotomous terms (writing/acting, film/theater, outcries/deadening) that this film—and I would argue most of Shawn's writing—will lend itself to this sort of critique. The "hellish eddy" in Shawn's writing might readily be associated with the Derridean *aporia*. The ambiguity of his works might be assigned to the unstable and contradictory metaphysical foundations he puts into play. Shawn is a minor master at putting a bug in the ear of the other, and I think it might indeed be valuable for someone to explore the pharmakology of Shawn's *Fever,* the brisure of *Marie and Bruce,* or the spermatic dissemination of *A Thought in Three Parts* straight into the debate it spawned in the British House of Lords. For the present study, I have opted for the most part to ignore that particular buzz. Shawn's plays afford unusual opportunities for what Gregory Ulmer called "applied grammatology," and what I aim to do here is trace out their undoubtedly poststructured ways in terms of what the plays look like and do.[23]

LIBERAL ARTS

➡ *I must say, though, I don't truly think that the world really needs more plays, in general. I mean, the world needs to be saved, actually. I mean, when you consider the suffering that surrounds everybody, and the evil, and the murder, and the threats of murder, and when you consider the fact that our own minds seem to be under some terrible assault, so that we feel our minds are dying, so that it seems people have completely forgotten how to live, I really don't think there is very much honor in a life devoted to writing, unless that writing can do something awfully unusual, something awfully necessary. Personally, I would rather work to alleviate human misery in some simple and direct way. I would rather devote my working hours to meditation and at least achieve for myself a sense of one-ness with the universe. Because writing is not only usually a waste of one's own precious time, but it's usually so harmful to others as well and just adds to*

the heap of stupidity and confusion and lies by which we are oppressed. I re-
ally do hope I'll stop writing, if I ought to.
                —Wallace Shawn, statement in *Contemporary Dramatists*

Certain stages in Shawn's history are worth knowing in detail. He recalls a fifth-grade teacher who encouraged him "first of all, to to- tally change my approach to life and secondly, to write a play and be in it. It was on the serious and philosophical side, on the tragic side. People were quite moved by this play and looked at me in a differ- ent way. I don't think it would take Sigmund Freud to figure out that this was positive reinforcement, a pleasant, even wonderful ex- perience, and I'm sure the rest of my life has been an attempt to crawl along behind that experience and repeat it."[24] His father gave him a puppet theater, and he and his brother created some elaborate mu- sical shows, which Shawn wrote, including one about the poet Ho- race, another called *Fins and Feet,* another that was on the subject of dynastic decline in China, an adaptation of *Paradise Lost,* and some- thing about Wittgenstein.[25] He and his brother also made movies. As he put it to me, becoming a writer was the most natural choice in the world for him, and the odd thing was, that for a time as he en- tered adolescence, he had decided he would *not* be a writer. Lucinda Franks reports that at this time he was reading Dostoevski, and "[h]e came out against order and for passion and anarchy; he was a kind of beatnik before his time. He proselytized on the uselessness of lit- erature, and tried to convince his classmates not to do their Latin homework (he later became a Latin teacher)."[26]

Late in his high school years, Shawn closely studied Henry Kissinger's ideas about global nuclear politics—ideas that were founded upon the imperative of anticommunism and were instru- mental in the evolution of the domino theory. These ideas were ba- sic to conservative foreign policy, and Shawn's strong interest in them was unusual given what we know of his background. But he reports that this interest had already begun to fade when he entered Harvard, and by the time he went to India, in 1965, on a Fulbright Fellowship, to teach English, he found himself growing daily more upset over what he was reading about the bombing of Vietnam. This was when he started to abandon ideas of "saving and civilizing the world à la J.F.K. politics."[27] His study at Oxford also served to put distance between himself and the war, just at the moment when he started to become a playwright. These were the years when his father took a strong interest in the counterculture, and it was his father who told him about Woodstock. Wally himself was "terrified" by the whole countercultural movement.[28] For him, the war was a shocking deviation from the ideals of this country, not, as he has subsequently come to believe, an inevitable sort of development for a capitalist, imperialist superpower.

Shawn was of course raised in an atmosphere of genteel liberalism. The *New Yorker* had, under his father's editorship, published such landmarks of liberal politics as Richard Rovere's columns on the Red Scare and Cold War politics (see his "Senator Joe McCarthy" and "The American Establishment") and Rachel Carson's "Silent Spring," although, of course, it was still best known for cultural reporting, fiction, cartoons, poetry, reviews, and casuals. Nevertheless, Tom Wolfe, with a shriek, pronounced the magazine distinctly "grim" compared to its original, perfect insouciance. Certainly, during the 1960s, the magazine spoke more directly than ever before to the political situation. Shawn himself recalls that his father was "radicalized" by the escalation of the Vietnam War, and some of the more pointed editorial pieces published by the magazine during those years were written by its editor-in-chief.[29] His mother, he says, became something of an expert on Vietnam.

In the late 1960s, the magazine began publishing the war reporting of Jonathan Schell, who had been Wally's roommate at Putney and Harvard. In the following years, Schell's political coverage of the Nixon era (collected in *The Time of Illusion*) and his widely influential analysis of the potential for global environmental ruin and nuclear holocaust, a sort of sequel to Rachel Carson's writings (later published as *The Fate of the Earth*), came out in the magazine and Schell was talked of as a possible successor to Shawn as editor. Meanwhile, Wally recalls, his own political consciousness awakened much more slowly. Schell had schooled his liberal impulse in the bombed villages of Vietnam and returned as an influential journalist, while

Shawn had used his student deferment to educate himself, also abroad, beyond the sort of manipulable stuff that the U.S. military could utilize. And, as a kind of confirmation of this inutility, he returned as a writer of unproduceable plays.

This contrast set in position one of the master myths by which Shawn's history can be interpreted—the parable of the prodigal son. Shawn was, in a way, the son who initially turned away from his responsibility, and from his literate and liberal and wealthy and wise and much-honored heritage, and who has subsequently struggled to understand why it is he was nevertheless welcomed home. His rebellion was evidently always contained by the love and understanding of his parents. Liberal tolerance has something to do with this; Wally was, after all, an example of freedom. No matter how defiant his plays became—and at their most extreme they were the antithesis of what could conceivably be published in the *New Yorker*—his father made no public rebuff of Wally: "I know that he never does it to attract attention or be sensational or for commercial reasons. His intent is so pure and it all has such deep meaning for him that I would accept whatever he wrote even if it fell outside the boundaries of what I usually like or even understand. I have great confidence in his work."[30]

Similarly, Wally has never expressed anything less than solemn respect for his father in interviews, while he typically rates his own achievements low. But then, liberals have traditionally made a strong separation between the public and the private realms, as well as between the political and the psychological. Surely one of the things that terrified Wally during the late 1960s (while perhaps intriguing his father) was the attack on those very same lines of demarcation by the New Left. Nevertheless, if there were erupting Oedipal tensions between father and son, one would expect a liberal reservation of them to the private realm. What shows up in public is a testament of Wally's respect for his father's politics, but phrased in such a way that it draws attention to the private task of living up to his father's example: "There are real disputes between nations, and it may be that we'll never get rid of wars until we end the nation-state as an institution. But it's also true that if every single person in the whole world were exactly like . . . *my father,* for example, somehow there would be fewer wars, because there's just something about his personality that, if everybody were like him, people would be seeking a peaceful resolution of their differences. Whereas if everybody were like Hitler, there would be wars all the time. So you think, well, what made Hitler like Hitler and my father like my father? It's the experiences they've had and the people they've met and the artistic works that have influenced them."[31]

Wally did not turn out like his father—different artistic works evidently led to that—and the result is that his personality is not one that necessarily leads to peaceful resolution of the differences between people. Indeed, in his own artistic works, there are moments when one senses that they want to go to war, which in a sense means they want to be at odds with his father. Why that is is hard to say, since of course it seems logical that one would want to honor and imitate such an eminently laudable man. Lucinda Franks addressed this paradox in a 1980 article in the *New York Times,* called "The Shawns—A Fascinating Father-and-Son Riddle." She compares the father's editorial style, especially his "technique of delivering soft, almost apologetic-sounding suggestions that pack the wallop of direct orders" to the "gentleness in the extreme" with which he raised his sons: "He believed, according to Wallace, that for a father to let slip something negative about a son's actions might deflect him from something valuable; he made it a rule never to be even constructively critical but accepted totally everything his sons did. That attitude persisted even when Wallace declared himself against everything his father represented." The father had thus given the son an unusually rich opportunity to experience individuality, the cornerstone of liberalism, in itself.

The result of this father-son, editor-writer collaboration is a powerful metaphor, a metaphor that works: "If the son creates himself from the father, so Wallace Shawn has, through a process of gradual selection, become the mirror image of William Shawn and the complete opposite of all that he represents."[32] Franks wrote this piece at just the moment when Shawn's other career, as a character actor, was taking off. In the following years, the other side of Shawn's artistic output would become a public fact, the carnivalesque side that abases itself as a comical character actor within the very same capitalistic mechanism against which his plays are arrayed in battle. This stands in contrast to his father, who maintained a strict, and some might say artificial, separation between the editorial and business affairs of the magazine, involving himself as little as possible in the latter. The liberal intellectuals were to stand *among* the advertisements for Van Cleef and Arpels but not *of* them. Yet Wally has probably made the flight from New York to LAX as often as he's walked the mile to the Public Theatre. His impolite playwriting is rare, in-your-face (and nonprofit), while his acting is omnipresent at the periphery of vision (and lucrative), both in contrast with "the inviolable aura of privacy" that surrounded his father.[33]

What happens to the prodigal son when his father never leaves it in doubt that he is welcome home? The whole scope of Shawn's career makes it clear that if there is a fatted calf involved in his return, the feast is one not easily digested. Increasing nausea becomes apparent, and finally, in *The Fever,* the fatted calf is thrown up in a third-world bathroom, with the hard-working other son (and perhaps Jonathan Schell, too) looking on in disgust. Shawn was proving himself not the conventional child of liberalism, but something weaker (in that his program is obscure) and diametrically opposite. Declaring his privacy public, mocking his own freedom, refusing to indulge his audience in any way, Shawn became a renegade. Of course, the world had changed significantly by that time (1991), and if Wally was no longer the child of liberalism, William Shawn was no longer, so to speak, its father (he had been removed from the editorship of the *New Yorker* in 1987), or perhaps "it" had in some sense disappeared. "It" was the thing that linked father and son ideologically, if only by the fact that they often stood in opposite orientation to it. Both father and son had felt the force of a historical trend that had complicated the idea of defining oneself as a liberal.

Liberals believe in generalizations, the universal offered to the particular.[34] Liberalism draws on a general belief in individual freedom, which is freedom of the sort most easily attained and most

readily experienced by those who are free enough to hold such beliefs, as well as those who would tend to lose freedom if others did
not hold liberal beliefs. It is inherently a kind of luxury, this freedom
to engineer the freedom of others. In the worst light, liberalism is
both a sign and a guarantor of power. Liberalism is founded on an
optimistic belief in the capacity of human beings to employ their rational powers and to act on the basis of essentially good natures to
bring about progress.

As an impulse toward action, liberalism is encountered when
someone else lacks freedom, and then it is experienced mainly by
those whose freedom is not directly under attack, and thus those
who are only ideologically motivated to action. Those whose freedom is directly under attack tend to seek not reform of the attackers
but redress. Liberalism prefers improvement to revolution, and in
this way it forestalls revolution. Liberalism sometimes devolves to
action for others *only* when it costs little or nothing, but it also might
lead to idleness when the cost to the liberal's own freedom rises too
high. Liberalism is a belief that structurally one cannot be forced to
uphold or maintain, because force entails authority, and authoritarianism erases freedom. Of course, authoritarianism can also create an
illusory freedom, at least for certain chosen beneficiaries, and liberals are often accused of using authoritarian means to fulfill their
goals.

In modern American liberalism—the legacy of the New Deal—
the state is the agency for enforcing the conditions in which progressive liberation might take place. The state is the device by which
the liberality of the "good" people who have the technology to make
conditions better for others is translated into programs and laws that
bring about those improved conditions. But it can also be seen as the
device by which one segment of the population imposes its will on
another, supposedly in the name of progress but actually out of self-
interest. Within the critique outlined here, liberalism has not fared
well in the 1990s. At its worst, liberalism has come to seem the pet
philosophy of a white male elite.

Shawn was raised in a family that could afford liberalism, optimism,
and a belief in the potential use of state power to enlarge freedom,

nationally and internationally. Of his family's wealth, Shawn has evidently inherited little or nothing to date. During the 1970s, he lived
a relatively impoverished life. Since his acting career began, his average annual income has no doubt considerably increased, but this
revenue is unpredictable, and he still appears to live very close to the
margin. He frequently mentions his unpaid bills. Of the luxury of
liberalism, Shawn inherited some fragment of the original confidence in the good nature of human beings, and some fragment of a
belief in the essential superiority of the American governmental
structure. Both of these beliefs, held in trust, have dwindled over the
years, to the point where the accounts have emptied. In 1991, he
came to a frank assessment of the bankruptcy of his earlier beliefs:
"Today I would say, well, there are reasons why America behaves the
way it does. I'm much more aware that our country consistently and
predictably and often brutally pursues its economic interests. Either
Reagan was a frank expression of what we were like all along or some
amazing aberration, and I came to think—I mean you'd have to be
mentally deficient not to see this—that the former was the correct interpretation. The assumption that we are basically a decent people
with good intentions—once you can face the fact that this is actually
untrue, that it's an illusion, well, it's quite liberating."[35]

Each of Shawn's plays can be read as a statement of debits and
credits in an ongoing account of liberalism. They are declarations,
made freely (in the sense that they have made little or no money for
him and in the sense that they seem to him, at least, to be voluntary
and undetermined self-expressions). But they exact a price, a toll, on
the audience in terms of the patience and tolerance and liberality
they are asked to supply, and on himself in terms of the extent to
which he wishes to impose his will as an author(ity) on that audience
and how he chooses to use their free time. Then too, these works are
also subject to the conditions of a certain sector of the cultural mar-
ketplace, specifically the nonprofit theater, which itself can be interpreted as a liberal mechanism. They are reflexive of the authority
vested in a cultural institution by the liberality of a certain class. At
the end of 1986, a year after the premiere of *Aunt Dan and Lemon,*
Shawn told an interviewer:

➥ *I believe that in order for the world to change, there must be people who devote themselves to assessing the situation that we're in, to thinking and to writing. The world can never change unless there are people who are trying to understand it and express their understanding. You might think that our theatre could be a place in which both that type of analysis and a dialogue about the way the world is run are attempted. It could be part of a thinking process going on in our society. . . .*

But here, quite honestly, I think it would be ludicrous to think that the theatre has that kind of role because most people interested in the way the world is going don't go to the theatre. They wouldn't think of it. Most of the people who go to the theatre are simply looking for a certain kind of soothing experience that will take their mind off their troubles. So if that's why a person has come to the theatre, I feel like an idiot grabbing him by the throat and trying to get him to worry about the things that are bothering me. My style as a human being is to indulge people who need to escape. Yet I insist on confronting them as a playwright. It's quite embarrassing, it's quite unpleasant, it's quite awkward.[36]

Theaters sponsor a private experience within the public realm, and so each person who has been bored or tormented by the play has felt the impact of that boredom or torment precisely in the area most sacrosanct within classic liberal doctrine—the private space. The play becomes a seizure of freedom, not a liberation. In the case of those audience members who expect to be hedonistically absorbed in the pleasure of the theater, Shawn finds himself the intruder upon their privacy, the one who takes charge of their leisure time and grabs them by the throat. There is, perhaps, another audience, the specifically liberal audience, who wants the theater to serve the very liberal program Shawn has just outlined, but he appears to have lost confidence that a liberal message sent to a liberal audience would have any effect. Perhaps such a communication would only promote an idle self-satisfaction.

It is hard to write about the dramatic tradition that functions by means of a refined liberal guilt without seeming to be rudely dismissive of earnest, well-intentioned artists, and yet it has become clear to Shawn that he must face a discontinuity with that tradition.

In 1986, in a roundtable discussion with three masters of that tradition, Athol Fugard, David Mamet, and Arthur Miller, Shawn said: "Sometimes there's an individual writer who believes passionately that his message of poetic insight could absolutely save society, but he can't get others to agree. I myself have felt at certain moments, my God, I have received this orphic, this profound, unconscious message that must be conveyed to the world immediately. But somehow the electoral process has very savagely returned the response, 'No, we don't want to hear the message.' " That is the historical rationale for the discontinuity with the liberal tradition in theater. Later in the same discussion, Shawn connected the historical with the personal in his own work: "I do think there's something about the current period—and I don't understand it—that makes it terribly, terribly hard for a writer to focus, in a truthful way, on the suffering of an individual person. I do think it's the most amazing thing in the world that there are millions of people living just outside the windows of this room who are suffering the very disappointments and personal tragedies that Willy Loman suffered, and it would be absolutely my dream to be able to write a play about that suffering, and yet I'm unable to."[37] Shawn typically does not conceive of his writing in terms of freedom of expression. By the mid-1980s, he had also essentially ceased to think of himself as a playwright because the word implies

⦿ *that you sit at your lathe and turn these things out one after another. I don't do that. I find it wonderful to be able to write anything. And I would be pleased to write more, pleased if it were to turn out in the form of a play. I know my way around theatre a little bit so there's always a feeling that it would be a shame just to throw that away and try to start again in a totally different form. But honestly, I'd be delighted if I ever wrote anything in any form. One has absolutely no choice about those things— at least I don't. I'll do whatever I'm able to do.*[38]

He said this at the time he was preparing to write *The Fever,* which would, by largely abandoning dramatic form, come closer to addressing that suffering outside the window if only by confronting the extremity of the gulf that lies between the performer and the subject.

The Fever was aimed initially not at the self-indulgent theater audience, but at the ruling class, the people who presumably could change the world in some progressive way. With this work, he had completed a cycle and returned from the public realm to the private, to the living rooms of the ruling class, where he performed this monologue for free. He had come home among the liberals as a true prodigal, someone who was prepared to take the fatted calf and fling it back in the faces of the overfed fathers and sons. The prodigal is someone who throws his riches away, squanders them, and Shawn had come to the point of returning to his childhood puppet theater and giving away his writing to groups of ten or twelve as they reclined on sofas and love seats. He had, as he said in the interview, thrown away what he knew about theater and started in a different form.

As he predicted, there would be shame involved in this giving it all away, but he had not then foreseen that his own sense of shame would be the very subject of *The Fever*. In the piece, he recalled all the things that had been given to him as a child and later on, and, in this work, he returned that liberality with a bitter twist. Shawn, the child prodigy, had turned prodigal, left the private, liberal home as public Person A and Person B, and then returned home as a prodigious, or rather monstrous, synthesis of all the contradictions: "the holy fool of the American theatre," as Ross Wetzsteon called him.[39] He now stands distinctly beyond all known liberal creed, all confidence that there is any sure foundation to the hope that progress will be realized or that the individual might find true fulfillment without undue cost to the Other. And yet his every gesture as a writer can be seen as a production of that hope, even if carefully balanced against an element of despair.

I believe he is now a good example of what Richard Rorty calls the "liberal ironist," the strong poet who acknowledges his ultimate contingency and yet believes in the power of redescription to create the conditions for solidarity, a common experience of human suffering with the aim of alleviating that suffering. In a world where people understandably long for something more certain, or more theoretical, such a strong poet as Rorty describes can hardly expect to be a culture hero. It is hard enough just to be human. Mark Strand

asked Shawn if he was satisfied being a character actor, and he replied
in words that ironize his role as a writer: "In a way I'm quite embittered about it because I sort of feel insulted that these people don't
think that I could be the father of the family, the husband, the lover.
Why, instead, do they see me as the bizarre priest who lurks on the
edges of life, the peculiar, sexless psychiatrist who skulks in the corner of the lives of the real people? On the other hand there aren't that
many roles of leading men that would be very appealing to me, because I think I would be too nauseated by those roles. But man's vanity is infinite. Man's capacity for being offended is infinite. The truth
is that I enormously enjoy doing these things."[40]

André Gregory did a great thing in 1989 when he gave Shawn the title role in *Vanya* (later filmed as *Vanya on 42nd Street*). Vanya feels insulted because people don't think *he* could be the father, the husband,
the lover. As Chekhov did for Vanya, Gregory did for Shawn, which
was the service of bringing him into the exact space and time and chain
of events from which he could realize how correct *and* inappropriate
his actions had been—how unheroic his impulse toward heroism had
proved. Vanya learns that his fate is not to be a star and that a certain
resignation to his less glorious status will be required of him, but also
that there is a role for him, every bit as good as any other on that stage,
in that life, a role worth fighting to improve at every turn.

Shawn has made it clear that he does not regard Vanya's final attitude as one of resignation: "People say Chekhov is preaching some
kind of resignation, that you have to accept your miserable lot, that
there's a heroism in just keeping on. That's all so repugnant to me
that I don't believe it was Chekhov's point of view and if it was it re-
pels me."[41] There is a restless dialectic in all of Shawn's work—between enjoyment and offense, heroism and resignation, command-
ing and serving, writing and acting, acting and reacting—but there
is no simple way to line up all the terms of these dualisms. The con-
stellation must be read, not for any one image but for the possibility
of revealing all. André Gregory gives a sense of what is to be discovered in the work of Wallace Shawn in a comment he made about
working with Julianne Moore, who played Yelena in *Vanya on 42nd
Street*: "What's beautiful about stars is that they are who we want to

be. But great character actors dare to be who we can't admit we are. Julianne reveals things about herself and women in general that most actresses don't have the desire, or the daring, to do. In a way, she's both Beauty and the Beast."[42] Person A and Person B (Beauty and Beast? or Beast and Beauty?), always in dialogue, dare to entertain us with who we can't admit we are.

During the years he was working on *Vanya* and bringing Person A and Person B into such close contact, such that the writer's words could be submerged into the performance of a character so well-suited for him, Shawn was writing *The Designated Mourner*. The main character of this play would, at the crisis point of his life, give Person B's point of view on being riven and creative, in lines that are perhaps Shawn's most purely Chekhovian. The character is talking about having seen two pictures of a "very nice, charming, good-natured actor." In one he's kissing his wife (picture Shawn with his long-time companion, the writer Deborah Eisenberg), in the other he is kissing a woman who played his wife in a movie (picture Shawn with the actress Julianne Moore). His initial impression is that the actor must be lying in at least one of the pictures, but then he reverses his opinion:

➺ *Jesus Christ—that actor wasn't lying, I'm the one who's lying when I keep on insisting that I am the same person, the same person I was this morning, the same person I was yesterday. What's that all about? And why do I do it? What is the point? Why am I struggling every day to learn my lines, to once again impersonate this awful character—this terrible character whom I somehow believe I've been chosen to play, this terrible character whose particular characteristics are impossible to remember? I feel exactly the way a criminal must feel, trying so hard every day to stick to the story he was telling yesterday, the alibis, the lies, the interconnected details—it can't be done, you can't remember it all. So why do I keep trying to pretend to be the same, when in fact my body is simply a shell, waiting to be filled by one person and then another?*[43]

Ironically, the answer to his question is that one maintains a sense of individuality as an expression of freedom; liberalism presupposes some capacity and opportunity for self-creation. The character in this play, Shawn's most recent, takes steps to free himself from the liberal world, from freedom itself, and will demonstrate the awful consequence of such a move. Shawn's career as an anatomizer of the liberal self and as a Hollywood icon of reduced man comes together in his most recent works, both of which came out well after I had begun this book. What's present is epilogue.

THIS BOOK

This book is not a biography of Wallace Shawn, although this introduction might have given that impression. Indeed, I have offered here an interpretation of some facts of Shawn's life, but what follows is more or less a critical discussion of his writings, with a certain historical, or even new historicist, twist. The fact is, I don't know Wallace Shawn as a person, or, not very well, although I have met him a few times and have had several conversations with him about this project. When I first proposed to do this study, Shawn agreed to give me some unpublished writings and perhaps to answer some questions, and I made it clear to him that a biography was not at all what I had in mind. As I worked through his writings, however, I began to realize the necessity of making sense of the self-reflexive quality of the later works in terms of the author's life, or at least in terms of some distinctive belief structure within that life. In *My Dinner with André*, Shawn makes many of the circumstances of his friendship with André Gregory a matter of documentary record, all for a higher discursive purpose than mere self-exposure, of course, but along the way producing a certain kind of autobiographical text. *The Fever* incorporates certain components of its author-performer's life, and I believe that *Aunt Dan and Lemon* does, too, as his accompanying essay, "On the Context of the Play," shows. The earlier writings, including the nearly opaque first plays, are more heavily coded, but for that very reason seem to insist on a reading in terms of context. The apparent trend in Shawn's writing—from the cryptic to the translucent, from the private to the public—is certainly more subtle than just that, but the confused signs of concealment and self-exposure are obvious enough to draw attention to the conflicted will of the author.

The incorporation of the autobiographical into the dramatic was something I was wrestling with in an ongoing project concerning Eugene O'Neill, and it is a dynamic that is familiar to anyone who reads twentieth-century American drama, especially Tennessee Williams, Lillian Hellman, Arthur Miller, Edward Albee, LeRoi Jones, Spalding Gray, and a vast array of contemporary playwrights and performance artists. In some ways, Shawn is not typical of this group, although I think his plays speak eloquently to that tradition. Very little reading is necessary to indicate that he does not like to talk about his creative process, that he is private about the circumstances of his life and family, and that the trend toward the openly autobiographical in his writing had to do with his *losing* confidence in drama. After further consideration, I began to realize that the terms of liberalism, at the moment of its historical disappearance as a political denomination, would be useful to get at the central issues of Shawn's writing. That is, I have invoked a belief system, which had an evolving presence in American culture over the last quarter of a century and beyond, and fragments of which could be detected in Shawn's interviews and plays.

In his discussion of "The Intentional Fallacy," one of the seminal texts of New Criticism, William Wimsatt insists on a radical difference between the internality and the externality of a poem, and he argues that the internal is the only proper foundation for criticism, as it is distinct from the biographical or genetic inquiry.[44] Shawn's writing certainly challenges the idea of a strict separation between internal and external, and, in fact, I am not greatly concerned about staying on the right side of Wimsatt's law. But I think it is potentially useful to think about Shawn's quest for a sense of purpose in writing and in theater in terms of the parallel development of literary criticism.

Shawn was three when Wimsatt's essay was published. He became a reader and writer within a literary ethic that valued the autonomy of the text while celebrating the service of the literary imagination to the ideal of a free society. The instruction he received in the privacy of his liberal family was a lesson in self-maintenance, a criticism of the person itself: "My parents brought me up to believe that there was something terribly important called morality—an approach toward life which was based on the paradoxical concept of self-restraint (or the restraint of one part of the self by another part)." What he is describing here is a formalist method of self-criticism, infused with the sense of righteous duty that was typical of that trend in literary criticism. There is demonstrated here an alertness to the self as object—its symmetry, its balance, its frame—as an object of value. He continues:

•◇ *Instead of teaching me merely to be alert to the threat of potential enemies outside myself, I was instructed to practice, in addition, a sort of constant vigilance over my own impulses—even, at times, a subjugation of them, when certain abstract criteria of justice (which lived in my own mind) determined that someone else's interests should be allowed to prevail over my own desires. Morality, this fantastic and complicated system (which a good many of my friends were taught by their parents as well) was, as we first encountered it, a set of principles and laws.*[45]

These principles included the idea that each individual has certain inalienable rights, and at that time, poems also were presumed to have a right to life, liberty, and the pursuit of happiness, without being subject to other agendas. Shawn, comfortable in the delicate textures of the life that had been given to him, was an embodiment of the well-wrought urn. But growing older he was to encounter such things as the seven types of ambiguity and later the self-consuming artifact, the reader in the text, the discontents of criticism and *différance*—finally, too, the critical considerations of race, gender, and class. These would have an alienating effect; Shawn was radicalized. He progressively fought his way out of the gift-wrapping, out of the poem itself, and into the faces of those (readers, audience members) who had disarmed him with terms of art. Shawn's writing now utterly resists closure. It falls and falls, and in its fall it calls for solidarity, which Richard Rorty defines as "the imaginative ability to see strange people as fellow sufferers."[46] I hope that my own compassion has been sharpened by this project to the extent that I can produce such a mediation. If not . . . "Forgive me. I know you forgive me. I'm still falling."

ACKNOWLEDGMENTS

I am grateful to the many strange people who have been fellow sufferers in this project, beginning with my students and colleagues. Shawn's plays explore the limits of teaching, and they bring teaching to its limit, and I am grateful to my students for usually going the distance and helping me with those extremes. I will begin with Delta Giordano, formerly an undergraduate at the University of California, Santa Barbara, whose interest in Shawn helped me realize what a good topic it was. A production of *Aunt Dan and Lemon* on this campus—with Delta as Lemon, Meredith McMinn as Aunt Dan, and Ellen Margolis as the Mother—shaped my thinking about this writer more than anything else I have seen or read. My colleague Robert G. Egan, who directed that fine production, has helped me often with his thoughtful advice and criticism on this and other projects over the years.

I want to thank Justin Isaac Ward and Chris Schloemp, whose production of *The Fever* showed the work's complexity. Thomas Whitaker, Barbara Bosch, Una Chaudhuri, Joel Schechter have all been very generous with their assistance. Many others have contributed in specific ways, including Genevieve Anderson, Eva Rosin, Stanley Kauffmann, Jonathan Kalb, Marc Robinson, Maud Lavin, Stephanie Sandberg, Mark Simon, Pamela Casey, Steven Nagler, Laura Kalman, Lee Kalman, Newton Kalman, Randy Garr, Kathleen Dimmick, Geoffrey Aronow, Melinda Halpert, Jeffrey Jamison, Sparky Jamison, Karl Kohn, Andrew Kull, Cecily Johns, Carmen Rendon, Paul Faulstich, Susanne Faulstich, Katherine Saltzman-Li, Ursula, Lucy, and Harriet.

I thank Mark Strand for generously allowing me to use his interview of Shawn, John Lahr for his encouragement of this book, and Allen Shawn for allowing me to interview him. Earlier versions of the chapters on *The Fever* and *Aunt Dan and Lemon* appeared in *Theater* and the *Journal of American Drama and Theatre* respectively, and the editors have kindly given me permission to reprint.

The series editor, Robert Dawidoff, has assisted this project in one thousand ways. Janet Francendese, senior acquisitions editor at

Temple University Press, has added another thousand. I would also like to thank Jennifer French, Jeannine Klobe, and Richard Eckersley for their work on the book.

My greatest debt, of course, is to Wallace Shawn, who has by his writing and acting focused my imagination in wild ways I could not have foreseen. I thank him also for the several forms of direct assistance he has given me.

Finally, I owe an enormous amount to my family. I begin with my parents who have been very often in mind as I explored this subject. Eva and Ruthie have been constant inspirations to me. My deepest gratitude goes to Rena Fraden who has, by her imaginative abilities, made this project and this world far less strange to me.

Early Writings

Four Meals in May
and *The Old Man*

In 1983, Wallace Shawn looked back sixteen years to the writing of his first play, *Four Meals in May,* and said, "I thought it was the answer to the war in Vietnam. I thought they would rename the country after me when people saw that play!" Instead (goes the other half of this rueful joke on himself), those who read the script reacted "as if they'd been given a handful of blank pieces of paper."[1] Somewhere between blank paper and an answer to the war—the play seems in all seriousness to aim for both—is the pure potential of the one and the definitive crystallization of the other. Like all of Shawn's early plays, *Four Meals in May* is an enigma, a riddle that seems to contain revelation.

Each of these plays is a puzzle, but they are not (a) clever allegories, (b) Masonic mysteries, (c) literary in-jokes, or (d) Ionescan imitations. Instead, they are parabolic, in a literary and even geometrical sense. The parables of Jesus Christ defined for the disciples, who presumably had the key, some important moral and religious teachings that could not be written out in terms of rules or principles. The parable itself was to be compared with or "cast alongside of" (the root sense of the word) one's life, so that one's life might be held in its path by the story.

The geometrical parabola, too, curves around a focal point but never actually touches that point. Here it comes close to the focus, while there it stands almost infinitely distant. This geometrical analogy fits the enigmatic quality of Shawn's early plays. At times, they are as incomprehensible as "a handful of blank pieces of paper." At other times, they bring the world into focus with such clarity that an "answer to the war in Vietnam" seems within reach. Such insights as they offer do not come at the climax of the work when finally the mysteries are resolved and a new wisdom is declared. Rather, these works are concerned with the *curve* of understanding, both toward and away from enlightenment. They develop in time and demand of the audience a constant process of comparative measurement, of inquiry, in order to disclose their forms. Indeed, world measurement (the root sense of "geometry") might be proposed as their main work.

Four Meals in May presents a highly ordered pattern of scenes as a way of analyzing the radical disorder of this world. The four scenes, each centered on a meal, trace out in succession each of the members of a family tree:

(1) Francis ─┬─ (unnamed wife, now replaced by Miss Altman)

   (2) Peter ─┬─ (4) Emma

      (3) Felix ── (4) Dora (fiancée)

The first scene shows Francis Pulciano, in his late eighties, alone in his flat at breakfast. The second scene shows his son Peter, the same day, at lunch in his art gallery. He is accompanied by two assistants, but he communicates with the world mainly over the telephone. The third scene shows Peter's son, Felix, on the same day, at dinner in a monastery not far away. The stage is sometimes filled with a constantly shifting population of monks—some thirty-three names of different brothers are mentioned, and twenty actually speak.

Breakfast, lunch, and dinner trace out a succession of generations and occupations, from a solitary grandfather retired from his bookbinding business, to a thriving father, in the thick of the art business, to a despairing son, in retreat from the world and in spiritual crisis.

The fourth scene takes place several years later at a hotel restaurant near the airport. Here, Emma, the wife of the art dealer, and Dora, the ex-fiancée of the monk, chance to meet after lunch. Dora is here to say goodbye to her uncle, the hotel owner, and Emma awaits the next flight out that will send an otherwise unidentified ambassador on his way home. With the departure of Dora to catch her plane, the play ends.

Each of these scenes places more detail into the bare family tree. The grandfather in the first scene, over his breakfast of cereal and orange juice, coffee and toast, tells of his devotion to Felix and Dora. The fact that the former has recently run off to the monastery troubles him greatly. Since retirement, he has found himself with less and less to do, more detached from his own past, progressively less able to read or watch television or listen to the radio. In this monologue, he tells of how his senses have begun cruelly to betray him. The needs of his life are attended to by a distant and never-seen caretaker, Miss Altman. The one delight of his life has been his affectionate interest in Felix and Dora, and now that they are gone from him (Dora having moved away from the city), he faces the decline of his powers in gruesome isolation. Recently, he recalls, in a rare moment of sleep, he dreamt of Dora and Felix, soon to be married. Now that that dream is shattered, he has little to live for except the arrival of Miss Altman, who will "sit on the kitchen stool and polish the silver and tell me what her sister's husband has said".[2]

Peter, in his art gallery, embodies success—the well-dressed entrepreneur, sure of his resources, vigorous, confident of his decisions. He makes expert use of his telephone to confirm one deal, to parry another, and finally to make arrangements for the weekend in consultation with his wife. All of this he accomplishes with much dexterity while eating a ham sandwich, salad, and orange and drinking beer. Peter's disconnection from his father is suggested in one brief moment when he asks his wife if she has heard from Miss Altman: "She said she'd call us two days ago. She's very lazy, isn't she? Or I suppose it's old age in her case" (25). Felix's name comes up only twice, and then only incidentally. Peter shows much more concern about a family servant, Felicia, who suffers from some illness.

While Francis, in the first scene, creates in the labored detail of his monologue a self-portrait of a life narrowing down to nothingness, Peter's scene works more like a Ruth Draper monologue, like "The Italian Lesson," indirectly giving an almost comical impression of a glib operator in the commerce of art and society. The use of the telephone in this scene conveys exactly the technological detachment from the world that is necessary for his manipulations. The audience never sees any of the art works to which he refers, and the suggestion is strong that he does not really see them either, that their importance to him exists solely in the market value. Thus, while Francis knowingly suffers from a sensory detachment from the world for physical reasons, Peter, too, lives at a distance from the world, hardly seeing or tasting or hearing anything other than the sensations of his will in action.

The third scene introduces the son, Felix, whose breaking off of his engagement and retreat to the monastery form the only suspense raised by the play so far. Why has he done these things? Most of this scene takes place against a background of activity, groups of monks engaged in various discussions before and during their supper. These conversations have mainly to do with the interactions and petty economies of the monastery, and Felix, who is a newcomer, is drawn into these affairs only sporadically. Meanwhile, in a series of private conversations in the foreground of the scene, he encounters three remarkable monks who offer very different sorts of instruction and counsel to him. The first shows him a new invention he has devised, a pair of ordinary looking spectacles, not to correct impaired vision but to improve normal vision: "The eye of man need not be limited, Brother Felix. Is there any reason why I may not see the world as a hawk sees it from the sky or as a fly sees it from inside a coffee cup?" (34). Felix is thrilled by the potential of enhanced contact with the sensory world.

After an exchange with a group of monks in which Felix protests at their assumption that his university education should make him more qualified than others to comment on a dream interpretation, he is taken aside by a monk who insists on addressing him as an intellectual despite Felix's declaration that he is not. This embittered monk preys upon what seems to be a latent sense of isolation in Felix. Here, too, the monk predicts, Felix will never feel a sense of belonging among this "herd of pigs" because his intellectual nature will not be able to stand the solitude. Finally, Felix responds in a way that silences the cynical monk and addresses the question of why he has chosen to enter the cloistered life: "We should expect to be solitary, if that's what befalls us. And really, I would have thought it was axiomatic that we should seek comfort from our loneliness in prayer and in our work, not in the company of others. And loneliness, in any case, I would have thought, is distance from God—is it not?—and not distance from men" (44). The victory is hollow, however, since the monk's silence confirms the loneliness of one capable of such clever rationalizations.

Another monk relieves him from the strain of this conflict, expressing pity for the cynical monk's misery. He then questions Felix, who claims that the despair he had earlier felt, which had left him unwilling or unable to eat, has now lessened. This brother then carries to an extreme the argument that Felix has just used. The pain of the monastic life must simply be endured and even celebrated because a monk lives for God, not the self. When Felix expresses his doubts ("Why does He send me one affliction after another, so that my heart is dizzy with hatred and sickness, so that I can barely go on with my life from day to day?" [49]), the monk calls him foolish for not rejoicing in these tortures. Those others, who have been there longer, would never have experienced the same anguish:

➥ *And why not? Because they've never even dreamed of the joys you have tasted in your life, that God has put in your mouth for you to taste. Don't you see? God's beautiful world, Felix! The world! You have experienced it. And do you still not see what He is doing? He sends you these pains to wound you and scar you as you make your journey out of the world, so that you won't ever forget—ever—that you once were there.* (49–50)

Felix can make no response to this. At last, the Father of the order comes in to say "Food, food, my children!" and the monks gather around for their supper.

Felix has tasted of life and love and has renounced those satisfactions for the world of self-denial. His grandfather has lost the physical capacity for sensory enjoyment; his father indulges vigorously in the world of sensations (aesthetics), but it is unclear whether he really tastes, sees, hears, or only responds habitually. Felix has put himself in a place where he must perpetually experience the loss of those sensations. And so these characters are all, for different reasons, cut off from the phenomenal world. The father and grandfather seem hopelessly locked within their conditions, either by physical incapacity or by self-satisfied ignorance. What is unknown is whether the son, Felix, has resigned or transformed himself on this May day, at a time of transformation and blooming.

If a series or progression is being traced out in these first three scenes, then its principle ought to become evident in the fourth scene. This does not happen, at least not in any obvious way. In fact, the fourth scene leaps several years forward in time, returns once again to lunchtime, and turns to the nonlinear figures in the family tree, Felix's mother, Emma, and his ex-fiancée, Dora. Unlike the earlier scenes, which each had a single focal character, the internal structure of this scene is comparative, as first one group is heard and then the other. The restaurant is divided in two by a wall, and until the end, there is no interaction.

Dora's effusive expressions of gratitude and affection for her uncle, the hotel owner, open the scene. One point of contrast to the earlier scenes is brought out at once. In all of these scenes of characters eating, Dora is the only one heard to express pleasure over the food she is eating. In the first scene, Francis remarks how his sense of taste now deceives him and makes his food taste bad. Peter expresses thanks for a gift of some strawberry preserves, but otherwise makes no comment at all on his food. The monks in the monastery conclude the scene by protesting the unappetizing food prepared by a substitute cook. Dora, on the other hand, gushes with praise for the "beautiful, *most* ravishing brunches" (58) she has enjoyed during her visit, as well as the "perfect coffee, which is to be found only here in the whole world" (58). When she is brought a pastry, her eyes fill with tears at the taste.

In contrast, Emma, who has chosen this restaurant to entertain the ambassador until he can catch the next plane, laboriously explains that while she has not been here lately, she has heard that it is still a fine restaurant. But when it comes time for her to order, she requests two poached eggs on toast and a small dish of spinach. She later mentions that she is on a special diet but then gripes at length about waiters who typically resist her wishes to order a few boiled carrots or toast without butter.[3] Meanwhile, on the opposite side of the stage, Dora recounts to her uncle, in images of taste, the memory of Felix's voice: "The clearest winter's wine cannot taste so sweet; the sweetest summer's night's liqueur cannot so enchant the mind as does that low, hesitant sound" (67). She recalls his unfolding of the secrets of his life to her, but not in terms of what he disclosed to her. Rather, she luxuriates in the remembered sensations — the wind, his white pajamas, her trembling. Her diction gains a peculiar floridity as she recalls her timid excitement at his self-revelation (reminiscent of Hedda Gabler's fixation on Ejlert Lövborg and the secrets he has shared with her):

➡ *I felt I didn't want to hear the things he so grimly, so softly, tried to say. But behind their curtains, the mansions of my spirit streamed with brilliant light; their chandeliers burned bright with all the thousand candles of pride. I was gay with pride; my face was hot; pride had filled me with bliss. I was proud because I was there, in my beautiful green dress, there in the golden presence of all that was private and amazing and marvelous.* (68)

These are the terms she recalls for the man who left her for a monastery. Soon, her cousin Michael arrives to take her to the airport. At the end of the scene, Emma is excited to discover Dora in the restaurant. The mystery of Felix's escape to the monastery is touched on briefly. Emma expresses regret that Dora has not stayed to visit Felix at the monastery, quickly adding: "But it's a hateful place, of course" (77). Dora agrees, and then in a flurry of activity, with waiters and porters carrying her baggage (all somewhat reminiscent of the end of *The Cherry Orchard*), she departs. Her uncle quickly returns, collects a forgotten umbrella, gives it to a lingering waiter to be taken to the car, then, as they both exit in opposite directions, the play ends in a blackout.

This, then, is the play about which Shawn wrote in the late 1970s: "I felt it was my statement about the war in Vietnam. I also felt that if people saw this play, the effect of those four seasons following one after the other would be to induce in them a sort of an enlightenment."[4] The repetition of the linkage between this play and the war in Vietnam suggests strongly that more weight is to be placed on *Four Meals in May* than simply to regard it as a handful of realist sketches of a dislocated family in some sort of crisis about contact with the material world. The reference to the four seasons helps make sense of certain elements in the scenes. The scenic direction at the beginning of the first scene refers to the dull white light that shines on Francis, in the winter of his life. A warmer and brighter light shines on the outburst of life in the art gallery, where new deals and plans are being made. A brilliant white light shines on the full flower of the monastery scene, and the dinner scene at its conclusion evokes the harvest. Finally, the departures of the final scene, set in a less bright but warmer light, associate it with autumn. If enlightenment is to follow upon this sequence, it must come at the end of the year. Will the pattern of dislocations and broken hopes then continue? (Is the war in Vietnam inevitable?) Or is there some resolution or instruction proposed here that will take the enlightened spectator out of the cycle and perhaps lead to a resolution of such problems as war.

Shawn's statements, and the play itself, suggest that some still greater weight might be placed on this collection of scenes, and the word "enlightenment" suggests a religious or metaphysical dimension. And yet the play finally resists most logical efforts to work out its terms. The third scene might be said to analyze the failure of Christian religion to work out the problem of man's personal relation to the sensory world, and the second scene might then be construed as an analysis of the failure of art to come to terms with the sensory world. But what then of the first scene? Francis was a bookbinder. Are we to read the demise of learning in this? And the final scene? . . . Or perhaps the play should be read allegorically. No evidence is given externally or internally as to where the play is set, but Italian surnames predominate. Perhaps in Peter's thriving art gallery we are to see a cynical image of St. Peter's Roman Catholic Church, while Francis might somehow be taken for St. Francis, and Felix as St. Felix, founder of another order of monks, or as any one of a number of antipopes. Felix = happiness, Dora = gift, Emma = Bovary? . . . surely, this way madness lies.

Perhaps, instead, an Eastern conceptual framework might be proposed. Dora, who alone *tastes* her food, perhaps exemplifies the disciple of Zen, or other sorts of Buddhism, who has attained the ability to live within the phenomenal world nonhabitually, in touch with its sensations. Lao-tse's warning that the five senses detract from one's nature, and Chuangtse's notion that life is a rotation through the four seasons, might also be brought to bear on this play. Just how far might this line of interpretation be taken? In conversation with her uncle, it comes out that Dora's cousin, who is to take her to the airport, customarily wears a yellow waistcoat and drives a yellow car. Dora has been staying in the Yellow Room of the hotel—with a canary. The scene she recalls, in which she was "gay with pride" in the "golden presence of all that was private and amazing and marvelous" about Felix, was interrupted by the grandfather, Francis, who took the occasion to tell them the story of a famous clown and the "Yellow Jugglers." In the first scene of the play, Francis had recalled a visit of Dora and Felix in which Dora wore a yellow dress, bonnet, and veil. And so on. All of this rings with especial emphasis since colors have hardly been mentioned in other contexts. Is the reason for this to be found in the color symbolism of the mandala, or in the Tibetan Book of the Dead, or in some other such master key?

I put this question directly to Shawn, and his answer helped pinpoint the exact difficulty of reading this and his other early plays. He had read the Taoist philosophers at Harvard, had taken a yoga class or two while teaching in India, but no esoteric source was used for this play, or for any other play he had written. Indeed, he said he had no recollection that the color yellow was used in any significant way, not even as a generalized reference to Eastern religion. Without being the least bit coy about it, Shawn suggested that he wrote at this time from an intuitive, as well as a logical, sense of rightness. Certainly the color scheme might be read as a means of making internal associations within the play. Late in 1986, Shawn spoke of the odd sources of inspiration he has sometimes received: "When I've seen a painting that has overwhelmed me, I've thought, 'Oh my God, maybe there's something in this that will give me a clue to how to organize my plays.'"[5] So, one might argue, while Felix's "golden presence" has turned to a monk's drabness, Dora has retained the brightness of yellow vitality, and both stand opposite to the navy blue worn by Peter. Beyond this, however, the formal system (if there is one) is difficult to figure, and the disproportionate emphasis on yellow in association with Dora and Felix (before his retreat from the world) is hard to interpret with any specificity.

All these efforts at a logical solution to the play's meaning seem to run out well before the goal is achieved, suggesting that the play engages its reader or audience in a translogical sort of thinking. Shawn actually wrote the play, which he calls a still-life and also possibly the strangest play he has written, while on a trip to Italy from Oxford. There for the first time he saw the frescoes of Fra Angelico and Renaissance architecture. He implies that he regarded himself in this context as a sort of Henry James, someone who could channel the profound experience of art into an intellectual, aesthetic message that could change the world.[6] But the message is oblique. Like a *koan* or a Nō play, *Four Meals in May* might be said to put the audience into a frame of meditation that is specifically aimed at transcendence of ordinary consciousness. The play gives the audience four moments in a world that has gone wrong in some subtle way. Each scene (or meal) supplies enough ingredients to generate some thinking about what is wrong, although no single problem is quite defined, and the series of scenes ends with a glimpse of happiness, in the person of Dora, but the key to that happiness is also not quite defined. This sort of hesitant, absolutely undogmatic approach to the analysis of human problems is to be found throughout much of Shawn's career, and especially in the early plays.

On the other hand, perhaps this play might be understood as the culmination of a frustrated quest romance, a *Portrait of the Artist as a Young Man,* with Felix as a sort of Stephen Daedalus. The Ulyssean Peter might be interpreted as a cynical portrayal of William Shawn—the broker of art and society, the father temporarily absent from the imagination of the son, as the grandfather is absent from the concerns of the father. Betrayal of "the old man" forms a linking theme between the first three scenes of the play, which work as a sort of tragic trilogy, exploring the fated catastrophes within a lineage.

John Lahr quotes Jacob Brackman, Shawn's college friend and a *New Yorker* writer, saying that Brackman modeled the character of David Staebler, in *The King of Marvin Gardens* (1972), on Shawn, describing him as "this little underground man who sort of saw everything and had it all nailed down but was keeping you at arm's length all the time."[7] The Staebler character is a radio monologuist, and the movie opens in the midst of one of his evidently autobiographical ruminations on "the old man," his grandfather, a man who exists obtrusively within the lives of his grandchildren, until they take revenge on him. How far might one take these lines of interpretation, and in which direction, toward the *Oresteia* or toward *The Life and Times of Wallace Shawn*? As if to answer this question, the character in Brackman's film says in the second radio monologue:

➥ *No one reads any more. I have been deprived of my literary right, and I crave an audience. The form of the tragic autobiography is dead, or will be soon, along with most of its authors. Goodbye, written word. So I have chosen this form, radio, to author my life, not because my life is particularly worthy, but because it is hopefully, comically unworthy. Besides, tragedy isn't top forty, which is just as well.*[8]

Four Meals in May was written in 1967, then somewhat revised in 1969, at which time Shawn also wrote his second play *The Old Man* while on a trip to Ireland. He was now putting to the test his new resolve to become a writer, and his second effort goes immediately to the outer limits of what anyone might identify as a play. This short and oblique monodrama might best be compared with the first scene of the earlier play. Here, too, an old man speaks of his present state of decrepitude and recalls images of pleasures past, along with dreams and bits of fantasy. He speaks from a hospital bed at night time and occasionally reflects on conditions in the hospital, but other nights and other beds, especially in hotels, also figure in his reminiscences. All of these memories are fragmentary and many are vague, so that finally it is impossible to assemble a portrait of this unnamed man as a character. The appearance of the script conveys its fragmentary, nondramatic organization—each of the forty-four reflections, or *pensées,* occupies its own page, and several consist of only a line or two. More than half of this script is blank. An anonymous hotel clerk and waiter are the only other human beings who get specific mention—and then only briefly and incidentally—while a variety of others are recalled only in collective form.

Some of the old man's memories contain sensory details that indicate one man's experiences; others suggest that he speaks from a collective or transcendental perspective. The shortest of all the fragments points to the possibility of the latter: "I was a human being." He twice speaks directly of death and at another point seems to refer to a transmigration out of the corporeal state. Referring to unidentified others, he says: "But I had to leave them sometimes, although they were good. I would stand near one of them, as he showed me his face and words before a meal, dressed in the clothes he had decided to wear, and then I would leave my body near him and go, suddenly."[9] In the next fragment, he recalls falling in the darkness: "I would travel through the fields where meteors grew like pumpkins, and then plummet through pure black, in the icy cold" (22).

Other fragments touch on a mundane level of existence: a memory of the texture of yellow cake, his dislike of a light orange color, a splinter in stockinged feet. Eight or ten of the fragments, beginning with the first, build from some observation of nature—an ant biting a blade of grass, fruit rotting, a mosquito smashed on a window. What links these, tenuously, is the impression that living things maintain a precarious hold on the little bit of vitality that is somehow contained within them. These reflections seem to correspond with a series of impressions about human blood, including an horrendous image of diving into a pool of blood. One particularly philosophical fragment draws these impressions together: "Nature keeps what is red inside. Occasionally she shows it forth—a clump of strawberries. But most of the time—within, within" (30).

Opposite these encounters with brute existence are a series of impressions that touch only on surfaces, such as a memory of the skin of young girls. He seems to recall watching sex films and having some sort of intimate relations with others, who are described as "good," but essentially his memories seem abstracted from the living. What survives at this terminal point of his existence is an extremely tattered remnant of experiences, ideas, impulses. And for every memory of sheets and blankets, smooth skin and folds of cloth, there are antithetical images, described in the present tense, of worms and ants, crushed bodies, and the skin of fallen fruit grown thin with age and split open.

The indistinct details of this old man's life appear against a background of an almost limitless replicability, the vanishing of the individual within a multiplicity that can be represented only in powers of ten, such as the ten thousand bed sheets he has used in his life: "The organ which a girl shows to us in a film seems to us like twenty thousand others. But when she was a child, in her home, and gently touched it in her bed in her wall-papered room, it was only her own which she loved. So we say, nature is plenteous, gives not one thing, but many things, a multiplicity endless and sweet" (16). Then, again, he envisions a hundred worms coming to the surface, and ten thousand ants, and near the end, he sees himself standing beneath a tree when a pear falls. As he turns to look, all of the pears fall from the branches: "But when the pears strike the ground, they are dying birds" (44). Somewhere between the one and the many human existence takes place, and it operates always in a tension between the perfect, containing surface and the force of nature that threatens to pierce or break open that surface and release the vital essence.

Given the epigrammatic quality of some of these fragments and the frank treatment of death as a fact of nature, including human nature, without any mention of Judeo-Christian teleologies, it is possible to hear in *The Old Man* an echo of Stoic philosophy. It is as if a latter-day Marcus Aurelius, now much older, were to meditate on a far more thoroughly corrupted existence: "Turn it [the body] inside out, and see what kind of thing it is; and when it has grown old, what kind of thing it becomes, and when it is diseased." Shawn creates in this play the speculative condition in which one might meditate on death as a fact of existence, or, as the philosopher advises: "Consider thyself to be dead, and to have completed thy life up to the present time; and live according to nature the remainder which is allowed thee."[10]

The final section (the forty-fourth) is also the longest and represents something of a departure from the pattern of the others. Here the play returns to its own setting, a man in bed on a moonlit night, but now postulates that setting at a mythic distance. It begins, "Whenever I travel far, I end up in the moonlit town" (45). Here he imagines a dusty, disordered, colorless community, pale in the washy light of the moon—white houses, white dogs, white milk bottles, white faces. The last sentence seems to call for an awakening from this death in life: "Then a marching band in red uniform comes down the main street, and we all wake up, put on our dressing gowns, and crowd to the windows to watch" (45).

These early plays are distinctly modernist in their violation of expectations about plot and form, in their allusiveness, and, especially, in their fragmentary quality. At the same time, they have what might be described as a paleographic quality, as if they were tokens of some highly elaborate, but lost, cultural system or form—a ritual, say, which would make each specific element of these scripts somehow essential. And in the best tradition of parable, they work as strangely unforgettable testimony to mysterious truth.

The "Plays"

The Hotel Play,
The Family Play, and
The Hospital Play

During the next two years, Shawn wrote three plays—*The Hotel Play, Play in Seven Scenes* (later retitled *The Family Play*), and *The Hospital Play.* These three "plays" make wildly different gestures toward dramatic form, but each also seems aimed at outraging the very concept of "play." *The Hotel Play* (1970) he later described as "a play with sixty characters about a hotel in the tropics. . . . There is a sort of malevolent hotel clerk at the center of this rather swirling tropical work." In *The Family Play* (1970), "a rather strange and passionate family—mother, father, and two daughters—live far away from everyone, in the mountains." Of *The Hospital Play* (1971) Shawn said what was quoted near the beginning of this book, simply that it "has a lot of weeping and vomiting."[1]

His comments on the plays, offered for an edition of *Contemporary Dramatists* during the mid-1970s, could hardly be confused with a producer's hype. Indeed, Shawn seems eager to undermine any illusion that these might be plays in a conventional sense, but he recalls that they were given to many to be read and were submitted to theaters for possible production. What he later called a "maniacal confidence" propelled him through any doubts that might have surfaced when he found that only two of his friends liked these plays.[2] They epitomize the *wanting to* and *wanting not to* write plays that, as a tension, defines much of Shawn's career. The same statement for *Contemporary Dramatists* contains his declaration of commitment only to those imaginary situations that "truly and totally absorb" him to the extent that

➥ *I have to take myself as I am, and if what I care about at that certain time is two elderly women having their tea, then that must be my subject, and if what it is at another time is a strange group masturbating in a dingy room, then I must write about that. And about each scene, there is always one true story to tell, I think; there is always one and only one thing which happened. . . . I'm not sure whether it's vanity or modesty that makes me assume that when I'm telling the most truth I can possibly tell about the thing that truly seems most important to me, I'm giving people something that they need to know.*[3]

The logic of serving his own needs to serve the needs of others puts him at a distance from those who would betray their values, falsify their ideas, or prostitute the art.

But the paired (or blurred) terms "vanity" and "modesty" mark a tension in the writer's attitude that has been frequently observed by writers on Shawn. He himself has recently said, "I'm very pretentious. I accepted that a long time ago," adding, "I rather boringly try to think through the details of my life as if it mattered."[4] So vanity and modesty, arrogance and self-effacement, cruelty to be kind, these paradoxes trace a tonal mode that is specific to Shawn. These early plays represent three extraordinary explorations of this mode.

With money he had saved as a teacher of English, Latin, and drama at a private school, Shawn traveled to Bequia, in the West Indies, and wrote *The Hotel Play:* "It was off-season, and for most of the three months I stayed there I was the only guest in this hotel. It was a strange island and a strange experience. At the time I thought I was a certain kind of writer; my first two plays were almost pure prose. But I soon learned it wasn't possible for me to write that way on that island."[5] What emerged was almost literally kaleidoscopic—many small, colorful fragments dazzlingly packed within an event that lasts little more than an hour.

The play begins at dawn with the Hotel Clerk and The Girl Who Plays the Game, undressed to their underwear in the clerk's bedroom, playing a game with wooden counters. She says "Dying," and he replies, "Yes. Everlasting—life."[6] She says "Knives," and he says, "Oranges," and with each term they put down a counter. She says, "Mouth"; he says, "Teeth." An enigmatic game that begins with

"Dying," it ends when the girl is out of counters, and then they madly embrace. When his embrace is not tight enough, she demands, "Why don't you let me die?" (10) and strikes him with her fists. The passion and fury of their engagement give way to her nausea and extreme desperation at the recognition that she is to leave on the next train. When the clerk draws the window curtain and lets in the cold morning light, the emotion drains from the scene, and they turn to the mundane tasks of preparing for the day. She dresses; he shaves. All of this takes place in about two minutes, and yet it forms a key to the extreme measures taken in the play, the bringing together of sex and death, mutual consumption and throwing up.

Shawn also introduces here the juxtaposition of the surreal and the mundane within "the games people play," as in the plays of Edward Albee, or the crossing of dream and violent waking, as in the later plays of Strindberg. Indeed, this play might well be compared with *The Dream Play,* about which Strindberg wrote: "Upon an insignificant background of real life events the imagination spins and weaves new patterns: a blend of memories, experiences, pure inventions, absurdities, and improvisations." Shawn's play introduces a similarly vast number and diversity of characters, and they have a similarly mutable reality to that which Strindberg describes: "The characters split, double, redouble, evaporate, condense, fragment, cohere. But one consciousness is superior to them all: that of the dreamer. For him there are no secrets, no inconsistencies, no scruples, no laws. He neither condemns nor acquits, only relates."[7] The hotel clerk functions here as the dreamer, but his implication in the events that unfold is more significant. He is a rather maleficent figure who toys with the hotel guests with the sort of impunity that only a servant can enjoy. From the unseen Miss Altman of *Four Meals in May* to the various waiters mentioned in *The Old Man,* Shawn has developed a mythology of the servant as a controlling figure, not unlike that which Strindberg evolved in such plays as *The Pelican* and *Miss Julie.* One fragment of *The Old Man* portrays a hotel clerk, "a sharp dealer," protesting the old man's sudden intention to check out.[8] Leaving that hotel takes on the resonance of dying, as it does

tender, helps shift the focus from one character to another, so that each is highlighted momentarily in a sort of vignette, and each of the vignettes helps obliquely to define the clerk as a central, largely silent figure. Shawn has said: "It's a play about a lonely seducer. By having so many people, you can detect the loneliness of the character."[9] The bar scenes are the photographic negative to the positive image of the first, third, and fifth sections of the play. While the latter are unnerving and perverse, the former are more or less wildly funny. In fact, the comedy of the crowd scenes is reminiscent of the sort of West Indian tourism humor to be found in a work such as Herman Wouk's *Don't Stop the Carnival*. The vignette style, based on character gags, albeit very twisted ones, is often not far from that found in such works as the Blake Edwards/Peter Sellers film *The Party* (1968) or even the television comedy series *Laugh-In* (ca. 1967–69).

The third section, which consists of three more of the blackout sketches, shows the clerk insinuating himself into the privacy of another woman, this time a married woman, under the pretext of fixing the haywire electrical system. As a clerk he has seemingly unlimited access to the guests' lives and can do as he pleases with them. This is in contrast with the He and She of the other sketch in this section, in which a couple's adulterous attempt to make love is suddenly interrupted by her husband, father, brother-in-law, and grandfather. Here, at the very center of the play, is the germinal scene of all bedroom farce, toward which, on one level, the play converges. People are seen to behave ludicrously when they get caught up in breaking society's rules about sexual relations. On another level, though, the play might be said to diverge from this central scene, extracting various elements of the farce—passion, the absurd, violence, sudden shifts—in order to explore them in isolation or in unfamiliar combinations. The clerk, who can shape these scenes according to his fantasies, who can know these characters' foibles and exploit them as he likes, might be seen as a figure of this playwright of deviant farce.

The last section of the play begins with the clerk and The Girl Who Broke the Bowl in his bedroom, where he is attempting to overcome her resistance and make love. Eventually, she responds to his caresses, and, as in the first scene of the play, a pause and shift of tone indicate the before and after of their lovemaking. Consummation of the sex act is not structurally a part of the classic sex-farce, which takes its energy from the frustration of all plans and desires toward that end. But this play, at the beginning, middle, and end, brings consummation, however elliptical, onto the stage. The first comes out of the first girl's sense of "dying" at the thought of leaving the clerk, and it leads to her feeling very cold, dressing to go, and his shaving. The second bridges the He-She classic sex-farce scene. The third reverses the terms of the first. She resists his advances, then gives in, then pulls away, mysteriously, to shave. Here is the shocking and enigmatic climax of this scene, and of the play:

CLERK. . . . So lovely. So good. I want to make love to you now. Yes. Yes. (*Pause.*) Are you awake? (*Long silence.*)

GIRL. (*In a slightly different voice.*) No. I'm sleeping. No. Get off. (*She gets up.*)

CLERK. Why? I— Wait—

GIRL. Please—please— (*She sits down at the table with the mirror. He stays on the bed.*) Not now. I'm sweating.

CLERK. You're— (*Long, long silence.*)

GIRL. Are you sleeping? (*He doesn't answer. Silence.*) What? What? I'm hot, I'm hot. It's time to shave. Here's my razor. (*She turns off the lamp. Total darkness.*) What if it slips?

CLERK. (*Sleepily.*) Careful.

GIRL. (*In darkness.*) Whoops—Oh—God— (*Silence.*) (41)

When the lights return in the second scene, her body lies under a bloody sheet on the sofa.

This is a mirror inversion of the more romantically conventional opening scene. The first girl was cold, and this one is hot; light was brought into the room when the curtains were opened in the first scene, and here the light is turned off; the clerk shaved in the first scene, and here it is the girl who "shaves." The first scene is an *aubade*, or song of lovers parting at dawn, while the latter scene places the clerk/playwright figure into an uncertain relation to the "song" that is being sung. What exactly has happened in the dark? The scene turns opaque at this moment, blacked out from consciousness. The slowness and long silences submerge the scene in the no-mindedness of a meditation or dream, but at the critical moment the dreamer's relation to the dream cannot be fathomed. Does the clerk/dreamer/playwright bear some responsibility for the accidental death ("Whoops"), as well as for the perversion of the farce that has occurred? Farce is about learning to stick to the rules; this play is about a slippage from those rules. Farce is about denial of the object of fantasy; this play grants the dreamer the desired object, and then shows the horrifying results.

When the fifth section resumes, the clerk is checking his account books and noting the supplies of shellfish. The girl's body lies under a sheet, and the room is spattered with blood. Hungry, he checks the icebox and finds nothing better than a can of peaches that he decides to eat anyway. Another appetite receives poor satisfaction. Blackout. In the final scene of the play, now in the depths of the night, the clerk decides to sleep. After a glance at the girl's body, he makes his only acknowledgment of her presence: "How disgusting. How horrible" (42). But then, as he turns out the light and looks out the window, he approaches the scene of dreaming. He sees by moonlight the clouds, leaves, birds rushing about in the wind:

➤ *And out there at the end, by the driveway, the pumpkins! No! The pumpkins are tumbling down the road! They're tumbling as fast as little carts! God! The pumpkins! . . . —It's really time for some sleep. It's time to sleep.* (He sits down in a chair.) *The pumpkins—the pumpkins, tumbling down the road. . . .* (He closes his eyes, and his head falls back. The curtain slowly falls.) (42)

The clerk's head falling back provides the only referent for this strange image of the pumpkins—heads freely, quickly moving, detached from their bodies by razor or dream. Then, too, perhaps this vision is a realization of one or both of the first words of the play—"Dying" and "Yes—Everlasting life." In the game, the clerk has chosen the latter.

The Hotel Play was produced at last in 1981, in a production at the La Mama Experimental Theatre Club. John Ferraro, who had come to know Shawn in the early 1970s when they both worked with

André Gregory's Manhattan Project, was the director, and it was his idea to persuade Ellen Stewart to sponsor the production. Shawn had expressed the wish that each part be cast with a different actor, rather than relying upon the usual gymnastics of double- and triple-casting. Ferraro, who saw it as "a one-character play with seventy-nine other people around," agreed, and so they appealed to Actors Equity for a special provision that would allow them to offer a token $100 payment for each Equity actor during the two-week run.[10] The agreement specified that they would limit the four-hundred-seat theater to no more than ninety-nine audience members, so this quickly became a hot ticket.

The cast, which was surely one of the larger in off-Broadway history, was also one of the more notable, with such actors as Griffin Dunne (as the clerk), Elizabeth McGovern (as the first girl), Linda Hunt, Tom McDermott, Mark Linn-Baker, and Larry Pine; and such nonactors as the writers Wendy Wasserstein, Christopher Durang, Ed Bullins, Dominick Dunne, and Ann Beattie; *New Yorker* cartoonists Jim Stevenson and Frank Modell; and many other luminaries. Maura Moynihan, daughter of the New York State senator, was The Girl Who Broke the Bowl. Shawn and his long-time companion Deborah Eisenberg also played roles. In an interview at the time of the production, Shawn said that he and Ferraro just started calling all the actors they knew to ask if they would like to be in the show. Finally, they even had to turn down some who were willing. Shawn identified one danger of this sort of showcase of showcases: "It will only be satisfying if the play becomes more important than the event."[11] In an "Author's Note," written for the Dramatists Play Service edition of the play, Shawn warned against the twin problems of actors overplaying their brief parts and the scenes losing focus within the general mayhem. He quotes the director's warning to the La Mama cast: "This is a play, not a party. Do your scene, do the play, don't perform for the audience" (7).

In the interview, Shawn and Ferraro agreed that the only way to get a show produced is by knowing somebody. This production became, then, a great display of "whom do you know." As such, the event extended to the audience. As Frank Rich put it, in his generally bemused review of this "mad theatrical stunt": "Even if you loathe *The Hotel Play*—and be warned, you might—you're unlikely to get totally bored. At the very least, you can kill the time reading the cast biographies in the voluminous program."[12] Indeed, the who's who business must have permeated the audience of friends and family and others who knew how to get a ticket. The production inevitably helped define a community, if only an extended circle of friends, by bringing all of these people, cast and audience, together into a public space, like a hotel, where they might become the substance of a strange but true dream.

The other play Shawn completed in the West Indies was the short *Play in Seven Scenes,* which was later retitled *The Family Play.* He had come to believe that he could only write when far from anybody he knew, and this was his reason for spending three months in Bequia.[13] While *The Hotel Play* in many ways "came from" this particular remote location, *The Family Play* ventured far from even this distant world to a place abstractly distant, described simply as "a valley far away." Here, just four people live, a husband and wife (seventy-five and forty-six) and their two daughters (seventeen and eleven). These people are only seen inside their house where they play out the final, untested variations on myths of the home. This is a play of the happy home gone nightmarishly bad when the children verge on adulthood.

This play comes back to the subject of family, now in an intensely concentrated state, in contrast to the refracted family in *Four Meals in May.* Here the family lives all too much together, on top of one another, and the baroque forms of politeness they have evolved to allow this concentration finally do not conceal the violence among them. The family name is Llaendrens, but the proper names are not Welsh—Karl and Andrá for the parents, Mála and Yúlè for the daughters. These are names of strangeness, of distance from the known, and they speak English in a way that sounds like a translation from a difficult language. Their world has characteristics of a quaint, bucolic setting, but notably softened, such as one finds in juvenile literature—more *Heidi* than Hardy.

The plot is at once simple and enigmatic—a doctor comes for a monthly visit, staying through the night. His presence triggers a jealous competition between the older daughter, Mála, and the younger daughter, Yúlè, who is just becoming aware of her sexual potential. The mother and father are gradually losing authority over the daughters, and the father is also losing power over the mother. The doctor makes some sort of advances on Yúlè, who at first resists then draws him on. Meanwhile, the father makes unsuccessful advances on the mother, and Mála seethes with jealousy and desire. The doctor leaves. The father suffers some sort of seizure. The two sisters are ambiguously reunited at the end. This summary is rather vague because the play touches only obliquely on events, instead concentrating on the subtextual, subconscious, indeed barely apprehensible, drama that is played out among them. This is a play that makes even such a masterpiece of subtext as *Uncle Vanya* (the plot of which it loosely parallels) seem grossly overstated.

At the beginning of the second scene, the mother gives a concise picture of the family's habitat:

➡ *Poor Mála, we live in such a place! No seasons, no fall, winter, or spring, and not the slightest change from week to week for the plants, the animals, or us. Our endless life is so similar to itself that we even find it somewhat strange each month to have a guest in our house, dear Doctor. Though our sad isolation adds to the pleasure of receiving one. For we do so love to see whatever may be slightly different, don't we Yúlè?*[14]

Yúlè replies in a way that defines the only agency of change within this world:

➡ *Indeed we do, dear Mother. And how wonderful, too, in this house of women—Father, Mála, you, and me—all rustling bees, to have a quiet, manly centipede pass through, treading his slow and handsome path through our quivering ivy walls.* (13–14)

Yúlè is just eleven, but she has sensed already the erotic fascination of a male presence among women, among whom she includes her emasculated father. The father seems to confirm the questioning of his masculinity, saying, "Though even if we were men, the Doctor would still be welcome" (14).

Both mother and father view Yúlè as a threat to their authority, and they are especially troubled by the way the younger sister has upset the preeminence of the older. They all try to diminish and objectify her as a property or toy, calling her "Elf," "pixie," "silly little pussy," "tiny little twig," "parasol." At the very beginning, after a saccharine breakfast scene in which Yúlè expresses sweet devotion to her father, she goes to awaken her sister, who is nicknamed Angel. The mother then says, "I'm sick to death of Elf, Daddy. She's a pig's liar. I hate to see her face." And Karl responds, "If she troubles our Angel, we'll choke her like a dog" (3).

Mála, in contrast, is the perfectly affectionate daughter, but it is for her that the doctor makes his monthly visits. (Yúlè asks how it could have been a month since the doctor's last visit, and Karl replies: "Because thirty elf-days have passed across your pixie fence—and scampered off into the soggy dark" [6].) Mála's sickness is never defined, but she is subject to strange visions. In the first scene, after the mother and father have left to do the milking, Mála starts suddenly and points to the door, saying, "Stranger piggies eat Death's apples. Piggie means Death. Death, sweetheart. Death, darling" (10). The father returns, saying that the piggies all want to come inside, and soon the doctor enters by the same door. The significance of this vision remains obscure for the time being, but, early on, Yúlè expresses her doubts about the idea that Mála is "absented from her little mind" (5).

While the doctor has been called to treat Mála, he also feels deeply drawn to the valley and expresses at length the sensual (or sexual) delight he takes in the visit. During the hot afternoon, he is left alone with Yúlè and in her presence becomes excited or delirious, at one point bursting out with "there is no question that physical beauty is the only thing that matters in this world!" (24). This sudden registering of Yúlè as an erotic presence takes him by surprise. At the very end of the scene, Mála reenters and takes note of the new state of affairs. In the next scene, after dinner, the mother reminisces about the cold house in a cold climate where she grew up, when, "in a strange

voice," Mála suddenly says: "And now you live in a house made of
sugar, where the floors are so warm that if you leave two seeds from
your vagina in the corner by your bed, in an hour they grow to a pe-
nis-tree" (28). A long silence follows. The tension between the sisters erupts at last when the subject of going to bed comes up. Mála
says to Yúlè: "Candy kitten—do you think you can fool your clever
sister? You've left your little pink scent on every pillow—do you
think we can't smell it" (31–32). Yúlè's response is simply to hug and
kiss her father, which inflames Mála still more: "You act as if we
don't know, you little pisser in your bed! Are you crazy? Do you
think Mother doesn't know? And Father? And do you think the
Doctor doesn't know, you little fucker? Do you think he can't smell
the poison you've spread on every sheet and under every chair to
catch his little mouse?" (32–33).

Mála's sickness might be no more than a desperation to escape
from the continuum of this stifling life. At seventeen, her life is the
perpetual, airless summer of staying home with her parents, with no
outlet for her desires, no exit from the family romance. That stasis is
what the parents work to preserve. It is a life of everyone remaining
in place, children as children, adults in control. But Mála also needs
to achieve separation—needs to be known otherwise—and her only
opportunity lies in the visits of the doctor, who both triggers and
constitutes a relief for her suffering and desire. In fact, the doctor
might be taken for a metaphor of the man who brings the daughter
release from the continuum of childhood by replacing the father as
an object of desire. He is the cure that a husband is supposed to be.

Yúlè is also at this time awakening to a recognition of the inhibit-
ing condition of her own minority. The fourth scene begins with her
praying to God to be released from this place, away from the Edenic
garden that is the happy home. She would prefer to be in contact
with the harsh realities of the frozen city—the fallen world—rather
than in a paradise overseen by her benign father and mother. A
knock comes at the door, and it is the doctor, who is soon overcome
by his passion and kisses her. The scene then proceeds with many
long periods of silence, during which one senses profound subtextual shifts of attitude and understanding between the two of them.

At first she protests at his lovemaking, but at the end she invites it. Just then, he turns from her and leaves, and she feels for the first time the suffocation and blinding of having lost a desired other. The passion she now knows is all-consuming: "And all through my body, from every vein and thick organ, a thousand endless tears press their painful way toward my helpless, burning eyes" (39).

The fifth scene begins with Andrá distraught because "everything here has come to an end" (40). She believes now that both children are becoming insane, that the family bonds must break, and at this point she blames Karl, calling him insane. The (rather insane) rationale for this requires explanation. The marriage of Andrá and Karl has been, seemingly, a joyful one for both of them, and toward the beginning of the play they express perfect devotion for each other. She calls him "pine tree," and he answers her with "Queen for my needles" (3). Andrá sees in Mála the perfect child, a replica of herself who acquiesces to her mother's desire that she remain forever a child. Mála seems, even at this time, torn between the status (or stasis) of being her mother's perfect child and the kinesis of being the woman who might leave with the doctor, thus betraying the father and mother. Yúlè has, in Andrá's eyes, introduced the rupture by questioning Mála's medical need for the doctor, refusing to ignore Mála's sexual need for the doctor.

When Yúlè, who initially expresses her dislike of the doctor, finds that she, too, can be a beloved object for another man, she discovers the basic replicability of the father. And Andrá makes a similar discovery, but she expresses it obliquely. She says that God has abandoned Karl and the house, and left all their souls sick and dying. God has become a stranger and is now too far away to give her release. She might have said that Karl has lost his godhood, his eternality, within this family because he cannot be the ideal father who would preserve the perfect childhood of his daughters. Instead, his daughters, first one and then the other, have discovered his replicability. In Andrá's eyes, this change in his status puts him at a distance from herself as well. When Karl seeks to make love with her, she suddenly breaks away from him, saying, "No! No! You're a stranger! I don't know you! I don't know you!" (43). He is not the man she married, not the man who became the father of her children. Instead, he has become the trickster replica of that man, who behaves as he did then but who cannot now be the God who could preserve that happy family configuration forever.

As noted above, at the beginning of the preceding scene, Yúlè prayed to God to take her away from this warm and sunny place to the cold cities "where it is always night, and the men live wrapped in paper, eating filth and brawling silently" (35). That is, she longs to leave her idyllic home for the real world, and of course Karl cannot be the God who would take her away. Again, in the scene with Andrá, he proves not to be the God she requires. Finally, in the sixth scene, Mála stands by the doctor, who is sleeping, and speaks to herself of what she wants from God:

➤ *It is only this: that Mother, Father, Elf, and I should live in this house forever, without end. . . . An hour of kisses would not be enough, nor ten hours, nor a million. There must be no hours; there must be no numbers. . . . I want them now, and now, and now, and now, till time shall run without concluding. I will hold them in my arms forever; our lips and hands will reach no end; and it will be for always.* (45–46)

Karl is not the God who can grant this wish either. Thus, the God of Andrá, Yúlè, and Mála proves not to exist in this house.

The seventh scene concludes this story of a "happy" family fragmenting. It begins with the departure of the doctor the next morning. Andrá seems especially sorrowful at his going—she had invested much of her hopes for Mála in him. He, too, has proved no God. Yúlè, on the other hand, exults in her increasing strength. Suddenly, Mála cries out at another vision, pointing to the window: "Pig— (heavy silence)" (49). As she is beset by this vision, associated earlier with Death, Karl suffers an attack of some sort, weakening severely. Mála cannot face his fall from power and instead turns to the ascendant Yúlè, asking her sister to kiss her. In the final line of the play, Yúlè returns the embrace, saying, "Mála, Mála, you cunt, Mála, how could you know? Eh? How could you know?" (49–50). Here, again, is the ultimate enigma of a Shawn play, just at the point where the dream conjoins a mystery. (Freud: "Every dream has at least one point at which it is unfathomable; a central point, as it were, connecting it with the unknown.")[15] How could she know what? Is she soothing her, challenging her, assaulting her? There is no simple answer to this question, which means that either the dramatic logic of the scene is unclear or there is a complex answer that must be sought. It is a platitude of modern playwriting that good dialogue should not require adverbial directions ("coyly," "desperately," etc.). The tone or attitude should be implicit. The final lines of this play seem to fail in this regard unless one proposes the indeterminacy as exactly the point in this moment. Yúlè has become at the end a paradox — an embrace, a sexually abusive term, a question of concern, and a question of challenge. At this crux (or point of dispersal), the play (refuses to) close(s).

I put the question to Shawn, how should the final line be spoken? Shawn himself directed a workshop production of this play with students at New York University in 1973, so some decision had to be made in this matter. He replied: "Yúlè's last line in *The Family Play*: She reproaches Mála because Mála somehow knew, and concealed from her, that Karl would die and the whole life in the valley was not eternal but would end."[16] So, it is reproach, but the sort of reproach that happens while embracing. How could I know? Eh? How could I know?

I turned to Shawn directly for help on *The Hospital Play* because here, among his enigmatic early works, I felt most at a loss to know what to say. This is an incredibly gruesome and unbearable play, a hopeless and hideous monster. Shawn made a series of statements that brought the play into focus and answered several questions about his early career. He told me that the play came to him incredibly clearly, "more filled in" than anything he had written then, or perhaps has ever written. He said it was a "turning point" and that "it is my only play that shows any compassion." I have described, at the very beginning of this book, my own sense of bewilderment at this last statement and the way I came to interpret it, as a particular sort of dramatic misfire, indeed a turning point but only because it represents a testing of the limits of modernist drama. There is a sense of old dramatic form gone wrong here, which is appropriate for the grounding of the play's history. Shawn explains this to me quite simply: "It *is* the Vietnam War."[17]

The play opens with the erotic image of a Boy kissing a Girl on the knees in the moonlight. She is in bed, and he is seated on a chair beside her, next to his own bed. These are the only two beds facing downstage in a setting not so erotic, a hospital ward, and they are not, as one would hope, alone. An Elderly Negro is brushing his teeth; a Self-Pitying Young Man scratches his hands. Also present are a man sobbing, a man coughing, a transfixed woman "fingering" herself, and several other patients, and behind a weakly illuminated screen two doctors and an unknown medical instrument provoke "gasps, moans, and stifled cries" from a Male Patient.[18] Two doors lead from this room to the Lavatory and the Vomit Room. "Everyone is cold, and many are shivering" (4). The agitated stillness of this scene is broken by the Coughing Man launching into what initially sounds like a speech of thanks or appreciation spoken to a colleague of some sort, named Carter. This quickly evolves into a long harangue, punctuated by coughing fits, against this unseen man, who is repeatedly addressed as "you God-damned shit-face hair-patting mouth-kissie, Carter" (7) and who is also called a killer or murderer. The Coughing Man and the other patients seem tormented by an awareness of the cruel inexorability of their mysterious diseases, and the doctors, who are unmistakably sadistic, offer no relief.

This hopeless and crowded scene shifts to an intimate scene of two black hospital staffers sharing a private moment in the Blood Room. It is a very tender scene. They speak of their love for each other in spiritual terms, but the middle-aged Bald Orderly is becoming aware of disturbing symptoms of disease in his body. He scratches his hands. The young Tall Nurse then recalls that when she injected the patients with their blood this evening, "the blood tasted so peculiar" (21). She had resolved earlier not to inject herself with any of it this evening. She samples some of the jars of blood stored on shelves in the room, sticking a finger in each to taste, and some of it seems to her spoiled. The Lady Doctor comes in, dismisses them, and injects some of the blood into herself. When the Black Doctor enters, she reads him a long excerpt from a mystery story. They, too, have been lovers. After a while, it becomes obvious that he is not listening, and soon, disgruntled and complaining of her own ailments, including irritated hands, she leaves. The scene revolves back to the ward.

Gradually, throughout the play, nearly every one of the twenty-two characters develops one or more of the symptoms—skin irritation, especially of the face and hands, fever or chills, deteriorating vision, nausea—of some enigmatic disease or condition. The next time we see the Tall Nurse and the Bald Orderly, he has just come from the Vomit Room and is in agony. They are all dying. The exceptions are the Black Doctor, the Head of the Hospital, and the Tall Nurse. There is a sense of the plague—a miasma—with no hero (no Oedipus) so committed to the truth to find out the true, insidious cause. The scenes alternate between group scenes (the ward) and intimate scenes (in more secluded rooms), as in *The Hotel Play* where there is also a sense of the world surreally out of control or in the hands of ludicrously bad forces seen alternately in close-up and long shot. In the fourth scene we come to the Office of the Head of the Hospital.

The Head philosophizes drunkenly about predestination, vaguely and incoherently evoking logical positivism. But he communicates these comically simplistic ideas about determinism (about whether or not one might say that the red boat will win the race tomorrow) to his Subnormal Orderly, and when the Black Doctor enters, it becomes clear that the Head is not really in charge of the hospital. They drink a liquor called Red Penguin, and later something called the Special, and then the "blue liqueur" in a mood of raucous celebration during which the Black Doctor seems to push the Head closer and closer to the brink of recklessness. If the riddle of the Sphinx is to be answered by anyone, it will not be by the Head of this particular state.

In the Linen Room, several of the staff members confer about the worsening situation. One of the orderlies has gone blind and foresees death. The squabbles among former friends or lovers begin to take on the air of finality, while the usual taboos break down. The Boy, in a delirious state, verbally seduces the Lady Doctor into his erotic dream, and she, weakening rapidly from the disease, appeals n't love me any more" (135). She apologizes, says she is glad he really loves her but he should not have killed everybody:

LADY DOCTOR. I know they're all dying. I don't mind, though. I know you did it for me. But we should have done it together. Everything is more fun together with you. That's why we love each other. Isn't that right?

BLACK DOCTOR. Yeah—that's right.

LADY DOCTOR. That's what I thought, you old rascal. I knew you just did it to tease me. (137)

Does she realize yet that she, too, is dying, and that he, perhaps accidentally or perhaps regretfully, has been the one who infected her?

There are three corpses present at the beginning of the next scene, including the Bald Orderly and the Girl (the one who was being kissed at the very beginning). The Tall Nurse, who loved the Bald Orderly, is kneeling over the dead Girl and blessing all the parts of her body. She more than any of the others shows true compassion for people, extending this even to some of the more corrupt staff members. She is an angel. In the final scene, she even brings her warmth close to the Black Doctor—the incarnation of mercy uniting with the essence of revolutionary rage. From a scene where virtually all are dead or dying, the Head of the Hospital has retreated, having come to no greater tragic recognition than this: "I don't know—I feel that something's going wrong here" (147). That leaves the Tall Nurse and the Black Doctor as the only two not dead or dying. She turns to him for human contact, asking him for warmth, and in the last line, he—the chronically disaffected and resentful terrorist—tells her to "snuggle in" (152). The statement here seems to be optimistic, that even in the presence of extreme cruelty, mercy can be extended and tenderness can be found.

This is a play about the fundamental breakdown of institutional structures (read political structures), a work in the vein of Ken Kesey's *One Flew over the Cuckoo's Nest* or Peter Weiss's *Marat/Sade*. The combination of sex and sadism and morbid humor is not unlike that in certain Pinter plays, especially *The Hothouse* (one of Pinter's very early plays, written in 1958 but not performed or published until

1980, although some material from this play was used in Pinter's revue sketches). But unlike those works, Shawn's play does not depict a specific link between power and cruelty. The mad master of Shawn's asylum is a careless and inhumane man, laughably out of control, not a tyrant like Nurse Ratched. His thoughts are fixed on the past—old medical instruments, a school play he was in, the liquors of bygone days. The cause of destruction here is an outgrowth of a failure of leadership and the vicious behaviors—betrayals and petty abuses—throughout the ranks of power. The tiny fragment of human contact that remains at the end of the play, ironically between the most trusting and the least trustworthy individuals in the play, seems to be a particularly mordant vision of the future.

The Hospital Play is a big play, a sort of symphony, with overlapping layers of speech and action meticulously scored. I have already suggested that *The Iceman Cometh,* which Shawn vividly recalls seeing in seventh grade, might have been an influence on him in shaping this (failed) masterpiece. Confronted with the Vietnam War, everyone had a different opinion about its strategy, or could we say, its dramaturgy? Recall that Shawn had taken a strong interest in Henry Kissinger's ideas about nuclear strategy around 1960. What he was reading at the time was an analysis of how a large nuclear arsenal, such as the Americans and Soviets possessed, paradoxically rendered these countries impotent. Kissinger called it "The Great Fallacy" to assume that "the use or the threatened use of atomic weapons of mass destruction would be sufficient to assure the security of the United States and its friends."[19] Since the consequences of total war would be so devastating, it had become a problem for the United States to gain credibility for a threatened use of power in any situation that called for something less than total war. In order for the United States to sustain its influence on global politics, it would have to find a way to exert itself through limited war, and this was, in essence, the justification for the fighting in Southeast Asia. Shawn had lost confidence in Kissinger's ideas by the time he was in India and England, when he found himself reading, with growing horror, the practical consequences of those ideas: "I woke up every day convinced that we were like Germans perpetrating the Holocaust. Ten thousand will be put into the gas chamber by dinner by my country."[20] This "limited war" suddenly seemed massive. Shawn's reaction to this war in *The Hospital Play* was, I would argue, something of a total war, an overwhelming, negative statement, a grandiose, Nobel Prize sort of drama, but incredible. After this play, Shawn would redirect his impulses to a much smaller-scaled, more precisely targeted drama, somewhat short of Armageddon and as a demonstration of power on the whole more credible.

"Inside Your Thing, But I'll Do It Quickly"

Our Late Night, In the Dark,
and *A Thought in Three Parts*

•➔ *Well . . . uh. The, uh, ordinary way that we modern Western people
tend to think of ourselves, um . . . uh, doesn't really . . . um, uhh . . . take
account of, uh, sex. That makes sex very interesting as a subject.*
— Shawn, interviewed by Don Shewey

In 1993, *Our Late Night* seemed to come of age. It had been eighteen
years since its opening, directed by André Gregory for his Manhattan Project, and twenty-one years since it had been written. During
all that time, it had not, so far as I have learned, been revived, despite
the fact that it won an Obie award in 1975. Its only publication was
in a limited edition of 1984, with an introduction by John Lahr.
Then, suddenly, it appeared again at the Powerhouse Theatre in
Santa Monica in a production directed by Karen Ludwig, a cast
member of the original production. Powerhouse had promoted this
as "an edgy comedy," but the two dozen or so people who gathered
on this odd weeknight in the rather cold little theater seemed grim
at the beginning of the show and subsequently registered (with a certain determined enthusiasm) the sheer horror—the right wrong—of
what followed.[1]

"Edgy comedy" is what you might have expected if you had come
to this production fresh from having read Brendan Gill's *New Yorker*
review of the original production, which was among the first published reviews Shawn ever received. This review represents Shawn as
transforming "his high-spirited view of the world into art," indeed,
creating a work that is "ribald and joyous" to the degree that Gill
promises to be "shocked and disappointed if it turns out to contain
a message."[2] As I watched the Powerhouse production, it was not so

much the question of whether the work did or did not contain a message that preoccupied my attention as it was astonishment that anyone could have found this play "joyous." Shawn has subsequently assured me that he had always regarded this review as some kind of gesture toward William Shawn—selling the son's show. Gill is, after all, the sort of man who "loves life" and must find that affirmative gesture in everything. Shawn himself recalls the production as, quite rightly, "upsetting and horrifying."[3]

The edge marks the spot beyond which something that is, is not. An edgy comedy presumably makes fun at that very edge. Gill began his review of the Manhattan Project production of the *Seagull* (in the very same issue of the *New Yorker*) with a confused nod to the devil, the tempter of his angel's (William Shawn's) son, in terms that perhaps apply better to the prodigal son himself:

➺ *André Gregory and his company, known as the Manhattan Project, bewilder me, and my bewilderment usually has an edge of irritation to it. Elegant in person, refined in apprehension, Mr. Gregory often strikes me as deliberately messing things up, as a delightful child might choose to deface a beloved doll. But to what purpose? Mr. Gregory is a man of considerable experience in the theatre; we are entitled to assume that his chase, however bizarre, has a beast in view and that the beast can be rendered visible. It is rarely visible to me.*[4]

In this way Gill demonized the director to save or redeem the son for his god, all in the name of virtue (i.e., what should be rendered visible to Gill). Thus, concerning the *Our Late Night* production, Gill declared: "Surely the author is secretly signaling to us that there is more to his salacious rhetoric than the wish to make us laugh? Are we not being offered a parable by which to gain salvation?"[5] For Gill, such style as Mr. Gregory evidently possessed became a mockery (of style itself)—a surface disturbance that prevented insight.

The fact is, the demonic, antithetical impulse that is evident in this play came at least initially from Shawn himself, who had been "messing things up" so successfully to this point that no one wanted to play with him. His plays were not done. The difference in this play and in the two that followed is that he turned to the "very interesting subject" of sex. It is not just sex, of course, that *Our Late Night* addresses. It is that whole realm of the human imaginary that is most vulnerable to the mockery or attack of others—desire in all its variety, nausea in all its variety, ambivalence and uncertainty, what Shawn calls "the intimate side of life."[6] But in an era when the whole notion of the "explicit" was becoming open for exploration, this play stood out for the way it provided access to the id. A writer for the *L.A. Weekly* in 1993 described the play arriving at the Powerhouse Theater "from a vanished time of baroquely excessive sexuality and self-centeredness. How refreshing his play seems, then, in our current age of Cromwellian propriety."[7] The question of just what the intimacy of 1972 or 1975 might mean eighteen or twenty-one or more years later is a complex and compelling one, at bottom a historical question. *Our Late Night* presents an associational fabric—a texture of relations—from the inner life of a past moment, and at this time, the effect of simultaneous immediacy and distance is dizzying.

The play begins with a couple in their thirties, Annette and Lewis, dressed for a party in their apartment ("high, very high, above a giant city")—kissing.[8] Their dialogue is erotically charged, with each phrase applied as a touch of the other, like a slow dance. At one point, just after the lights momentarily dim and come up again, the characters dip just below the surface of consciousness with Lewis asking, "Do you think I should be a woman tonight?" Annette replies, "Is that what you want, Lewis?" (1). Gender and sexuality are pathways they are trying to find with each other. These are positional questions—how *are* we toward each other?—and they soon connect to other positional questions, such as, how are we toward other people and toward the city? They look out the window. Lewis asks, "What are you looking at?" The lights go out. Annette answers, in the dark, "The buildings stiff to stiff—." Lewis says, "That's all right." Annette continues, "—standing below us like stiff children, with swollen knees and crabbed-up knuckles—can't move" (2–3). The image compacts voyeurism, superiority, relative age and relative youth, relative mobility—a shifting and complex relational structure. The dialogue here and at the end of the play has this specular closed—and she had a sharp mustache, and almost a beard! It was terrifying!" (25). Afterward, though, he remained aroused and next accosted his wife, twice. Cold water would not reduce his erection, and so he ran screaming through the woods, masturbating, and finally came by rubbing into the slime at the edge of a lake. Even this did not completely relieve him, and it was his wife who managed to bring out, orally, his final drop: "After that, I covered my face with my pillow and emitted some stifled sobs; I felt dizzy, as if I was hurtling through a misshapen darkness, but I knew that when I landed, it would start again, that feeling of the juices in my prick, and never stop, never leave me alone" (29). The speech is a tour de force of sexual paranoia, but it provokes from Jim only the hilarious reply, "My God—and to think that I planned to go to the tropics on my vacation!" (30). Producer Joseph Papp recalled, "The audience went crazy at that scene. . . . Some were shouting and one man got up and walked around in a menacing way—they didn't even know they were doing it. Wally was looking around the theater, very perplexed—he didn't realize he had gotten rid of his own sexual mania and given it to everybody else."[10]

Later, Tony fingers Samantha until she begins to feel ill and turns on him: "Little weepie man. Little chocolate man. Little hamburger Tony. You only got yourself lost and wet in those great big hairy old doors down there" (35–36). Kristin tells Jim of her use of a burning jelly in sex, adding that such techniques are necessary because she hates enjoyment. Grant talks in horrifyingly suggestive fragments of some masturbatory procedures involving children, needles, vomiting. He also tells Tony of an episode when pink fluid poured for an hour from the nostrils of his wife, right in the middle of dinner. Kristin asks Jim if he knows about gagging. He answers, "No! No! Why don't you protect me? Let's go out. Let's leave. Let me walk behind you, just to press on you, to press against your legs, but not to fuck you. Help me! Help me! You're trying to make me sick!" (44). Kristin begins crying and puts on her coat; she goes toward the door, but does not leave. She remains weeping there until the end. Tony goes into the bathroom and can be heard vomiting through the next scene, in which Grant tells of a recurring dream he has in which his daughter kisses him under his eye: "And then I always

The play ends with a series of momentary, alternating tableaux—first Annette asleep, Lewis awake, then Lewis asleep, Annette awake, then Annette asleep, Lewis awake. . . . "And so on ad lib till the final blackout" (53). They are dream and reality to each other.

In 1975, the play was described by a *New York Times* critic as having "a defiant stylishness" that Gregory had underscored by suggesting a "ritual pattern" to the action.[12] Shawn himself recalls that production as "more stylized" than the 1993 Powerhouse production: "with unbelievably elegant costumes (which were in some cases borrowed from the designers by our costume designer, Ara Gallant, a famous hairdresser and member of Andy Warhol's 'family,' introduced to André by mutual friend Richard Avedon). Yes, the acting, after three years of rehearsal, was very sparkling and crackling."[13] These terms, including the emphasis on costume and the fringe association with Warhol, all might suggest that the production worked within the context of a modernist juxtaposition of cultivated form and shocking content. The play outrages a certain expectation about class (or elegance). The play also outrages a certain expectation about romantic love, and about verisimilitude and decorum and linear development and closure. In all these ways, the play, via Gregory's production, operates satirically, or at least by answering the audience's question with a Warholian nonanswer. The play declares a newness clearly and loudly enough to upset permanently certain values.

Interestingly, though, this view of the play, which I merely pose here as an alternative, is not really consistent with the view of John Russell Brown, discussed above. Brown puts the emphasis on the frame story, preferring to read the party as a complex means of precipitating the consciousness of those two characters, so that interior and exterior are made equally available to theatricalization: "*Our Late Night* presents both the outward facts of living and also the tireless, sexual, fantastic inner facts of being."[14] Ritual patterns and stylization have only incidental relation to this aspect of the play's interpretation; Brown's phrases could, indeed, be applied to that very different and unwilling modernist, Chekhov. Karen Ludwig's 1993 production was, Shawn observed, "more melancholy in feeling," and the costume designer did not even get a program biography.[15]

Chekhov was very much to the fore in this production, which seemed to test the Method capabilities of the performers to "make it real." I am supposing that the 1975 production had a bit more to do with "make it new." Staff members at the Powerhouse told me that after seeing their production Shawn said to them, "I thought I wrote a play that actors couldn't act, and you acted it." Depending on how you look at it, this statement could work as praise or blame, or merely as a curious observation. Certainly they had played every bit of Chekhov that was to be found in the script, and the moment when Kristin is off weeping in the corner and Tony is vomiting in the bathroom as Grant goes on in his meandering way about obscure linkages of pain and pleasure was in their production as emotionally disturbing and funny as, say, the fire scene in *The Three Sisters*. You drink it in even as you notice a very bitter taste. The scene is textural; it asks an audience to feel its contours.

Possibly, though, by pushing the actors in a stylized or "sparkling and crackling" way, this same scene might prove more estranging, more aggressively gestural or even assaultive. Shawn tells me: "In my view at the time, *Our Late Night* was upsetting and horrifying."[16] The sad fact might be that the eighteen years between the two productions might have provided the foundation of truth to make outrage actable. Eros has never before been so intensely in dialogue with Thanatos. This is what I meant by suggesting that the play might have come of age. The profound linkage between libidinal and death instincts now seems much more obvious.

At just about this time, Shawn wrote the libretto to a one-act opera, *In the Dark*, with his brother, Allen Shawn, as composer. This little interlude, in the *Pierrot Lunaire* vein musically, recounts the discordant notes of a first date between coworkers identified simply as He and She, leading to an awkward night "in the dark" together. What happens is not explicit—no nipples stiff, no hairy doors—but instead is figured by the bed itself and the duet woven around it:

In the dark room
the bed
stands

on four legs
while our four
lie twisted on it.
White sheets
and scratchy woolen blankets
protect us from
the cold
but get tangled
between the legs,
and arms,
between us,
bending feet and elbows,
while underwear and socks,
discarded, and nightgowns, shirts, ribbons,
and towels
from other days and nights
climb to the surface
to confuse us,
and from a window
sudden icy winds
run suddenly across us.[17]

Later, perhaps, these two will purchase an electric blanket (see *My Dinner with André*), but for now they are bound together in that most awkward (delicious), most vulnerable (exciting) position—coupled. In that space, abrasion unites with stimulation, and discomfort comes with ecstasy. The world around them is harsh and alien and encroaching. There is nothing melodic or harmonic about their duet—they are rarely even in unison. Only a rough, formal congruence puts this generic couple in any specific relation to one another, while discordance suggests the violent tendency within the impulse to sing of love.

In some ways, the subject of *In the Dark,* which is also the subject of *Our Late Night, A Thought in Three Parts, Marie and Bruce,* and Shawn's second operatic collaboration, *The Music Teacher,* is a very narrow subject—the psychic space where pleasure and warfare unite in intimacy, in intercourse. How does one get to that desired space? And how does one deal with the unexpected violence that is found there? These are the plays that established Shawn as a dramatist of human obscenity, as a brutal satirist of romance and urbanity, and they represent his most consistent trend as a playwright: Shawn as a modern Juvenal.

Clearly, Shawn is working in a mode that is close to expressionism (or possibly even surrealism) at this point in his career, trusting only the most compelling perceptions, and then realizing those compulsions in a way that must prove upsetting to an audience:

➼ *One thing that I think I can say about my plays (to date) is that I always seem to write about imaginary situations and places and characters, but only about those that truly and totally absorb me. I think that perhaps at each moment in one's life there is only one such totally fascinating imaginary thing (one picture, let us say, of one unknown person in one unknown room), and to find that one thing inside my head is always incredibly difficult, because it is always something I have never really seen or thought of before, and often it is something that I don't really want to see or think about too much at all. But there is really no hope, no chance, of changing myself before I write; I have to take myself as I am, and if what I care about at that time is two elderly women having their tea, then that must be my subject, and if what it is at another time is a strange group masturbating in a dingy room, then I must write about that. . . . I may not understand why my characters do what they do (and I usually don't, just as in the same sense I usually don't understand why real people do what they do in life), but I can still, at least, watch, listen, and tell the story.*[18]

The extreme example of this trend is *A Thought in Three Parts* (initially titled *Three Short Plays*), which was written with the financial support of Joseph Papp in 1975 and given a workshop production at the Public Theatre in 1976. It was produced by the Joint Stock Company at the Institute for Contemporary Arts (ICA) in London in 1977 under the direction of Max Stafford-Clark.[19] Here is to be found the actual "strange group masturbating in a dingy room." The group also performs just about every other possible heterosexual act, with relatively little evidence of what Republicans call love and Democrats call respect. This enormously displeasing play, a tour de force of gratification denied, was predictably greeted with the horror and disgust of many critics. It quickly drew the attention of the vice squad (or the London equivalent), who examined it closely for violations of the laws permitting simulated sex acts on stage. Soon it was the topic of debate in the House of Lords over Arts Council funding, with Lord Nugent of Guildford saying, "Most people expect government ministers to protect the public against this sort of pollution. When the taxpayer is required to pay towards protecting it, it adds insult to injury."[20] Lord Nugent even talked of curtailing funding to the arts, if you can imagine such a thing.

The state ultimately declined to prosecute over *A Thought in Three Parts,* but the event led to extensive debate about obscenity and its aesthetic value. John Barber of the *Daily Telegraph* wrote: "Squalid squirming on beds, accompanied by the obligatory oohs and aahs, becomes monotonous sooner than might be believed possible. No story, no character, no situation and no social relationship engages attention. There is no attempt at anything that could be called aesthetic endeavor." And Irving Wardle of the *London Times* declared: "This is definitely a show to confirm any life-hater in his view of sex as a graceless and messy amusement, bringing out the worst in all concerned."[21] Other critics concurred. A horror show. *Clockwork Orange.* Everything that is decadence.

Certain critics dissented, but the most forceful response came in a letter to the *Guardian* by Howard Brenton, Caryl Churchill, David Hare, and Barrie Keefe:

•➤ *As working playwrights we note that the latest victim of the arrogance, indolence and carelessness of the English theatre critics is a visiting American, Wallace Shawn, whose trilogy of plays* A Thought in 3 Parts *opened at the ICA this week.*

We believe him to be a writer of outstanding talent exploring love and sex with great linguistic and theatrical insight. On the whole he has received only mindless and prudish abuse. We want to express our support for our gifted colleague and hope the public will ignore the grubby obstacles put in their way to a pleasurable evening.[22]

Ned Chaillet, whose initial review in *Plays and Players* had declared the play "comic but loaded with comment and manifestly not pornographic," later was forced to declare, "the reputation of the three one-act plays that made up the evening was invisible for the outrage that had been engendered." Chaillet's observations on this play (before its occultation) are important: "What actually occurs is enough to alarm both the sexually repressed and the honestly sensual: sexuality is expressed as a driving force in men and women, but close to the love of its pleasures and comforts Mr. Shawn places a revulsion and alienation."[23]

The play has not been revived and stands as a permanent challenge to anyone who has the attitude that *anything* can be revived. Recent cultural history has so radically changed the proximity of the erotic and the pornographic, and recent pathology has so radically redefined the fulfillment of desire, that the play can now almost not be read. It was an amazing sunset (such as only polluted air can produce), now dark.

The first part (called "Summer Evening," a two-hander) is a foreplay, all about not being at that moment yet. A couple in their late twenties, in a hotel room, prepare to go to bed after a night out. Finally, just as they turn the lights out, "they touch."[24] The second part (called "Youth Hostel," for three men and two women who seem to be "youth," i.e., considerably younger) is about "acts"—jerking off and fucking, mainly. (No other words are quite right.) The couples are variously in each other's beds and bodies. The third is a monodrama (called "Mr. Frivolous," for a man in his early thirties) in which a man seems to reexperience either his love-making or his fantasies of love-making of the past. He verbalizes the elements of his experience, much like a sense memory exercise, while sitting at his breakfast. Most of what he says is in the narrative present, but at the end he relates his experiences in the past tense, ending with "Then we gathered up our clothes, long since discarded as we lay in the grass, and headed for home, to wash, to dress, to have dinner, and then to bed, and tuck you in, and lights out" (57).

Thus, the play gives three temporal perspectives on sexual relations—before, during, after—but at its end, the man (Mr. Frivolous) is just beginning the day, with his first cup of coffee, whereas at the beginning of the play, the man (David) muses: "Well dinner was not so bad, in fact" (31). The cyclicality of desire and satisfaction is thus clearly evoked. On the other hand, the fact that the couple in the first part must go through an elaborate verbal preparation for their touching, unlike the minimalist, almost zipless, relations of the youth in the second part, but yet less verbally involuted and onanistic than the older Mr. Frivolous in the third part, suggests a progressive frustration with increasing age that accompanies the cycle of desire and satisfaction.

Shawn has found strong verbal correlatives for the three sorts of nonrelationship in these little plays. The first part offers dialogue on the verge of complete discontinuity, as if subject to an extreme interference but at base high modernist. This is degraded, riven speech, but echoes of an old romanticism are apparent:

SARAH. Yes, I'm *quite* content, love—

DAVID. I'm glad, my darling—are you happy, with—?—

SARAH. —how they *find* fruit so ripe—

DAVID. I—

SARAH. —the napkins, and look—

DAVID. —and just always be happy?—

SARAH. —these toothpicks—

DAVID. —and—

SARAH. —starts sort of flat and then round and then comes to a point—

DAVID. Your teeth are so pretty—you bite those things—

SARAH. Do you like my teeth, love?—the saucers—I wish we—

DAVID. I—

SARAH. Wait, though! You still haven't seen my—(*She goes into the bathroom and shuts the door.*)

DAVID. Quietly I watch her dress, undress. Incredible, incredible, she has no idea the trembling in my heart as I lie in bed and watch her clothing, falling to the floor, softly to the chair. (*She enters in a new dress.*) My God—did you get this dress—today? Your breasts—

SARAH. I—yes—

DAVID. —the color—

SARAH. I was thinking—

DAVID. —that rising—

SARAH. —this top with the very same dress—it seems almost too thin, but I like the arms—

DAVID. —through those sleeves—

SARAH. —it seems—

DAVID. —they slip right through the sleeves—should lie down a bit after eating?

SARAH. Yes—(*They lie down on the bed. Silence.*) (33–34)

There is a kind of accidental imagism to this dialogue, and the contrapuntal rhythm is always strongly controlled. In this way the play registers some recollection of wholeness and harmony.

The banality of the dialogue in the second part is occasionally reminiscent of that heard in a porn film, which is what the action of the play mirrors, although accelerated. Most of the speech, however, is strongly abusive, even violent. The bodies, both male and female, are compliant and almost continually in action (the stage directions mention at least eighteen orgasms), but the characters are, without exception, nasty to each other. All of this is ironized by patterns of language that evoke a second-grade reader:

HELEN. I wish I were dead.

DICK. Is that right? Why is that, Helen?

HELEN. Go fuck yourself, Dick.

DICK. Gee thanks, Helen.

HELEN. "Gee thanks, Helen." You really are an asshole, Dickie.

DICK. Yeah, thanks. Thanks a lot, sweetheart. Why don't you leave me alone?

HELEN. Well why the hell should I?

DICK. Because I want you to. I'm sick of you.

HELEN. Really? Really? (*She lifts up the bed covers.*) Are you sick of this?

DICK. Oh come on, Helen.

HELEN. Come on, Dick. Just finger me, Dickie?

DICK. Why should I?

HELEN. Well why don't you, Dick? Please? Please?

DICK. You're just sitting there, Helen! (*He goes to the bed and fingers her.*) I'll feel your asshole too.

HELEN. Oh God.

DICK. Is that okay?

HELEN. Okay! Okay! Oh! (*She comes. Pause.*)

DICK. Yeah—Well—Look what you've done to my fingers. God!

HELEN. Well—so what?

DICK. Yeah—so what for you. (*Wiping his fingers.*) You've fuckin' wrecked my whole time, God damn you fuckin' shit—

HELEN. Yeah—Well—Thanks, Dick.

DICK. Yeah—thanks for nothing. Get the fuck out of here.

HELEN. Yeah. Okay, Dickie. See you around.

DICK. Yeah. So long, Helen.

HELEN. So long, Dick. (*Exit Helen.*) (47)

This is a relatively mild segment of the play, but it gives a sense of the zero degree of empathy and understanding between the characters. The more tolerant critics recognized a wildly comical effect (one called it "maybe the first real sex-farce to reach the British stage"),[25] but the main impact came from the audacity of so much simulated sex taking place in less than half an hour. Shawn's play was, of course, not the first to incorporate total nudity or explicit sex. Of particular relevance is Andy Warhol's *Pork*, which was a notorious exploration of (among other things) the effect of actual sex on a theatrical audience. The play was created in New York in 1971 and performed in London in 1972, at which time Leonard Leff underscored how unmistakably different it was in the framing of its satire:

➥ *In truth, there is much in* Pork *to offend the squeamish: overt displays of homosexuality; simulated douching, masturbation and intercourse; graphic discussions of flatulence and feces, penes and pudenda. Yet the concentration upon bodily processes and fleshly pursuits highlights Warhol's theme, the vulnerability of man. Not only are Pork, Vulva, and*

B. [characters in the play] mocked by the society in which they live (represented by the audience at each performance), but also by the simple fact that, like everyone else in that society, they are mortal beings. We share with them a sense of death, theirs and ours, which obviously trivializes existence.[26]

The careless and even disorderly coexistence of cock, cunt, whatever in *Pork* defined a certain intersection between self-exhibition and celebrity—the underside of pop imagery. Shawn's play is simultaneously less campy than Warhol's, less a mockery, and less vested in a philosophy of sexual fulfillment. It is a gross text, hilarious in its own way but notable mainly for the way it makes youth, love, and pleasure itself seem delusions.

The language of the third part moves into an unforeseen lyricism, as the lone character reviews a sexual experience in terms that begin with conventional romantic imagery but then take on a poetic intensity and finally even seem to evoke the "Song of Solomon." A segment from the middle of this monologue gives a sense of the movement toward a metaphysical dimension:

➡ *I ask you to love. I ask you to love me. I ask to be taken, out to the toilet. And washed. And cleaned. And washed. And cleaned. I ask. I ask. I ask. I ask. For your arms. To be there. And your shoulders. There. And for you. To open. And for you. To hold. To take. Me in. To hug on me. Hard. While I. Am sliding. While I. Am pressing. While the hours. Pass. And our bodies get wet. Our bodies get slippery. And cold. And cold. And cold. And cold. These truths, beam fresh, to me, tonight, with the moon, coming in, my window, as I speak. Come get me, come find me. I lie here naked, I lie here waiting. Now. Now. Now. Now. I want, to be pulled, and looted, and ripped, by your nails, and strangled, with your stockings, and painted, like a placard, with your lipstick, on my back, on my legs, on my ass, on my asshole. And these things, these, lying around—these sheets, these bits, of clothes, of brassieres, of panties—I think, these are an easel, for all that work.* (57)

Shawn recalls reading *Ulysses* at the age of fifteen, specifically so he could talk to an expert on Joyce who was coming to the house.[27] Here, unmistakably, one can trace that influence. The difference is that Joyce's novel turns at the end to the experience of the woman, giving voice at last to her desires, but Shawn's play, indeed arguably all of his writing at this stage of his career, foregrounds the experience and the capability of the male characters.

Other thematic patterns should be factored into this interpretation. The couple in the first part are in a "pleasant hotel room in a foreign country," while the group of characters in the second part are in two sparsely furnished, dimly lit rooms, also abroad. All that is said of Mr. Frivolous's environment is that it is an "appealing room," but the allusion to going home in the last line and the imaginative venturing of his monologue complete the sense that all three plays explore the strangeness outside, the adventure from the familiar. As in *The Hotel Play* and *My Dinner with André,* tourism operates in part as a metaphor for knowing the other, exploring. André himself studies this metaphor in the final minutes of *My Dinner with André,* taking careful note of its infra-theatrical (as opposed to metatheatrical) connotations:

•◇ *You see, I think that's why people have affairs. I mean, you know, in the theater, if you get good reviews you feel for a moment that you've got your hands on something. You know what I mean? It's a good feeling. But then that feeling goes very quickly. And once again you don't know quite what will happen next, what you should do. Well, have an affair and up to a certain point you can really feel you're on firm ground. There is a sexual conquest to be made. There are different questions: Does she enjoy the ear being nibbled? How intensely can you talk about Schopenhauer at an elegant French restaurant, or whatever nonsense it is. It's all I think to give you the semblance that there's firm earth. But have a real relationship with a person that goes on for years—well, that's completely unpredictable. Then, you've cut off all your ties to the land, and you're sailing into the unknown, into uncharted seas.*[28]

In a sense, one might say, the "sexual conquest" was made with *A Thought in Three Parts,* but history has posed to Wallace Shawn the question of how such a work becomes historical ("a real relationship with a person that goes on for years"). How does the shock of the new—in this case a direct assault on normative expectations about what should go into a play—translate into something enduring and meaningful, "a real relationship"? Easy enough it is to scandalize the public, horrify the House of Lords, but how does one convert that impulse into a sustained career?

In 1976, Shawn only knew that feeling of getting "good reviews" (i.e., being well-liked, in the full, ironic, Arthur Miller sense) as a rare experience, and this play particularly begged rejection for its caustic portrayal of modern dysfunctional relationships. Here was Shawn, thirty-three years old, exposing the genital organs of a group of actors to the direct scrutiny of the audience—one step short of Annie Sprinkle—and asking, in effect, the audience: Is there any way you could love me (or I you) after I've fucked you over this way? Perhaps not since Alfred Jarry, Tristan Tzara, or indeed Warhol has such a fuck-you attitude prevailed in the latter-day theater (i.e., the whole tradition of theater-is-dead theater). But Ubu, Dada, and *Pork* operate with the uproarious effect of the farce/satire tradition, whereas Shawn's play functions more as a form of torture with excruciating effect, bleak and unerotic.

In terms of age sequence, the ready sexual access of "Youth Hostel" deteriorates into the verbally obstructed engagement of "Summer Evening" and then further degrades into the solipsism of "Mr. Frivolous." In this sequence, the material conditions improve, from hostel to hotel to an appealing room where breakfast is perhaps served. But there is less and less substantiality or richness to the other with whom the subject must deal. The outlook, then, is for increasing alienation, as well as a retreat into self-isolation and neurotic dysfunction. The woman in Mr. Frivolous's fantasy is no more than a figure of his desire. If one thinks of Mr. Frivolous as a degraded version of the man in "Summer Evening," who could, in turn, be seen as a remnant of one of the youths of "Youth Hostel," then the play works diachronically as a cautionary tale—the history of a postmodern Prufrock. In contrast, *Our Late Night* concentrates more on the synchrony, the anatomy, of a relationship in crisis. With his next play, Shawn was to combine the synchronic and diachronic effects with extraordinary success.

"A Powerful Smell of Urine"

Marie and Bruce,
The Mandrake, and
The Music Teacher

Marie and Bruce, written in 1978, returns to the structure of *Our Late Night* with intimate scenes of a modern, urban couple at the beginning and end and a party scene in the middle. *A Thought in Three Parts,* with its three-part structure and its crowded middle play, also makes use of this formal pattern, but there it is the discontinuity—of character, place, and action—that seems foremost in order to set off the radical theatrical gesture of the middle play. *Marie and Bruce* has the social satirical edge of that play and, though it involves no nudity, manages to be just as shocking. Yet it also reverts to the more realistic and continuous dramatic foundation of *Our Late Night.* Indeed, it might be seen as an effective synthesis of the two earlier plays.

A great deal of critical attention, most of it favorable, came to the play, with, for instance, Jack Kroll concluding that Shawn "is a true original, one of the most deeply seeing, sharply writing playwrights we have."[1] The most significant point of similarity among these three "middle" plays, which established Shawn as a playwright with a distinctive voice and subject matter, is the movement from private to public and back to private. An intimacy is tested against the world at large. In effect, the personal is studied at just that point where it becomes the political. Characters in these worlds struggle against various sorts of confinement, ideological and otherwise, that keep them locked in unhappiness. But getting out, in many senses, proves hard to do. With the very first line of *Marie and Bruce,* Marie announces to the audience that she intends to get out of her marriage to Bruce because, as she then shouts to him, "I'm sick of you!"[2] In the spirit of throwing him up (or out), she tells the audience that on the previous day she tossed his old and filthy typewriter out the window, and yet her aggressive gestures provoke only the mildest of replies.

Whereas *Our Late Night* had begun with the central couple in all their vulnerability—asking, in their habit of submission to each other, 'what are the limits of mutual submission?'—*Marie and Bruce* begins in the condition of utter subordination. Marie vilifies Bruce in terms as extreme as words allow. She addresses him as a "God damned worthless piece of filthy shit, you idiot, you asshole, you God damned filthy idiot cock-sucking turd! (*To audience*) I'll tell you frankly I'm fed *up* with this God damned fucking incredible pig, I've had it with him, I've *had* it up to *here,* and I'm going to fuckin' well leave him and see how he likes it" (2–3). To this he replies: "Darling, don't be angry. I'm a nice guy—I am—I'm not so bad. All right, I'm worthless, I'm nothing—I know that. But why can't you accept me? I'm only a person" (3).

It turns out that Bruce has a drive to get out as well, to venture from the marriage, but they are constrained by each other. The marriage is a kind of territory that they both seek to retain and to escape. It is the unlovely space of private life, carved out by a history of liberal individualism, where the self in its most cancerous form eats away at life. De Tocqueville predicted that in a democracy such as he found in America, predicated on equality and individual liberties, the outcome might be a dangerous isolation of the self and a detachment from inherited mores, such as ideas of civic duty, political responsibility, and even an undermining of such institutions as marriage. Marie and Bruce's marriage might be interpreted as an image of the endpoint of that evolution.

It could be said that they are chimerical to each other—he the epitome of the spineless man and she the specter of the castrating woman. They do not exist in the same space as full beings but only as expressions of dysfunctional relationship. A feminist reading might see Bruce as an image of the phallus. Remove the masculine encoding of power in language (i.e., throw out the filthy typewriter), and the man suddenly seems ineffectual—the phallus becomes a limp penis. Marie reports that after she threw out his machine and he was unable to find it, he "came upstairs in his torn little sweater, and he put his head on my chest, and he cried. And he cried and he cried and he cried and he cried, and I finally thought, well, I really have to leave you. I mean, you're a fine little man, you're not a bad little man, but, I mean, I really have to leave you, and I really have to leave you, and there's really just nothing else to say. And that's when I decided that I had to leave him" (9–10). The difficulty, or perhaps impossibility, of this resolve is underscored by the stage direction and dialogue that immediately follows, "*Bruce enters*" (you can't keep a good (little) man down):

BRUCE. Hi, darling.

MARIE. Hi, Bruce.

BRUCE. Do you think we should throw out this coffee? Or keep it one more day?

MARIE. Oh, I don't know, Bruce. What would *you* say about it? Let's hear *your* opinion. Keep it for a day?—or just toss it out?

BRUCE. Well, why don't I make a fresh pot right now—just so you'll have some?

MARIE. Why, Bruce, how thoughtful! I didn't know you were a saint—that's really just terrific—you make a *perfect* saint.

BRUCE. Oh well—thank you—er—darling—I'll just do this quickly. (*He starts to make the coffee. Silence.*)

MARIE. Bruce—darling—I think you smell of urine, sweetheart. (*He keeps working on the coffee.*) I say, sweetheart, I believe your trousers have urine on them, dear. Do you think you should change them?

BRUCE. Darling, I'm trying to concentrate on making this coffee. Is that all right with you, sweetheart? Please don't disturb me.

MARIE. But, darling—your trousers have urine on them today, dearest. I think they should be changed—don't you?

BRUCE. I'm doing my best, darling. I'm doing my best. Simply the best that I can. Simply my best. Simply the best that I can. Now these *aren't* the trousers I'm planning to wear. I'm *planning* to change them. But I need my concentration. I need to pay attention to the thing that I'm doing. Do you follow me, darling?

MARIE. Yes, Bruce. I think I do, dear. I think I do, dearest. (10–11)

She characteristically throughout the play represents him in de-meaning and diminutive terms, often associating his sexuality with excretions. In the intimate, domestic scenes at the beginning of the play, Bruce remains generally constant within his weakness, an eter-nal nebbish, while Marie in her exertions of strength constantly changes aspect. She is the Protean (or Medean) kvetch. She has, in a sense, acquired the fictive power that Bruce lost with his typewriter; she controls his representation and her own. At one point, address-ing him, she parodies a newspaper story, "quoting" the following words: "Yes, a horrible episode happened today. A disgusting, nau-seating animal was seen wandering around in a person's apartment. A revolting dick protruding from his open pajamas revealed the filthy beast to be a male shit of the most disgusting variety. The in-truding filth was immediately chopped into bits, and his revolting member was thrown into the stove where it was roasted. A neigh-bor's baby, coming upon the member and tasting a bite of it, devel-oped an incurable plague and vomited his guts out" (5). With such terms she circumscribes Bruce's existence in her life.

By "a powerful smell of urine" a male dog marks its territory, sig-naling its dominance. That is an image of private property and its do-main of individual prerogative, though not one that the philoso-phers of liberal individualism would particularly esteem. Marie's eruptive response toward that philosophy is continually absorbed within his complacency. This might be seen in political allegorical terms as an image of the revolutionary impulse absorbed—and de-fused—within liberal "goodwill." Bruce's plan for the day is to go out to lunch with his friend Roger, who, according to Marie, will probably deliver his usual boring lessons "about the history of urine and feces in the nineteenth century" (7). This image of the male validating his power by publicly affirming a connection with history ("I know you men need time to yourselves, just to suck each other off in your own little ways" [8]) stands in contrast to Marie's day.

In a long monologue, she tells the audience that she stayed home, preparing herself to go out to a party that night (showering, putting on makeup, etc.), then eventually she left, still too early for the party. A large male dog with a face like a person's somehow led her into a strange garden where, overcome with sensations, she lay down on the ground and fell asleep. When she awoke it was with a powerful desire to have intercourse with the dog, but it ran away before she could carry this out, so she proceeded to the party in this state of ungratified desire. At the party, she encounters Bruce again, and now they see each other from the point of view of their availability to others' desires, and in this way they become desirable to each other. Bruce is a version of this male dog she has encountered, strange but also natural, who intrudes upon her but whom she would allow in. At the party, Bruce tells Marie that every male in the room is looking at her and wants to have her, and in turn Marie calls Bruce beautiful, handsome, attractive. The violence from their private life persists in this public arena, only now Bruce becomes the aggressor. After Marie calls him attractive, he says, "I *like* that, darling. I really do *like* it. Only—aha ha—you should *fuck* me more often then, darling, if you find me so handsome."

MARIE. Oh Bruce—really—

BRUCE. No, really—I mean it—you should *fuck* me more often—I mean, because you can be sort of a *cunt* at certain times, darling, when you refuse to fuck me—I mean, I'm just saying that you really should *fuck* me more often—

MARIE. I hear you, Bruce—

BRUCE. Well, of course I'm being an asshole—I know that, darling. I mean sometimes that's just my way, I mean I seem to be an asshole. I mean, some people aren't, but I just happen to be one somehow—an asshole, I mean—I mean, you know me, darling—(23–24)

He is an asshole in that he shits on people, while she is a cunt in her refusal to be receptive.

Marie becomes more and more delirious and incapacitated during this party scene, which is a landscape of power in its modern guises. The scenes between Marie and Bruce are interspersed among blackly humorous fragments of conversations of the other guests, which encode such themes as class privilege, snobbish intellectualism, the venal ways of polite society, and human exploitation. The scene is a modern *Satyricon*. As this world comes more clearly into focus, with

Bruce fitting in perfectly, Marie recedes, becoming more and more detached and passive, lost in a dream.

Toward the end of the party scene, Bruce recounts to the audience his own experience of coming to the party, in a long monologue that is the counterpart of Marie's story. On his journey to the party, he encountered not a dog but a young woman, who was absorbed in reading a newspaper. He initially resolved to seduce her, but after deciding, on scant evidence, that she was insane, he decided instead to masturbate. So he checked into a hotel room from which he peeped on yet another woman in an apartment across the street. He observed her cleaning the apartment and later reading. He saw her remove her shirt and then, through a tiny crack, glimpsed her continue to change clothes to go out. The spectacle leaves him drenched in sweat in the darkness of the hotel room, but he does not come to orgasm, realizing that he would be late for the party and must set out. Thus, like Marie, Bruce has an extended fantasy that comes to no fulfillment, provoked by an image of the opposite world—for Bruce, the private, and for Marie, the public world. The image that compels Bruce is a window onto interiority and the (self-)absorption of a woman at home alone—with the implicit sexuality of a woman unaccompanied. For Marie, the fantasy image is of the exterior—the garden, with its lush, overstated plant-life—amid which is to be found a phallic, but impersonal, creature.

At the conclusion of Bruce's monologue, Marie awakens, still at the party, feeling really sick. Bruce speculates that she has perhaps become mentally ill, then he rhapsodizes about the lives of servants and the imagined joy of working within the houses of the wealthy, and finally he tells her about a sexual experience he had with another woman at a party some eleven years ago. The balance of power is here the reverse of that in the opening scenes of the play, although Marie had been positively aggressive, while Bruce is here more passive-aggressive. The upshot, however, is to throw Marie into a state of extreme anxiety, in which she is overcome with nightmarish images of being beaten, murdered, raped.

They have been alone together in private, in their apartment, with Bruce the victim of Marie's hostility, and then together in public, at the party, with Marie the victim of Bruce's hostility. Next, they go to a Chinese restaurant, a space where they can be alone together in public. Here, Bruce eats, while Marie is drinking many cups of espresso and becoming, as Bruce notes, very nervous. Marie explodes into an incredible tirade of abuse, telling him over and over in a variety of ways that she hates him. Bruce calmly continues eating through all of this, occasionally making efforts to stir her into small talk or some semblance of civility. Finally, Bruce withdraws: "I know you'd rather have me be quiet. I know how you feel. I was trying to talk, but I can see that it's better to be quiet. It's all right, darling. I'm just going to sit here, and we'll just be quiet, and we can finish our meal" (49–50).

At that moment, two men enter and sit at the next table. One of them describes at great length and in vivid detail an especially horrendous episode of a bloody bowel movement. Bruce goes over to them and tries to get them to change the subject, or at least lower their voices, but is rebuffed in such a painfully humiliating way that Marie goes to the outer limit in her abasement of him, telling him he is not a living person and that she is leaving: "And so because you are now nothing and you are now dead, it means nothing to me to leave you, because you are now nothing. You are death. And I don't know anything about you, because you are meat. You are only meat. God help me—I know what it means to be sitting with nothing. You may say things, but I don't have to listen, because you are death. You are filth. You are only meat. You are filth, You are only filth" (58). There is a silence. Then Bruce tells her that he has bought a new typewriter and is very pleased with it. A pause, and then Marie asks if he will miss his old one. He says no, there is a silence, and then Marie describes bringing him home from the restaurant, drinking some hot milk with him, putting him to bed.

The cadence of her speech becomes drowsy as she describes how she sat and listened for a while to the rain begin to fall, then sank into the bed and slept. That is the end, a sudden submergence of the raging inner life back into the cyclical routine. Brendan Gill described this ending in his review of the play: "To our astonishment, Marie has been transformed into a sort of Manhattan Molly Bloom, speaking a long and poetic soliloquy, wifelike and motherlike, over her little Bruce. There is a sadness in the innumerable 'little's that big Marie has uttered; the marriage is terrible and will last forever."[3] The stream of consciousness of Mr. Frivolous, at the end of *A Thought in Three Parts,* has a similar Molly Bloom quality, while the concluding moments of *Our Late Night* use the series of blackouts, with alternately Lewis or Annette sleeping, as a metaphor for the regular rhythm of sex, of night-time breathing, sun rising and setting, dualism itself, as well as for the emotional discrepancy between two partners within a marriage, the synaptic gap across which some discharge of consciousness might occur. Shawn: "My plays are stylized, I guess, but my dream is total realism. At least that's what I think I'm doing when I'm writing."[4]

The published script of *Marie and Bruce* does not, apparently, tell the whole story. When the play was first done in New York (after having been first produced in London the year before), Shawn declined to provide stage directions with his script in order to encourage a certain sort of experimentation: "If there are no stage directions, the play will never be inert. I went way out on a limb writing the two main characters, and it will take absolutely virtuoso brilliance even to take a stab at acting them. If they're not acted truthfully, this whole thing will just be garbage."[5] This production was directed for the Public Theatre by Wilford Leach, who had three years earlier cast Shawn in his first professional acting role in Machiavelli's *The Mandrake,* for which Shawn also provided the translation. Something must be said of this production and of Shawn's acting in it before the ending of *Marie and Bruce* can be interpreted.

The Mandrake was the play that established Shawn as a performer (a job he has infinitely preferred to that of shipping clerk, which he had held earlier), including drawing the attention of Woody Allen's casting director, which got him cast in *Manhattan.* This was long after the time Allen split up with Louise Lasser, who was to play Marie in *Marie and Bruce,* and after she had virtually defined media iconoclasm as Mary Hartman, the original low-concept, antisoap star. Lasser's divorce from Allen was especially bitter, and it is not inconceivable that she might have put some of her anger into her performance of Marie. The fact that Shawn, who plays the current lover of Woody Allen's former wife in *Manhattan,* provided the vehicle for Lasser to express her hostility works well in the chain of substitutions. In fact, Foster Hirsch says that Lasser's appearance in Shawn's play "aroused speculation that *Marie and Bruce* was a dark, a pitch-black, comedy version of the short-lived stormy Allen-Lasser marriage." Hirsch glimpsed Allen in "the scrawny husband's [Bruce's] deceptively mild manner that is as lethal as it is self-protective."[6] Shawn's part in this equation came in his playing of Siro, described by Brendan Gill as "a servant . . . of unparalleled obsequiousness; when he bows, one fears for his forehead, and only a trifle less for the floor."[7] This Shawn did well enough that suddenly the Xerox-machine operator was a character actor and getting a lot of calls.

Yes, Shawn was able to "get a life" from *The Mandrake,* but it is worth looking closely at what role, and what life, that performance got him. Papp was the one who commissioned Shawn to translate the play, and it is no great stretch to imagine that Papp (and Leach) saw Shawn as a natural for this role and as a surrogate for Machiavelli himself. Machiavelli had introduced into the play an element of his own self-abasing arrogance and manipulative ineffectuality, in the character of Siro, the classic comic parasite. The role is described as follows in Shawn's text of the play: "The basic fact about him is that he has no life of his own; his life is just an instrument to be used by his master; he therefore represents a stunted, degraded form of humanity, despite his intelligence." It is also observed that "he doesn't take himself seriously enough to adopt an ethical position on any issue, even in his own mind, although of all the characters he may be the one most capable of moral awareness."[8] An element of ironic self-reflection becomes visible here. That is, as a partial payback for the play he had commissioned (*A Thought in Three Parts*) and could do nothing with, Papp might have insinuated Shawn into translating (as a writer) and speaking (as an actor) the words of Machiavelli's prologue:

➤ *And if this frivolous material seems unworthy of a writer and a man who would like to be taken seriously, who would like to be considered to be a person who might just possibly have something important to offer to the world—you may say he wrote this pitiful and silly little play simply to make his dull, unhappy days pass a bit more pleasantly. He has no other recourse, no choice, you see, because all other doors have been repeatedly slammed in his face, and the opportunity to show in more important types of work his more valuable talents has been consistently denied him, there being no respect paid to him and no reward offered for the years of dedication he has given to the world.*

The reward that he expects this evening is that each one of you will sit in your little seat and sneer at his play, ripping to shreds in your minds every line and every scene. And of course that's the most common thing in the world today. Everyone loves to criticize and destroy. But unfortunately the consequence of this tendency is that artistic activity happens to be dying out in our world today; and the end result of this is that our world is growing very ugly and debased; because do you really think that the few people of talent who are alive today are going to spend their hours ripping their guts out and smashing their heads against walls trying to produce works of art? Well, they certainly are not, because they know very well that the work they produce will immediately be torn to bits by gales of envious and ignorant vituperation, or else—what is even worse—it will be instantly buried by a thick and sickly fog of total neglect. (11–12)[9]

This was the first bridging of Person A (Shawn the actor) and Person B (Shawn the writer). In this vivid theatrical paradox, the actor (a "sunny presence . . . insistently exuberant," as Walter Kerr described him) struggles to survive in a text (a "witheringly iconoclastic comedy," as Kerr described it)[10] that he had "written" only through the medium of a man who had stood his ground with Cesare Borgia and later written *The Prince*.

Machiavelli was a somewhat impoverished and hard-working aristocrat, like Shawn, someone who tested the ways of civil service, balancing political interests and rights and expediencies, a sort of Kissinger, and he ultimately lost his position when the Medicis came to power. Cesare Borgia was the object of his fascination: the quintessential Renaissance politician, ruthlessly opportunistic and treacherous, yet also remarkably effective at gaining the goals of his faction. In later years, Machiavelli measured his own failure against a theory of the corruptions and advantages inherent in power, using Borgia as his exemplar. His writings pose notable difficulties of interpretation in terms of the layers of irony they involve, such that they might be taken as both a theory or how-to of tyranny and a critique. Machiavelli makes it clear in all his writing that power is the one indispensable and unmistakable term in interpretation, whether it be in analysis of political formations or in the unfolding of a dramatic plot. Indeed, the thing that confuses the political formation is plotting, and what complicates dramatic plotting, when Machiavelli turns to art, is an unresolved political ambiguity. What does it mean to put the Renaissance twist on an essentially Roman plot? What does it mean to exercise pagan values in a Catholic world? Furthermore, what does it mean for Shawn to put the modernist twist on an essentially classic play? And what does it mean to place a postmodern lens on a modernist production? These are questions of how or under what auspices the words and actions of others are to be used.

Late in his life, Machiavelli wrote several plays, including adaptations from ancient drama and new plays, arguably in order to look at just such questions. How should the modern stage (or world) adapt inherited forms, traditions, models to current uses?[11] To what degree are the roles that are inherited from the past appropriate to the present? Machiavelli was a philosopher who insisted that no single standard could be used to evaluate all human actions. Instead, at least two categories must be recognized, the private and the political. He argued that a well-founded moral code might indeed be the most productive for happiness of the individual but that a certain expediency should take precedence in political affairs, even at a cost to individual liberties, and even if it means the state must control by means of fear. Of course, this political philosophy stands diametrically opposite to liberalism, which puts the highest value on individual liberties, and, in its modern form, demands that the state act benevolently toward those who suffer from a deprivation of liberties. Machiavelli spoke both for a more pessimistic attitude toward human beings as political creatures and a much harsher view of the state.

Such was the "master" to whom Shawn/Siro, the translator/parasite, had attached himself. But it should be added that *The Prince* represents Machiavelli decidedly in his Person B aspect, while *The Mandrake* reflects Person A, the antic figure who, as his prologue relates, "wrote this pitiful and silly little play simply to make his dull, unhappy days pass a bit more pleasantly," because, "the opportunity to show in more important types of work his more valuable talents has been consistently denied him" (12). The play is thus a crossover point, in different ways for both Machiavelli and Shawn, in which they can indulge their counter-selves and pose for themselves the question of which of their aspects is the more authentic.

Shawn is sensitive to the ambiguity in the play and his duty to serve that ambiguity. He begins his foreword by asserting that "*The Mandrake* can be seen as a dark, grotesque play or a sunny, delicious one; it is arguably a cruel satire or a joyful tract in praise of human behavior—harsh or kindly, disturbing or delightful, depending on one's point of view" (4). That is Shawn the translator; later in the foreword he speaks on behalf of the performer: "The style of performance may be severe or casual, naturalistic or caricatured, farcical or witty, intellectual or passionate. And the characters too are subject to all sorts of interpretations. In any case, I have included very few stage directions in the text, in order to allow directors, designers, and actors the greatest possible degree of interpretive liberty" (4). Again, one finds this hesitancy about stage directions and the restrictions they impose. Perhaps more significance might be read into this insistence on the interpretive liberties of the individuals within the company, here and also in *Marie and Bruce,* in terms of the Machiavellian and liberal political philosophies. What sort of a "state" was it that Wilford Leach was attempting to direct in this Public Theatre production?

Consider that the core of the cast of *The Mandrake* came from the Manhattan Project. Tom Costello, John Ferraro, Angela Pietropinto, and Larry Pine had played roles in *Our Late Night,* and the same group, more or less, would later appear in *Marie and Bruce* and *The Hotel Play.* These were among the performers who developed *Alice in Wonderland* under the direction of André Gregory, a production that Shawn mentions as one of the theatrical works that meant most to him when he returned to the United States in the early 1970s and resolved to continue playwriting.[12] *Alice* became a legend for the extreme physical expressiveness and risk-taking improvisational style of its acting, and also for the collective or collaborative authorship by which it was created.[13] Perhaps more than any other production of the 1970s, *Alice* defined the liberal ideal in American experimental theater in the sense that here artists operated as equals in a community where sensitivity toward others was of supreme importance, and where authorship (authority, authoritarianism) was distributed among the members of the collective.

Shawn had approached this politic/aesthetic as an author (*Our Late Night*), but they took their time (two and a half years) to accommodate him, and then some years after that they made him a citizen, by making him a servant (Siro) in *The Mandrake*. In the meanwhile, André Gregory, who had taken especial care *not* to be the author of the Manhattan Project's version of the Lewis Carroll conundrum, had fallen out of community with those people. They were, one supposes, among the people he felt were not seeing him for what he actually was during the years described in *My Dinner with André*. Shawn, during those same years, was having the opposite experience, getting his plays produced and happily acting in *The Mandrake* and later in Leach's production of *The Master and Margarita* and Robert David McDonald's *Chinchilla*. Shawn acknowledges in *My Dinner with André* that he had occasional doubts about this community, but these were the years when he was indeed beginning to feel some sense of belonging to the theater community and to feel that he had work to do, that he was a worker.[14] For a guilty aristocrat like Shawn, this was an accomplishment.

Gregory was also born an aristocrat and also discovered work in the theater, including travel to Poland to bring back the lessons of one of the great autocratic philosophers of modern theater, Jerzy Grotowski. In other words, Gregory might be seen as a Machiavelli and Grotowski his Cesare Borgia. The relatively unalienated labor of the Manhattan Project did, however, give way to a crisis in which Gregory experienced the inauthenticity of his life, and like Machiavelli he retired into a kind of isolation where he attempted to make sense of his personal history. Is it sheer coincidence that the project

André explores as a means of getting back into the theater (the world) is Saint Exupéry's *The Little Prince?* Ultimately, he abandoned that project, because the book struck him as "fascistic," latent with an "SS totalitarian sentimentality."[15]

So, Gregory was attempting to deal with the loss of that luxury to which he had been born—a sense of autonomous self—while Shawn was discovering the possibility of belonging in the theater and submerging his own arrogance in the collective purpose. Shawn had literally found a new director in Leach, and he celebrated the fact in his notes to the Dramatists Play Service edition of *The Mandrake.*[16] If you read these words broadly, rather than narrowly, they represent Shawn's purest expression of liberal optimism:

➻ *Though frank, unsentimental, and at times quite unpleasant, the Leach production clearly interpreted the play not as an attack on the world and its ways, but rather as a jubilant and unrestrained celebration of life in all its many manifestations. The production seemed somehow an expression of the health and abundance of the Italian Renaissance, and one could glimpse in it some of the same freshness and freedom, and the same sort of luscious, ripe, and generous sensuality that we see in so many paintings of the period. The acting style employed—this is hard to describe—was both subtle and broad, in a way naturalistic and yet at times quite farcical; the characters seemed larger than life, and yet their behavior from moment to moment seemed truthful and believable. No character was played as a caricature. Every actor was sympathetic to the character that he played, and the effect was that the audience felt a sympathy and liking for each one of the people portrayed.* (62–63)

Concerning the use of some anachronistic touches in the staging, Shawn adds:

➻ *In effect, these anachronisms were like little windows into the reality of the play; they helped to make it clear that the characters were to be seen as real people, involved in real situations and tormented by real passions. And they also conveyed the point that those putting on the play were alive as well, and shared a world with the audience. The actors and all those asso-*

ciated with the production were actually human beings themselves, in other words, and they were trying to have fun and survive and find happiness, like the people in the audience. (66)

This vision of a free, non-exploitative, egalitarian production is suffused with the language of the Declaration of Independence. Leach had provided an environment for "life, liberty, and the pursuit of happiness." Shawn was obviously filled with admiration for this production and its Thomas Jefferson, but also aware of certain risks to which it was subject. In particular, he writes of certain lines that were added to the script by the actors in rehearsal or in production:

➡ *I would caution very strongly against any such improvised lines in general. If injudicious or inappropriate, they can easily destroy an entire scene—or, in fact, the entire play. However, I must admit that my own opinion is that the spirit of the play and the nature of the play—added to the fact that while the original may be a "classic," no translation can be one—do permit the very occasional use of such fundamentally dangerous improprieties. (66)*

It is an author's instinct to resist the actor who goes beyond the script (the contract), just as it is frequently the tendency of authority to be leery of "free speech." The strict constitutionalist enforces the letter of the law and resists improvisation with the social contract.

Nevertheless, when Shawn had his *Marie and Bruce* produced a couple of years later at the same Public Theatre, he seemed quite happy to have Wilford Leach as his director, and he made much of the fact that he left out the stage directions from his script.[17] The party scene, for example, was meant to be a multilayered conjoining of fragmentary bits, and the directors of the New York and London productions accomplished this in quite different ways. Leach used a double revolve and a number of what were described as Duane Hansen-like *papier maché* figures to increase the number of party goers.[18] It would have been silly to record in the published script the exact moments of entrance and exit of all the characters in a scene staged in this manner. As Shawn puts it in his prefatory note to the play,

"Characters and things should be present when they ought to be, and not when they shouldn't be, but the appearance and disappearance of characters and things should be accomplished in a way that does not detract from the smooth and continuous flow of the play" (xii). In other words, the play rules, but the director and actors (who move the characters) will exercise under that rule a certain latitude.

How far can they go? One incident, reported in several reviews of the play, but not recorded in the stage directions, raises insistently the issue of the "dangerous improprieties" to which the liberal "state" is vulnerable. Walter Kerr reports that after Bruce has been humiliated by the man in the restaurant and again proven himself someone who "infinitely prefer[s] cowardice to valor," and presumably after Marie verbally castigates him, as quoted above, the performance then took a turn that is nowhere indicated in the published script: "Enraged beyond endurance, she gets to her feet, doubles her fists, and clobbers the living daylights out of him, mercilessly. The beating is most persuasive, and so—for the moment—is the savage soul behind it."[19] Marie is already the embodiment of dangerous impropriety in this play, the barely contained threat to the weak-kneed liberalism of Bruce, but in this moment her hostile impulse toward that sort of paternalism springs forth "from the smooth and continuous flow of the play." In the midst of the liberal theater establishment, Shawn's insurrectionary play, inspired by Leach and fueled by Lasser, became one great dangerous impropriety.

Perhaps, on some level, this is why a critic like Robert Brustein would call the play "one of the most savage assaults yet on the failure of the American promise." He adds: "Lasser's characterization has all the strengths associated with 'private moments.' At times, we feel we are invading her soul; at others, we are witnesses, and sharers, of unbearable anguish. I can understand why people would have strong negative reactions to this performance; I can only tell you that I personally found it more overpowering than anything I have seen in the theater this year."[20] It would be interesting to know how the experience of Lasser's performance "overpowering" Brustein runs parallel to the spectacle of Marie "overpowering" Bruce. Several other male critics registered the "power" of her performance and of the ending. Brendan Gill, for instance, wrote: "It is a daring chance that the playwright has taken, and I find it imperfectly realized, but what an ending it gives us!"[21] I wonder what ending he means. Is it the spectacle of the ultimate unleashed fury, or is it the quieter "over-powering" that evidently occurs, as Marie relates that she brought Bruce home, made him chocolate, put him to bed, and so on, while the rain fell harder and harder outside.

The whole structure of this play, the very germ of its plot, might be Tennessee Williams's well-known one-act play, *Talk to Me Like the Rain and Let Me Listen.* This is a play about a man and a woman in Manhattan, and the woman has resolved to go away. Independently, first the man and then the woman, go into a "private moment," an intimate narrative of oblique relevance to the immediate scene. Both are deeply shaken by their sudden feelings of distance from the other. Even as they drift apart, they reach for each other. At the end, as the rain falls harder, the woman gradually stops sobbing and calls to the man to come back to bed. In the final image, the man "turns his lost face to her as—THE CURTAIN FALLS."[22] This is a tragic vision that Williams opens in a remarkably short space of time, and a surge of deep feeling answers this scene of unfortunate but also necessary sorrow. Quite opposite is the feeling that responds to the end of Marie's long day's journey into night: "Then it started to rain. Then it rained and rained. It began very gently, very lightly; then the sound of the rain grew stronger and heavier, and I sank down farther into the darkness of my pillow, and my face went down into the pillow, and my mouth opened wide, and I drooled into the pillow, and I sank down farther into it, and farther, and farther, and I slept" (60). Shawn hits just the right wrong notes here, emphasizing a messiness and a suffocation, so that Williams's tragedy seems all at once like a ridiculous anachronism. This "translation" of that "classic" sets "dangerous impropriety" free, even as it goes to sleep.

One further work by Shawn seems relevant to what might be called his male hysteria plays. In 1983, Shawn wrote the libretto for another opera, *The Music Teacher,* composed by his brother, Allen. Allen Shawn followed his brother to Putney and Harvard, then stud ied piano with Nadia Boulanger in Paris. Back in New York, he continued his studies while teaching, composing, and playing in a variety of settings. He was a musician or composer on half a dozen shows at the Public Theatre, including *The Mandrake,* and he also wrote some of the incidental music for *My Dinner with André. The Music Teacher* was given a couple of readings, one at the Public Theatre and the other at the New York City Cultural Center, but has not been produced.

The story is narrated and enacted by Jack Smith, a music professor at a large university, and Jane, a former student. Ten years earlier, Jack tells us he was a music teacher at a New England boarding school (it could be Putney), and he describes himself as a hedonist and "a collector of experiences. A collector of pleasure."23 Jane was about fifteen and a member of the chorus, and she was the one who persuaded him to compose an opera for her to sing. "She was a talented girl. But what a slavedriver she was!" (8). The experience of composing and staging the opera proved such a torment to him that he flew to the city the weekend after the performance and resolved to quit his job. Jane recalls that he became "a complete maniac" and that she "was a prisoner, chained to his piano" (9).

The scene shifts to the opera, and now Jane and Jack are costumed in the roles of adulterous lovers in a pseudoclassical tragedy. Alcimedes (Jack) has come to visit his war buddy, Chronilos, who is played by an unnamed student. Chronilos's wife, Aeola (Jane), serves breakfast to Alcimedes. In keeping with the usual Shawn breakfast motif, the quality of the coffee comes up for discussion. That night, when neither of them can sleep, they happen upon each other, and eventually fall into each other's arms. Chronilos, also unable to sleep (he's so thrilled with the beautiful night), comes upon them and stabs them both with Alcimedes's sword, then stabs himself and goes off to die. The lovers awaken, soon discover that they have been wounded, and eventually die.

It seems no boy on campus was suitable for the role of Alcimedes, so Jack had to sing the role, and thus had the experience of dying in Jane's arms. And so, the opera stages yet another sort of illicit relationship—a faculty/student affair, so far only realized within this musical fiction. Jack flees to the city, but it is clear that a sexual obsession has overtaken him and interrupted the dull monotony of the teaching life. His experience with students had been of nonspecific, interchangeable, constantly replaced faces in the chorus. Suddenly, one person, Jane, has taken on a supplemental identity. There are several vignettes of his school life, in which it becomes increasingly apparent that he is vulnerable because of unresolved desires. Jane recalls on the night before the opera finding herself unable to sleep and setting out for a walk, only to find that Jack is also out walking (as in the opera), but instead of meeting him, embracing, and so on, she simply watches from a distance as he masturbates beside a lake.

Jack recalls going to a hotel dining room, the day after the opera, and then setting out on a sexual rampage (reminiscent of those described in *Our Late Night* and *Marie and Bruce*), first with the hotel dining room singer, later with a waitress—a mad, multiorgasmic plunge. At the conclusion of this rampage, he remembers his life seeming to pass before his eyes: "Without any effort of will at all, my years at the school seemed to have assembled themselves in a neat single file in order to pass before me in some kind of review or inspection. It was a wonderful performance. It was enjoyable, great. In fact I was doing what collectors do in the silence of the night—I was gloating over my piled-up horde and running my treasures through my fingers, so to speak" (71). It is the covert aspect, the private property aspect, of his hidden desires that he indulges in: "I had kept my life a secret because I had wanted no one to be hurt by me, and no one had been. . . . I had been very happy, but I had hurt no one, I had harmed no one" (72).

But the sort of self-indulgence that is involved in these covert pleasures does imply some harm, or at least pain—especially in the distance that is enforced upon both him and the students by the rules that forbid contact between teacher and student. He knows himself to be an undeveloped, unrealized man—a man of immature and uncertain feeling—and senses that among these students is to be found something he desires and also fears: "Every teacher knows the same secret. It explains why most of them are teaching. It's that every year all the teachers get older, but the students don't get any older"

(46–47). The fantasy of remaining eternally young and irresponsible and ripe with potential is what students represent to him.

The next flashback he has begins with him sobbing in his room, presumably because he knows he cannot have Jane. A boy knocks at the door, having heard him crying. Jack is disconcerted at having been discovered in this emotional state, and the boy cannot express just why he is there, except to say, "Sir, I think you're a wonderful man—" (76). With that, the possibility of still another illicit desire that student might have for teacher, and teacher for student, is intimated. Back in the hotel room, as if to test this other avenue of development for himself, Jack asks a bellman who has brought coffee if he is homosexual and then propositions him. They embrace.

The opera turns to the experience of Jane for its conclusion. Just as she represents for him a fantasy of the youth and beauty he would like to retain for himself, he represents for her a fantasy as well, though less distinct. He is, perhaps, a figure of the world she would like to live up to and please, as a student wishes to please a music teacher by performing well. She relates how she got permission to go home for the weekend but instead tracked him down to his hotel room. She presented herself as "a gift to him" (79), naked and willing. He found himself in a frenzy of emotions—panic, reluctance, desire. He made love to her, badly, finally just masturbating next to the bed. She describes how they ate breakfast in silence. Happy with the breakfast, at least, she thought to herself, "Oh, yes—if I ever want to have a really nice time with someone I really really like, I'll come back here" (82–83).

Then they return to the school, and we see her resume her place in the chorus while he conducts them in the song they always sing and have always sung for him, all those interchangeable choruses:

Inside the trunks of trees,
Beneath the frozen streams,
Life lies curled up, sleeping, waiting.
Life lies curled up, sleeping, waiting. (83–84)

It turns out that he was not Jane's fantasy but instead just another man, not notably a good one, and Jane was not Jack's fantasy, just another student, another voice. We know from Jack's narration near the beginning of the opera, though, that he did change his life. He left the school, got married, left his old sublimations behind, that is, except to address them in the opera he is at that moment narrating. The opera, then, functions as a sort of moral tale (in some ways reminiscent of the moral tales of Eric Rohmer).

The opera is formally odd, as might be expected. There are lengthy narrations by the two principal characters and several shorter scenes of dialogue that involve no music at all. Allen Shawn tells me that he recognizes a formal connection between this piece and his and Wallace's childhood collaborations, in which they would together make puppet figures of the characters, hang them in a little theater, and then have them speak long monologues. He also tells me that, as with their boyish inventions, the words come first, the music follows. The music in this opera often makes the bridge into the past, expressing directly the discordance of that distant time with the present. The vocabulary is eclectic, evoking for me Ravel and some American modernists, such as Ives and Nancarrow. On the recording I heard, Allen Shawn plays the piano, and it is easy to discern the virtuosic, sometimes improvisational method one would need to compose incidental music for the theater. At certain points, the music becomes illustrative or parodic, such as in the song of the school chorus, which has clearly an "anthem" sound, or the sleazy piano bar quotation in the restaurant scene. Allen Shawn "hits" his target consistently, with the sure kind of make-your-point theatricality one would expect of a musical technician experienced at trying to figure out what his brother was getting at. The parodic impulse is heard at length in the pseudoclassical opera, which musically and dramatically evokes Debussy's *Pelléas et Mélisande,* although twisted just enough to make it slightly tacky. The longest extended musical statement is in this parody, which is just on the verge of mockery and expresses both a distancing from some outgrown enthusiasm and a deep respect for a perhaps now lost sincerity.

Although this little, untitled opera-within-an-opera is musically quite different from the Shawn brothers's *In the Dark,* which was basically atonal, both of those "earlier" operas (about a decade old) concentrate on the feelings of a couple who meet and unexpectedly make love. Danger, potential or actual, surrounds this act of loving, which is vividly characterized in *In the Dark* as

> *trying to warm the one*
> *whom we hold in our arms,*
> *the one who holds us,*
> *who has no face,*
> *whose weight presses heavily upon us,*
> *lifeless in our hands,*
> *to whom we don't speak,*
> *whom we cannot see,*
> *the dead and dying stranger in the darkness,*
> *whom we don't know,*
> *and who doesn't know us.* (15–16)

The music in both pieces illustrates the confused and anxious—and also lustful—emotions that surge through this act of loving. But in *The Music Teacher* that expressive impulse is now quoted as an example of what the artist figure created ten years earlier, at a time when he was dangerously out of control. Since then, we are made to understand, he has gotten a grip on himself and now has a perspective on that early work.

Something had changed in Wallace Shawn to allow him to take that distance on himself, and the work he created between *Marie and Bruce* and *The Music Teacher* helps explain this change. Shawn begins his preface to *My Dinner with André*:

➡ *I'd been working as a playwright for ten years. My plays had been intense, extreme, even maniacal. That was fine, but now I wanted to do something else, and I didn't know how. The world of my imagination was becoming a prison—I knew every inch of the walls, the floor, and the ceiling. Meanwhile the real world, with its bounteous profusion of fascinating everyday-ness, was lying resplendent outside the gates, winking at me, beyond my grasp. I had generously shown on the stage my interior life as a raging beast, but my exterior life as a mediocre being and dilettante of normal intelligence remained unchronicled. And although my conscious, rational self had cried for expression for years, my unconscious self still kept a brutal grip on my pen. I knew—I knew—that beneath my work's primeval, hysterical facade there was a calm little writer in an armchair just waiting to burst forth, but I didn't know how to reach him; he'd been repressed too savagely for too long.*[24]

My Dinner with André was the astonishing work that began that examination of the calm little man in the armchair—a version of the music teacher, or Bruce with his typewriter—coming to some sudden realization of himself.

"In the Way in Relation to the Others"

My Dinner with André

5

The beginning of *My Dinner with André* tells the story of the beginning of Wallace Shawn's dinner with André Gregory as a diffident, reluctant, even resistant beginning. The film ironically suggests that it begins in spite of itself. Wally did not really want to go to this dinner. He actually dreaded it, and yet now the film's audience finds itself following him to that very dinner named in the title. Fortunately, audiences tend not to be diffident, reluctant, or resistant at the beginning of a film. They want to see what's coming next and know that it's not to be avoided, so they hear the narrator's words across a certain distance. And in fact Wally's words are whimsical, even when he's recounting his anxieties. This is Wally as Woody. He appears on screen wearing a Woody Allen overcoat and a muffler, making his way through the streets of Manhattan to the restaurant as comical and adorable as can be. Only later does the audience recognize that there might indeed be something to dread in this dinner, only after they discover that the paradox of an author repelled by what he is about to experience will be expanded and echoed throughout the work.

The plot of the film—or one of them—is the story of how the film got written, how a dinner became *My Dinner,* and how, in the present, an audience gets hooked into attending that *Dinner*. This story entails leaving home, overcoming obstacles, facing danger, and enjoying a well-earned happy ending, an ending that is unexpected but welcome. It is a kind of melodrama, and like all melodrama it opens a window on hell itself, if only briefly. The particular hell it uncovers is the Sartrean one—other people—which is the hell specific to playwriting: the stories of the other.

The first words of the film are spoken as a voiceover: "The life of a playwright is tough."[1] Wally refers here to his own experience as a writer: doing countless errands, getting rejected, struggling to pay his bills. Financial pressure has even made it impossible on this evening to go home and have dinner with his girlfriend, Debby. She is working as a waitress, just to pay those bills. All this trouble is as nothing, however, compared to the fact that he has agreed to have dinner with a man he has been avoiding "literally for years" (18). André, he tells us, was the man who had "discovered" him and first put on one of his plays on the professional stage.[2] Thus, instead of a comfortable evening with Debby, he must look forward to an evening with someone who has been a guardian and guide in his career, a father figure of sorts. The trouble is, André has stopped putting on plays and has evidently adopted strange beliefs and practices: "It was obvious that something terrible had happened to André, and the whole idea of meeting him made me very nervous. I mean, I really wasn't up for this sort of thing. I had problems of my own. I couldn't help André—was I supposed to be a doctor, or what?" (18).

The question of just what Wally is supposed to be to André—or to himself—is, it turns out, perhaps the central question of the work. Along the way, the film certainly ponders such topics as the collapse of civilized society, the dubious function of art, and the uncertain goal of spiritual quest, but by the end, the practical inquiry has pretty well been honed down to the question of what one human being can *be* to another. At some point during this dreaded "dinner," Wally has evidently come to the recognition that one thing he can be to André is a writer. The screenplay they have just enacted, cowritten by the two of them, serves as proof of that, and indeed the last line of the film sets this up. Having gone "out" to dinner with reluctance, Wally returns home in a better frame of mind to tell Debby "everything about my dinner with André" (113). That telling, which begins at that moment with the introduction of the title, somehow evolved into the production of the movie so that the audience could also hear "everything."[3] Having attended the dinner, having witnessed Wally's discomfort, having heard all the questions and all the answers, the audience might wonder, in retrospect, what change did Wally undergo. Who administered healing to whom?

Wally is, he says, a playwright, not a doctor, but in the course of the evening he will hear from André a good deal about the shortcomings of doctors, those other observers of suffering to whom the world turns for answers, and he will also hear about the inadequacy of the theater, and he will hear things from André that possibly a doctor ought to hear. Signs of a crack up? When André finally arrives at the restaurant, Wally thinks, "He looked crazy to me" (20). And at a certain point, yes, Wally does his best to supply the healing words, make things normal and healthy, cure the disease. Certainly, the situation that presents itself to him is a pathological one, a scene of suffering, and by a certain empathic capacity, Wally comes to share this suffering himself.

No real doctor will attend to this situation, except perhaps, in a way, Chekhov, who stands for a certain capacity of drama to examine real symptoms of human pathology, in the broadest sense. Indeed, the example of Chekhov is invoked often enough and in such a way in Shawn's writings and interviews that he might be taken as the very emblem or standard of playwriting.[4] According to the way Shawn later recalled it in his preface to the work, quoted earlier, the "dinner" was the occasion for Wally to break through the "primeval, hysterical façade" and become the sort of playwright he admired, a realist or even a naturalist, who could finally grasp "the real world, with its bounteous profusion of fascinating everyday-ness" (13).

Ironically, the "calm little writer in an armchair just waiting to burst forth," the man who had been "repressed too savagely, too long," accomplishes his breakthrough by writing not a play but a screenplay, and that only in collaboration.[5] Even though he and André would test the script initially by performing it on a stage, the work was intended from the start as a film. Then, too, Shawn's first step in making this transition to realism would be to invent the dinner. Shawn recalls that they had never, in fact, had such a dinner together before the completion of the script.[6] The simple dramaturgical device of organizing the film around a dinner liberated Shawn from his role as playwright: "He would say absurd things, I would say absurd things, and we would just talk, as people really do. And instead of just writing it myself out of my imagination, André and I would really talk for a while, and then my script would be based on our real conversations, and I would use his words and his ideas— It wouldn't just be me! And the piece would say what he wanted it to say, as well as what I wanted it to say. It would be his piece too" (13–14). Thus, Wally accomplished his goal as writer at this moment by discovering a way *not* to write. The paradoxes multiply in this reminiscence when Shawn acknowledges that he recognized that his job would be to sharpen the conflicts between them, to define their "characters," and to get André to be "the hero." In other words, becoming Chekhov means using the tools of Scribe—the well-made play.

André remembered the origin of the film in a somewhat different way, but also in terms of a transcendence of old roles:

⟿ *[Wally] came over to see me and said that he felt that either I had had a complete nervous breakdown over the last few years, or else a creative block, or a spiritual awakening, or a combination of all three, but whatever it was, when he reached my age (Wally is ten years younger than I am) he didn't want to go through the same thing. And then he proposed that we should sit down together a few times a week and talk and that I should tell him about all the things I had experienced since leaving the theater, and that we should create a fictional piece—a film—based on our talks, and performed by us. I loved the idea, first because there were certain feelings and thoughts that for a long time I had strongly wanted to share with others, and this might be my opportunity to do that, and second because here was a chance for me to return to my old activity of making something for an audience to see, while at the same time surprising myself in the new adventure of being a writer and an actor instead of being a director, and third because it immediately struck me that the most necessary and appropriate piece that one could possibly do at this particular moment in history would be a piece about two friends sitting and talking to each other. So Wally and I immediately began to discuss what kind of a work this could be and what might be its themes. And then when Wally left my apartment, I was struck by a peculiar sensation. I had felt all along that*

the road I'd been traveling in the last few years was sure to end up in some
fascinating city. Suddenly now I had the impression that I could see spires
glimmering just ahead. (10–11)

André is, in fact, "going through hell," and so, very soon, is Wally
by the fact of his being drawn into this dinner. But a glimmering
city, a heaven, seems to await them both.

As a defensive strategy, more than anything else, Wally decides to
adopt the role of a sort of private investigator for the evening, just
to ask questions and find out what he can about this other. This he
admits is a means of avoiding his responsibility as a friend to give
compassion; it is attention without implication. Something happens
along the way, though, and eventually he recognizes himself on the
hellish journey as well. André is Virgil to Wally's Dante in the passage through infernal modern life, life with all its temptations and
pitfalls, in pursuit of some redemption, some answer, some Mount
of Joy. Gregory is a decade older than Shawn and was in his late for-
ties at the time the film was made. In the preface Gregory wrote to
the published version of the screenplay, he comments on the significance of this:

➤ *A few weeks ago I had dinner with Twyla Tharp in her kitchen, and*
we were talking about the problems of the artist, or for that matter the in-
dividual, maturing in our society. Why do we have so few mature artists?
Trying to answer this question, we began to speculate that your early
years, say your twenties, should be all about learning — learning how to
do it, how to say it, learning to master the tools of your craft; having
learned the techniques, then your next several years, say your thirties,
should be all about telling the world with passion and conviction every-
thing that you think you know about your life and your art. Meanwhile,
though, if you have any sense, you'll begin to realize that you just don't
know very much — you don't know enough. And so the next many, many
years, we agreed, should be all about questions, only questions, and that
if you can totally give up your life and your work to questioning, then per-
haps somewhere in your mid-fifties you may find some very small answers
to share with others in your work. (11)

Ten years of trial lie ahead of Wally just to arrive at the uncertain station where André is now. There will be the years of losing conviction, and then the years of questioning will follow, and perhaps at the end (which is also the beginning) "some very small answers" will come out of the dinner that is *My Dinner*. There are passages in the film when the roles of quester and guide, questioner and respondent, are reversed, and ultimately it becomes clear that neither one quite knows the way. They are both lost, somewhere midway on life's journey, in a dark wood, but both have also found some sense of purpose in cowriting this screenplay and acting it out.

Like a Socratic dialogue, the dialectic of Wally and André aspires toward the light of reason, a clear emergence from the dark cave into a recognition of truth. They are both intent on living without illusions, on loving honestly, on knowing why they ought or ought not to make art. (The issues are those of Plato's *Symposium*.)[7] And the film makes clear that it is only by the process of the dialectic, by attaining some synthesis or agreement of ideas, that they do make progress toward understanding. Again, as in several Socratic dialogues, this understanding is represented as being achieved only by their managing to become honest and even loving towards each other, and so the drama here centers on Wally's confronting and overcoming his suspicions and anxieties, his deep mistrust of the world. For André, the drama lies in his trying to cope with the evasions—imaginative and real—to which he has resorted in his life, the fantasies and long journeys and hocus pocus which have, like dream work, partly diverted his attention from the real sources of trauma. At the beginning of the film, Wally admits to the strategy of behaving as a detective or investigator, merely asking questions. At a certain point, the tables are reversed, so to speak, and André becomes the inquisitor. The dinner comes to an end with questions— "Where's that son? You know?"—without answers, reminding the audience of the unresolved nature of this dialectic, the questions that go on unanswered.

What has happened, though, in the course of the film is an engagement of the audience in the dialectic, with one or the other of its participants presumably standing in for the questions the audience might wish to have resolved. But, as in the Socratic dialogues, the pathway of the dialectic is now fixed, written, acted out, photographed. In the *Phaedrus,* Socrates cautions his beloved ephebe against such a fixing in writing of the dialectical process, because a written teaching cannot respond directly to the living questions of its student. So, Plato in writing the Socratic dialogues simultaneously preserves and undermines the scene of instruction, and the result is something that looks like drama (tragedy without the music, as Nietzsche says) but operates much more coercively on the reader.[8] A similar sense of manipulation (Socrates leading his interlocutor by the nose) can be felt in this film, and many have experienced this work as a severe trial, a test of patience. David Denby, for example, writing for *New York* magazine, comments: "If I could have spoken for Shawn, I would have said that dabbling in madness strikes me as asinine, and that Gregory, for all his charm, sounds at times like one of [those] articulate acid-trippers of the sixties who loved to boast of how closely they had come to spinning out of control forever. . . . At last Shawn rouses himself to protest. . . . Yet he never says the one thing that is thunderingly obvious: that any reasonably candid person would have to admit, before calling everyone a robot, that he had bought his way out of his own particular prison with a private income."[9]

Other examples might be cited, tracing other patterns of dissonance with the film's dialectic, but the point is that the film must inevitably prove agonizing to some degree—agonizing in the literal sense of throwing the audience into the contest or debate (*agon*). Perhaps this is why Socrates (or Plato) takes such care to find an amenable place (*locus amoenus*) for his dialogues to take place, such as in the shade of a plane tree for the *Phaedrus.* For Wally and André, this place is an elegant Russian restaurant (another trace of Chekhov, especially in the figure of the aged Russian waiter who in many ways oversees the meal).[10] Both seem to enjoy the food, which looks delicious, but both also register the difficulty of being in this place. Philosophically, if not financially, for both of them this amenable place is impossible, but philosophy is, of course, not all that is happening here. Despite the agonizing quality of the philosophical debate, the audience recognizes, with salivary certainty, that this is a dinner (like *Babette's Feast*) they would love to attend.

Both Wally and André work hard for a time to define, in the Socratic way, the good life. In general, André seems inclined—philosophically—to believe that the way (to "a strong or meaningful experience") is at the top of Mount Everest or in retreat from modern urban life, while Wally seems more inclined—philosophically—to explore the cigar store next to the restaurant or his electric blanket, the proximate realities of daily living. But André has discovered that life and art at the extreme (such as his experience of being buried alive on Halloween) can prove horrifying and not entirely fulfilling. And Wally has discovered that daily living is a tricky business; he sometimes defines his happiness as narrowly as waking up to find that a cockroach has not died in his coffee cup overnight. In this ironically, doubly anti-Candidean, worst-of-all-possible worlds, both comedians in this "intellectual vaudeville"[11] find out that there are "more things in heaven and earth . . . / Than are dreamt of in [Horatio's] philosophy." Those "things" are not Horatio's but Chekhov's, who represents precisely the knowledge that Horatio does not have. Between asceticism and Epicureanism, between metaphysics and empiricism, stands a precise sort of measurement and measure that tolerates ambiguity and indeterminacy.

Ultimately, philosophy is not what this film is all about, and the progress made in the course of the film by the two characters is toward a revelation of what it is to live, not how one should think. Shawn is getting at this when he describes the film as "more intimate" than the staged version in London: "People who saw it there said they saw it as a philosophical dialogue. The movie is totally personal."[12] This is a crucial observation. The philosophy, such as it is, is an effect which the film sets out specifically to transcend or ironize. Concerning the choice of Malle as director, Shawn writes: "We wanted someone who would know how to satirise us both—who would see us clearly as men who had grown up with privilege and money, two lazy dilettantes philosophising over a meal while the world outside was toiling and suffering—and yet who could also portray us with the human sympathy that would be necessary in order to interest an audience in our fate."[13] Note that Shawn refers to a single fate. By different pathways, both Wally and André come to a realization comparable to Roquentin's in Jean-Paul Sartre's *La Nausée:* existence, the life of sheer contingency, without freedom. They discover this independently along quite different pathways of agonized experience and quite apart from all the convenient theories and ideas that pass as philosophy.

In the same novel, the spectre of the Self-Taught Man serves as the exemplar of the humanist who has digested all philosophies. Roquentin finally sees himself in this man and hurries to detach himself from this image of intellectuality. The Self-Taught Man is also depicted at one point as the ultimate humanitarian, and this, too, Roquentin cannot abide. He leaves the library, which is the compendium of that humanism, and in the park, at the roots of a chestnut tree, suddenly, "the veil is torn away."[14] He sees the tree in its existence and knows that the "Nausea" he feels *is* his own existence. He awakens to the challenge of transforming his mere existence into "Being." Likewise, near the end of the film, Wally recognizes that this is the goal (or fate) to which André seems to be driving him, an end which André seems on some level to know without having himself yet experienced it. Wally expresses his resistance toward André in words which seem to answer Sartre as well:

➡ *You know, the truth is, I think I do know what* really *disturbs me about the work that you've described — and I don't even know if I can express it, André — but somehow, if I've understood what you've been saying, it somehow seems that the whole point of the work that you did in those workshops, when you get right down to it and ask what it really was all about — the whole* point, *really, I think, was to enable the people in the workshops, including yourself, to somehow sort of strip away every scrap of* purposefulness *from certain selected moments. And the point of it was so that you would then be able to experience somehow just* pure being. *In other words, you were trying to discover what it would be like to live for certain moments without having any particular thing that you were supposed to be doing. I mean, that was the purpose of these workshops, really. And I think I just simply object to that. I mean, I just don't think I accept the idea that there should be moments in which you're not trying to do anything. I think it's our nature to do things. I think we should do things. I think purposeful-ness is part of our ineradicable basic human structure. And to say that we ought to be able to live without it is like saying that a tree ought to be able to live without branches or roots; but actually, without branches or roots, it wouldn't be a tree. I mean, it would just be a log.* (103–4)[15]

At this point, the pragmatist has answered the transcendentalist, say-ing that the latter's quest seems "absurd." This comes after the tran-scendentalist has questioned the real utility of the pragmatist's work. This point marks the philosophical impasse, after which the film moves toward the personal in a way that categorical figures—the philosophers—cannot follow. The first step toward this comes when Wally calls up the image of himself alone in his apartment; he says he would not just sit, he would get a book. André asks, "And if Debby is there?" Exasperated, Wally declares that that would be just the same; they would both find something to do and not just sit there, which is a concept, Wally admits, that makes him nervous be-cause it seems ridiculous: "I mean, is there really such a thing as two people doing nothing but just simply being together?" (104). This question inevitably points back to the circumstance of Wally and An-dré together at this dinner, apart from their families, doing nothing ("two lazy dilettantes," etc.), "being together."[16]

After all the bad faith and the detours, Wally and André come to the fundamental circumstance of the whole dinner—their coexis-tence—quite apart from Platonic ideals. Roquentin, recollecting his vision of the chestnut tree, gives an extraordinary description of this state:

•• *In another world, circles, bars of music keep their pure and rigid lines. But existence is a deflection. Trees, night-blue pillars, the happy bubbling of a fountain, vital smells, little heat-mists floating in the cold air, a red-haired man digesting on a bench: all this somnolence, all these meals di-gested together, had its comic side. . . . Comic . . . no: it didn't go as far as that, nothing that comic; it was like a floating analogy, almost entirely elusive, with certain aspects of vaudeville. We were a heap of living crea-*

tures, irritated, embarrassed at ourselves, we hadn't the slightest reason to be there, none of us, each one confused, vaguely alarmed, felt in the way in relation to the others.[17] (Sartre's ellipses)

In the way in relation to the others, including each other, Wally and André come at last to the intimate or personal dimension of this "floating analogy" and experience this fated end as a series of questions about what or who they are "in relation." André (Virgil), a crucial decade older, leads a very nervous Wally into this line of inquiry by uncovering the deepest level of doubt about his own authenticity, a doubt that is explicitly phrased in terms of theatricality:

➡ *And I mean, it's a very frightening thing to have to realize suddenly that, my God, I thought I was living my life, but in fact I haven't been a human being. I've been a performer. I haven't been living. I've been acting. I've acted the role of the father. I've acted the role of the husband. I've acted the role of the friend. I've acted the role of the writer or director or whatever. I've lived in the same room with this person, but I haven't really seen them. I haven't really heard them. I haven't really been with them.*[18] (106)

Wally, sitting right beside him, quickly agrees: "I know what you mean. Sometimes people are just existing side by side" (107). Whether one sees this theatrical conundrum in terms of existentialism or neo-Platonism or Gnosticism is immaterial. What we have here is the spectacle of two theatrical creators, appearing "in person" to work out the question of how in a theatrical context they can be authentic to each other and to themselves.[19] André spells out the final, infernal or hellish (Sartrean) questions: "And I mean, people hang on to these images of father, mother, husband, wife, again, for the same reason, because they seem to provide some firm ground. But there's no wife there. What does that mean? A wife. A husband. A son. A baby holds your hands, and then suddenly there's this huge man lifting you off the ground, and then he's gone. Where's that son? You know?" (112–13).

The son, who is Wally, is the man who is soon pleased that André pays for the dinner. On the taxi ride home, he passes the place where he recalls his father taking him to be fitted for a suit, but it's years later and his father is home or somewhere else, and it's hours after the store has closed, and indeed it's late enough that when he gets home, Debby is there, and he can tell her the story of "my dinner with André." That story is the story of a man coming from a lazy dilettantism into a sort of engagement, and the final, transitional turn to the impulse to tell. At the end of Sartre's novel, Roquentin seems to emerge from his dark night of the soul with a new project, something that might, in art, carry out his project of acting in a way that expresses the freedom of his noncontingent "Being." He knows that it would have to be something in a new form:

➙ *It would have to be a book: I don't know how to do anything else. But not a history book: history talks about what has existed—an existant can never justify the existence of another existant. . . . Another type of book. I don't quite know which kind—but you would have to guess, behind the printed words, behind the pages, at something which would not exist, which would be above existence. A story, for example, something that could never happen, an adventure. It would have to be beautiful and hard as steel and make people ashamed of their existence.*[20] (my ellipsis)

Readers of his book disagree over whether Sartre means to imply that this novel in some way *is* the book Roquentin proposes to write.[21] Forty years after Sartre's novel came out, in a moment after existentialism, Shawn and Gregory confronted a sense of absurdity in their lives comparable to what Roquentin faced and looked to a new form for an answer. *My Dinner with André,* which is, in a sense, the history of that impulse, returns critically to Roquentin's assumptions. They look again at the question of whether "an existant can never justify the existence of another existant," and between themselves—two existants—putting shame aside, they ask us.

Sartre, of course, later supplied a more definite answer to Roquentin's half-formed question about how he should make use of his own freedom, that is, in political engagement. In recent years, anyway, Gregory has insisted that Shawn was aiming at a similar commitment. In effect, Gregory says that (Shawn's) "personal" is

(Sartre's) "political." He points to the fact that Shawn has been political all his life and especially alert to the political exigencies of the totalitarian state. Thus, André's many references to Nazism in the film call up for both of them a latent "dark" side, which, despite their common Jewish ancestry, they might find themselves unable to confront. Gregory says that Shawn knows Wally is a person who might find that his business is more important to him than the Jews crossing Warsaw in a trolley. And Gregory acknowledges that he himself is the sort of extremist who might become so involved with his own religious search that he could accede to totalitarianism.[22] Una Chaudhuri takes this dualism even further, seeing in the film a contestatory debate between the ideology of the 1960s and the 1970s—in effect making the film into an allegory in which distinct political attitudes come to terms with each other.[23] This political line of interpretation might seem initially to conflict with the "intimate" reading promoted by Shawn himself. But the truly remarkable achievement of the film is that it brings these different points of view into direct contact—the intimate with the parabolic. The film puts Chekhov into the exact same space as Brecht.

In the film, André invokes Brecht in terms that amplify the subject of coexistence, discussed above:

•◦ *And then when you think of Bertolt Brecht—he did something that was perhaps the most amazing thing of all. You know, he somehow created a theater in which people could observe, that was vastly entertaining and exciting, but in which the excitement didn't overwhelm you. I mean, he managed to allow you the distance between the play and yourself that in fact two human beings need in order to live together.* (85)

Then, immediately following this statement, come words that were published but not included in the film, words which Shawn did not need because there is enough Chekhov in this scene that their point is implicit and unmistakable:

•◦ *You know, people say that [Brecht] was against feeling, but that's just not true. I think he was looking for a kind of clarity in the theater that would*

Beyond "A Certain Chain of Reasoning"

Aunt Dan and Lemon

An hour or so into Claude Lanzmann's film *Shoah,* one first sees the shot that, repeated over and over through the next eight hours, has become its signature shot. It is what is known as a tracking shot, where the camera is moved in order to move the searching eye of the viewer. It is a questioning shot: To what does the eye lead? Here the camera appears to move on the long-disused railroad track leading from the station of Auschwitz, Poland, to the death camp, and again and again the camera advances toward and eventually enters the gate to the ramp where Jews were unloaded to be gassed. At first, Lanzmann cuts away before the "train" (of which the viewer is both passenger and engineer) crosses the threshold. Then, at last, one passes through the gate, and one listens, involuntarily, for the click that signifies the passage into a world of despair and death.

During another scene in the film, Lanzmann insists upon a witness pointing out precisely where the wall of Treblinka had been, and Lanzmann walks across that perimeter, which is now invisible in a grassy field, as if to feel for the knife edge at that border. He says: "This is the Polish part, and over there was death."[1] *Shoah* is a film that might be described as a single nine-and-a-half hour tracking shot in search of that edge.

The many near-victims whom he interviews at length knew that border too well. Their stories help bring the edge into focus. Otherwise, thirty or forty years later, there is dismayingly little to show that such a demarcation ever existed. The camps look like parks. The Nazis planted one camp with pine trees after it was shut down, so now it is a forest. The camera passes smoothly through the archway into what was Auschwitz, and there is little difference now between the place where the trains rolled up on death and the place just out-side, where farmers worked their fields all those years. There is no actual click at the threshold, no signal that what happened here was anything radically other than the natural landscape. The fact is that even the harrowing testimony of these blessed/cursed survivors and the words of a few sympathetic others do not register that the atroc-ities are anything other than historical—meaning, of the historicized past. The recurrent, smooth tracking shot into Auschwitz resounds with awareness that not much separates "normality" from genocide even now.

Wallace Shawn's play *Aunt Dan and Lemon* opened the same year *Shoah* was released, 1985, and it, too, explores the landscape of hu-man atrocity in search of significant borderlines. Here, though, the long "tracking shots" are through a psychological landscape of life in the Anglo-American 1960s, as recalled from the 1980s. In the rea-soning of his character named Lemon, Shawn listens for the click that would signify passage from innocent or normative thinking to fascistic amorality. But what one hears at that borderline is silence. A sort of grass has grown over the death camps in the memories of those who were never threatened, and now it is hard to tell just when one passes from sweet reason into inhuman rationalization. The play engages its audience in an extraordinarily complex dialectic, trap-ping them in certain dangerous habits of perception and judgment conditioned by the usual handling of political message within con-temporary drama.[2] A certain self-conscious antitheatricalism thus defines Shawn's approach to his subject and becomes a strategy for revealing the dangerous myths of the basic theatrical contract, what binds an audience in a submissive relationship to the very power of drama. While the play might seem a continuous field of grass at first, the knife edge cuts through at last, reminding one that nowhere, cer-tainly not in the theater, can there ever again be a simple walk through the countryside.

Lemon (a nickname for Leonora) is the character who addresses the audience at the beginning and end of the play. She is a woman in her mid twenties, "weak and sick."[3] These long speeches—of fif-teen and twenty minutes respectively—frame a series of flashback scenes from the childhood of Lemon, when she came under the influence of a charismatic friend of her parents, whom she knows as Aunt Dan. Dan, short for Danielle, was "one of the youngest Americans to ever teach at Oxford" (21). There she had befriended Lemon's English mother and her American father, both students, and had remained close when the father became a businessman and the mother gave birth to Lemon in 1960.

Lemon introduces these scenes from her past by saying that her most intense memories "go back to my childhood, but not so much to things that I did: instead I remember things I was told" (5). The audience hears long speeches from the father and mother, in which their personality flaws become apparent—the father's overbearing anger and the mother's insubstantiality. There are also snippets of remembered scenes in which one sees their endearing characteristics, their playfulness and intellectuality and zeal for life, only then to hear that one by one these qualities have slipped away. At barely ten years of age, Lemon awakened to a steady dislike of her father and a contemptuous pity for her mother:

➻ *My mother was a saint—she loved him very dearly. But my father was a kind of caged animal, he'd been deprived of everything that would keep him healthy. His life was unsanitary in every way. His entire environment—his cage . . . was unclean. He was never given a thorough washing. So no wonder . . . his fur was falling out, he was growing thinner and thinner every day. His teeth were rotten, his shit was rotten, and of course he stank. He stank to hell. When we sat at the table, as if everything was normal, everything was fine, there was an overpowering stench that was coming from my father. My mother ignored it, but you have to say, she did get sick and die at the age of fifty. (14–15; Shawn's ellipses)[4]*

Meanwhile, Lemon has turned more and more to Aunt Dan for instruction and example in adulthood. When Lemon was eleven (in 1971), Aunt Dan spent an entire summer with the family and each evening visited the girl before bedtime, telling her "about every complicated subject in the world" (21), including lurid stories of her own life and that of her friends. The upshot of this for Lemon is a radical altering of her parental configuration, such that "my mother and father had other friends, and they had their own lives, and they had each other, and they had me. But I had only Aunt Dan" (22).

In a series of long speeches, Aunt Dan tells Lemon first about her former lovers, and then, with much the same zest, about her idol, Henry Kissinger. Dan had never met Kissinger, only once observing him in a restaurant, but she has evolved an elaborate vision of him as a lonely genius who bravely takes on the most solemn and thankless task of being a world leader. Lemon, who becomes enraptured by these Homeric evocations of the secretary of state, is troubled to find that her mother does not like Kissinger.[5] The long speeches culminate in a series of dialogues in which Dan simply bowls over the too-polite liberal protestations of the mother. Lemon has heard Dan speak of Kissinger in terms at least as inflamed as those used for her lovers. Indeed, Lemon imagines herself running away to live in a flat with Dan, where Kissinger would drop in frequently for easy-going intimacy, and there Lemon would offer herself to him as a "personal slave." From this point of view, her mother's vaguely expressed reservations about Kissinger's involvement in the bombing of Vietnam seem like typically repressive parental qualms—doubts about a leather-jacketed boyfriend who smokes.

Dan also personalizes the politics here by defending Kissinger on the basis of an imagined intimate knowledge of his private thoughts and intentions such as only a lover might have. Dan comes to associate the mother's protests with the criticisms advanced by journalists, to which she exclaims: "They're out to stop him! Defying the father figure, the big daddy! Worms! Worms! How *dare* they attack him for killing peasants?" (46). In answer to this torrent of abuse against the children who would overturn the "big daddy," the mother musters only a feeble, metaphorical question of whether Kissinger has "a heart" that is capable of deciding correctly. Dan construes him as the master who longs to be a slave or a little child rather than face such terrible decisions, if only he were not the one best suited to the awesome task. Lemon, the child who would offer her body to this hero, takes a lesson in idealized romantic passion from this debate, and the lesson tells her that her own parents must be replaced. They seem all too abstracted from real feeling and action—the father obsessed with "orders" in a closed system, the mother preferring a philanthropic compassion to Dan's political/erotic passion.

This debate is followed by a series of fragmentary scenes that are enactments of stories told by Aunt Dan about a circle of friends, including some shady figures and one extraordinary libertine, named Mindy, who held a particular fascination for Dan. Indeed, Aunt Dan tells Lemon what she has *heard* about Mindy's way with sexual relations and what she herself, as a voyeur, has *seen* of Mindy in a sexual relation, and she tells her more than a little of what she has *experienced* in a sexual relation with Mindy. All this is a sensational awakening to the eleven-year-old girl. In the slow tracking shot of Lemon's memory, which is what drives the play, one listens to the stories that are retold and reconstructed for the moment when they pass over the threshold, from spicy tales to corruption of a minor.

This structure, analyzing through flashback the course of evolution through successive layers of memory, from personal memory to a sort of collective memory of a whole generation, to some degree resembles Eugene O'Neill's *The Emperor Jones*. Both plays begin and end in the present moment to show where this developmental process, which is outlined in the flashbacks, has arrived. Both plays reveal the "guilt" of the main character to be the consequence of a systemic failure. But where O'Neill points to a social cause of Jones's self-alienation (i.e., the whole pattern of appropriation implicit in capitalist enslavement), Shawn points to a psychological, as well as a social, moment that has produced Lemon. Jones, in his journey into memory, goes back through successive generations, passing from personal memory to race memory. Lemon, too, goes back through generations, retelling or reanimating scenes from her own life and from Dan's life and from the stories Dan tells of other lives, all of which are relatively contemporaneous but generative of one another. In its search for origins, the play explores a complex series of parental configurations among the play's characters.

Kissinger, whom Dan idolizes as a perfect man—sensitive but firm, supremely conscientious, and infallible in his judgment—and Mindy, whom Dan also idolizes as a "gorgeous, perfect" woman,

desirable but detached from her own desires, supremely opportunistic, and masterly in her execution—form a sort of dream image
of an ideal marriage, with Aunt Dan who "loves" them both as the
agent or *copula* of the love-making between them. Dan, by revealing
her sexual passions for these two, thus brings Lemon indirectly to
what Freud calls the primal scene, a witnessing of the sex act between
mother and father. This "scene," which might be actual or imaginary, propels the child into unappeasable Oedipal conflict with her
own parents. Dan has assumed singularly the role of Lemon's dual
parents, and she has brought her "child" to a recognition of the desires that bind her (Dan) to each of them, in their idealized forms as
Kissinger and Mindy, as well as the antipathies that repel her from
their debased forms, Lemon's real mother and father. Dan herself,
who can love the father (Kissinger) for his distance and the mother
(Mindy) for her availability, has gone so far as to transgress the
taboo by actually consummating her relationship with Mindy.
Lemon, in turn, by a clear transitivity of affect, has been brought to
the point where she discovers her own desire to transgress the taboo
in a sexual relation with Dan. Lemon's desires, however, were never
gratified, but in beautiful restaurants where they met she recalls that
they would both be thinking, "Well, why not?"

Early in the play we see Lemon in a dinner table scene with her
parents, being pressed to eat when her impulse is to die rather than
swallow their meats: "Mummy, it's raw" (13). As she puts it, "There
was a problem about that family table for me" (12). Several years
later, with her surrogate or vicarious mother/father, she fixes on
"some odd moments, some crazy moments" in those restaurants
where they met, when the full feast lay open before her. "There you
are sitting right next to me," she recalls musing, "and isn't this silly?
Why don't I just lean over and give you a kiss?" (75). Shawn here, as
in several of his earlier works, plays on the strong association of sexual appetite and hunger. Indeed, the first words the audience hears
from Dan come when she is saying grace at a picnic in what she calls
"this garden of life" (17). Lemon imagines herself as "a beautiful apple" (75) that Dan might have plucked but did not. The Edenic innocence that was thus preserved has led to corruption of a different

sort. In her opening speech, Lemon declares, "Most of my 'sex,' if you can call it that, has been with myself" (4). She sustains herself in this unfruitful, unplucked isolation mainly by drinking fruit and vegetable juices. She has rotted on the tree.

Dan has been formed as a child-woman by her passions for Kissinger (seen once in a restaurant) and Mindy (seen first in a restaurant). They are the figures, male and female, whom she honors above all others and who do most to shape her way of being. They are the ones who have given her appetite, of both sorts. They have, in this sense, generated her, and yet she has transgressively corrupted those feelings by overriding the taboo in her sexual relation with Mindy and somehow also by excusing the killing of innocents on the part of Kissinger (i.e., of North Vietnamese peasants). Lemon comes to her own primal scene (and to her desire for Dan) by way of the feast that is laid before her by Dan, which centers upon the ultimate food, Dan herself, whose stories are laden with references to big meals she has eaten, especially after sex. Lemon would like to partake of this feast, for once overcoming what has made her "weak and sick," but holds back because her anorexia extends beyond an attitude toward food to her whole outlook on life and love:

➤ *But of course Dan would never have touched me first. I would have to have touched her. Well, neither of us really took those moments seriously at all. But sure, there were moments, there were silences, when I could feel her thinking, Well, here I am sitting on this nice lawn, under this lovely tree, and there's a beautiful apple up there that I've got my eye on, and maybe if I just wait, if I just sit waiting here very quietly, maybe the apple will drop right into my lap. I could feel her thinking it, and I could feel how simple and natural it would be just to do it, just to hold her face and kiss her on the lips, but I never did it.* (75)

Freud's notion of the primal scene has been applied to literary influence by Harold Bloom, who identifies a kindred "scene of instruction" that binds a later poet in an Oedipal relationship to a precursor poet. The later poet operates under an "anxiety of influence," a painful sense of belatedness, in which the poet longs to return to the scene of the precursor poet's act of creation—the artistic moment that in some sense defines the tradition that, inescapably, the later poet can never originate.[6] This metaphor of poetic tradition bears direct relevance to the series of relationships depicted here, because these characters know one another largely by acts of reading and discernment of personal styles. Lemon's mother studied English poetry at Oxford, feeding on it rapturously without regard to other appetites. Lemon recalls as one of her happiest memories the sound of her mother reading poetry out loud. The audience hears a fragment of one of these readings—earnest, latter-day romanticism. Lemon's perception of the loss of intimacy with her mother is a realization that the readings had come to an end: "There was one evening, some evening, which was the very last time she read to us all, but no one remembered that evening or even noticed it" (20–21).

What replaced the poetic readings were the stories that Aunt Dan began to tell her in the little outbuilding from the house, which Lemon had converted to her bedroom when she was eleven. These stories are first about the sensational incidents in Dan's love-life. Later they are the testaments to Kissinger and retellings of stories she has heard from Mindy. Lemon has thus been vicarious witness to Aunt Dan's "poetic" scene of instruction, her reception of influence from Kissinger and Mindy, and Lemon has in turn received instruction or influence from Dan. But Dan, in defiance of the so-called Electra complex, which governs mothers and daughters as the Oedipal complex governs fathers and sons, has actually come into the arms of the "mother" figure, Mindy (who, of course, is merely a friend and lover, except within this mythic parental configuration). But Lemon, outside of the lineal pattern (like Electra herself), does not fall prey to the desires.

Clytemnestra succumbs to the vengeful tradition of the House of Atreus by murdering Agamemnon to revenge the killing of Iphigenia, and she is regarded as unnaturally manlike for this deed. Dan, too, succumbs to a masculine "tradition" in her desire to possess Mindy. In thus embodying the male, Aunt Dan becomes the "perfect" androgyne (as the terms of her name suggest) for Lemon to adopt as a single parent. One might note that the context for this "unnatural" gender-shifting and parental replacement is the moment when the "father," Agamemnon/Kissinger, is off at war. Dan's stout defense of Kissinger against the womanly doubts raised by Lemon's mother further associates her with the masculine heroic tradition.

It is a pulp sort of literature that Lemon hears from Dan, in contrast to the refined dullness of the mother's readings, but filled with apparent glimpses of the ultimate mystery of love and also steeped in mythic tradition. The Oresteian correspondences that have been cited become especially strong in the stories that Dan retells from Mindy (from the tradition) and suggest that the motherlode of poetic material from which this play draws is to be found neither in the lyric genre of the mother nor in the pulp narrative genre of Dan but in the dramatic genre. The two most theatrical scenes of this play—indeed, the *only* theatrical scenes in the sense that all other scenes might be presented with little loss as a radio play—are enactments of the stories of Mindy.

The first is a scene in which Mindy brings Jasper back to her circle of friends, including Dan, and manages to seduce him into spending an enormous sum to have sex with her. This is done in the spirit of open challenge—he has won the money gambling, and he has freely offered her ten thousand to start. Dan has early on resolved to watch this scene to its conclusion, offering five pounds for her seat at the show (a likely theater ticket price for the time). After Mindy has literally screwed an astonishing sixty thousand pounds out of him, and Jasper has fallen asleep, Mindy, stark naked, then tells Dan other remarkable stories of her life: "There wasn't much that she hadn't done, and there were things she didn't tell anyone about, but she told me" (59).

One of these things is a story of Mindy conspiring to kill Raimondo, a Latino con man who had "been working with the police for some time against her friend, Freddie" (72). The scene is enacted for the audience, and both Dan and Lemon are on stage for most of it to watch what happens, though Dan has only heard the story from Mindy, and Lemon from Dan, and we in the audience of this staging are presumably "hearing it" from Lemon. Mindy seduces Raimondo (and Dan and Lemon and the audience) in a slowly developing series of acts of the sort that turn audiences completely silent with throat-tightening erotic fascination. Using a false identity, she beguiles him with coy talk in a restaurant, wrapping herself around his Latin flirtations. When they arrive at her apartment, he confesses that it had been the sight of her lavender stockings that had enticed him. Like the purple cloth spread on the ground before Agamemnon, this sensuous indulgence becomes his downfall. In her bedroom, "the light from the window falls on the stockings" (71). She dopes him then strangles him with the stockings as he cries out. In his "Note on the Set," Shawn reports that in the Max Stafford-Clark production, Lemon appeared in every scene (as an observer, at least), except at the beginning of this bedroom scene. During this scene, "the back flat parted at one point, and the whole garden could be seen, with Aunt Dan and Lemon in it, watching."[7] This inversion of the *pathos* scene in Greek tragedy, such as the revelation of the body of Agamemnon, slain in his bath, underscores the theatricality of this core scene. It is an audience, inactively, impassively watching, that represents the ultimate horror disclosed by this tragedy.

Attracted by—what?—the cold-blooded executive style of this Clytemnestran deed, Dan could no longer resist reaching out from the "theater" to make contact with the mythic figure that Mindy has embodied. At the conclusion of the story, Dan says that she touched the rose lipstick of "this naked goddess," who "grabbed my hand and gave it a big kiss, and my hand was all red" (72). For a "wonderful week," they engaged in a Dionysian orgy, feasting and making love. Then Dan's story comes to an end. After a charged moment, Lemon asks, "Why only a week?" (73). Dan answers this question—the only words until now spoken directly by Lemon to Dan—with a speech that is the crux of this play, a speech that seems to bar Lemon from deeper intimacy with Dan and to answer the question, "Well, why not?"

•• *Lemon, you know, it's because . . .* (Pause.) *Because love always cries out to be somehow expressed.* (Pause.) *But the expression of love leads somehow—nowhere.* (A silence.) *You express love, and suddenly you've . . . you've dropped off the map you were on, in a way, and onto another one—unrelated—like a bug being brushed from the edge of a table and falling off onto the rug below. The beauty of a face makes you touch a hand, and suddenly you're in a world of actions, of experiences, unrelated to the beauty of that face, unrelated to that face at all, unrelated to beauty. You're doing things and saying things you never wanted to say or do. You're suddenly spending every moment of your life in conversations, in encounters, that have no connection with anything you ever wanted for yourself. What you felt was love. What you felt was that the face was beautiful. And it was not enough for you just to feel love, just to sit in the presence of beauty and enjoy it. Something about your feeling itself made that impossible. And so you just didn't ask, Well, what will happen when I touch that hand? What will happen between that person and me? What will even happen to the thing I'm feeling at this very moment? Instead, you just walked right off that table, and there was that person, with all their qualities, and there was you, with all your qualities, and there you were together. And it's always, of course, extremely fascinating for as long as you can stand it, but it has nothing to do with the love you originally felt. Every time, in a way, you think it will have something to do with the love you felt. But it never does. It never has anything to do with love. (73–74)*

This speech leaves Lemon permanently no more than a spectator to the mythic drama that Dan has *seen* and *enacted* and *passed on* in traditional form, the drama of human contact itself, and Lemon's testimony shows that she has remained largely detached from life ever since, never more than a spectator. It says that to express love is to lose it. Containment within the self is thus the safest course, a maintenance of the isolation that comes of nonparticipation in discourse or, in all senses, intercourse. The temptation to enter into the world of actions, to become an actor and not just a spectator, must be resisted or one faces the sort of loss that comes of "spending" your life in love.

The "expense of spirit in a waste of shame," as Shakespeare called it (Sonnet 129), is the sort of "spending" to which Lemon has turned for her sexual appetite, while for her other appetite, "I spend all my money on these wonderful drinks—lime and celery and lemon and grape—because I'm a very sick girl, and these juices are almost all I can take to sustain this poor little body of mine" (1). This restrictive attitude toward "spending" can be traced not just to the lesson that Dan gives her, but also to the first test of her mistrust of the consequences of expression. Lemon tells of a visit to Dan's flat when Dan was sick and dying. In the bathroom, Lemon faces all the legible and tangible evidences of the mortal being she has never really touched: the medicine bottles "with labels I don't want to read" and the "well-worn towel, bearer of the imprint of her nose, her mouth—I feel no need now ever to see her again" (76). In this moment, she has literally washed her hands of Dan. In the room with Dan and hearing of the "wonderful woman" who has been caring for her "as if she were a nun," Lemon speaks—spends—only five words: "An older woman? . . . A nun?" (76–77). Dan has given her a kind of instruction in the ways of being human, including the expression of love, but that instruction has resulted in a Lemon incapable of compassion even for the chosen surrogate parent. Dan has seemed a self-willed phenomenon in her prime, after the examples of Mindy and Kissinger, but in her decline, she requires the care and intimacy of a "wonderful woman." Where Lemon has found a substitute in Dan for her inadequate parents, Dan has found a substitute in this nun-like woman for the inadequate Lemon. Indeed, the girl has proved a lemon in her capacity to make contact, as well as in other respects—intelligence, general health, productivity.

Lemon's most profound appetite that requires satisfaction in her adult life, once Dan, like Lemon's real parents, proves out of reach (and indeed all have died), is the filling of her imagination with sensation and story. Her life is largely occupied in the effort to make the time pass or in sleep. Once detective stories had the role of satisfying or stupefying her sensibility, but lately she has been reading instead about Nazi death camps, so she tells the audience, near the beginning of the play. To an extent, she admires the skill with which they accomplished their goal of exterminating Jews, not because she approves of (or even morally evaluates) that goal, but because, in the abstract, the clever and ruthless obliteration of an "undesirable" seems to stimulate an almost erotic fascination within her. What fantasy of Lemon's, one might ask, does this historical example serve? Whom would she like to kill? Her father (who "stank")? Her mother (who doubted Kissinger)? Dan (who passed beyond the need of her and died, but not beautifully)?

Shawn has said that the "unifying theme of the play is clearly the education of Lemon," and Lemon's first speech, in which she declares her keen interest in the Nazis, is the first glimpse we have of just where this "education" has taken her. The puzzle posed by the play is just how she has been brought to the point of admiring the actions that constitute one of the more repugnant atrocities in history. Shawn has posed the over-arching question explicitly in a preface to the Dramatists Play Service edition of the play: "Lemon, in *Aunt Dan and Lemon,* doesn't say the same things Aunt Dan has said, and you, in the real world, don't say the same things Lemon has said. Lemon's attitudes are different from Aunt Dan's in certain ways and different from yours in certain ways. But there are also similarities. Is Lemon a bad disciple of Aunt Dan or a good disciple? Is Lemon a million miles from you, or me, or is she somewhat closer?"[8] These are the questions that hang, somewhat oppressively, over the play. In fact, as the integumentary history of Lemon's character unfolds throughout the flashback scenes, one can hardly forget the sponsoring vision, set forward in this opening speech, of a woman to whom genocide is a process to be admired. She wonders at the genius of the mechanism at Treblinka that drove people theatrically to their deaths, in deluded complicity, under the willing suspension of disbelief. When the illusion broke down on the "Road to Heaven" outside the gas chambers, the whip—direct contact—insured compliance.

Lemon, too, was led through a chain of theatrical illusions, with her parents and later Dan giving her a false image of love and then stripping her of the capacity to experience it. Dan has misled her in her instructions in the nature of love, replacing the deeply reciprocal, hence generous, feeling with a selfish sensationalism. Lemon's discovery that she is unwilling and unable, finally, to touch or love Dan, the one person who has offered her most in the way of instruction in touching or loving, seems to have propelled her into the radical isolation evident in the character at the beginning and end of the play. Lemon was led down the garden path, so to speak, toward an apple or "Heaven" that turned into death and the fall. Theatrical illusion has led her down this "Road to Heaven" to the point where, in the presence of Dan, she feels the whip, the physical disgust at the fact of death, which turns her permanently from direct contact with life. Hereafter, she will embrace and be thankful for whatever mechanism intervenes between her and death, and especially between her and killing. These are the mechanisms that free her from the burden of compassion or sympathy—the "feeling with" emotions that demand contact.

In the final, long speech, spoken just after the brief scene with the dying Aunt Dan, Lemon translates her "education" into an instruction for the audience. Here is where the "moral" of the play might be expected. She begins with a defense of her interest in the Nazis and gets at the element of fictional creation in the life of an empowered individual or group. She says, "The thing is that the Nazis were trying to create a certain way of life for themselves" (77). The final phrase of this sentence recurs in this peroration as the ultimately vague phrase describing the end that might justify virtually any means, including the extermination of anything or anybody threatening the achievement of that way of life. While she concedes the Nazis might have been "wrong" in their beliefs and "ruthless" in their tactics, she resists the tendency to interpret their actions as inhuman, because "the mere fact of killing human beings in order to create a certain way of life is not something that exactly distinguishes the Nazis from everybody else" (78). She advances three examples to support this contention—the killing of criminals, Communists, and American Indians. Each of these categories of human beings has, in certain contexts, so threatened the "certain way of life" of another group that killing has been adopted as a moral right, or at least as a practical necessity beyond moral review. She then advances another succession of three sorts of killing in order to speak from her own experience and to establish (a) that the spectacle of death, of however lowly a creature, is not pleasant, and (b) that the larger the creature, the more unpleasant the death. She begins with the experience of killing cockroaches so numerous as to threaten a way of life. Then she recalls the experience of killing a laboratory rat in an experiment. Finally, she speaks from acquired facts about the unpleasantness of killing a human being, by hanging or gas chamber. In this series, she gives human beings no special status at all.

At this point, the rhetoric of her speech manages by trickery and sheer force to fuse some apparently logical connections that will not stand up to closer scrutiny. The browbeating method of her argumentation (for which, in rhythm and method, compare Aunt Dan's defense of Kissinger) involves a particularly devious use of the first person plural in the following crucial passage. Note the shift of pronouns:

➡ *Now when people say, "Oh the Nazis were different from anyone, the Nazis were different from anyone," well, perhaps that's true in at least one way, which is that they observed themselves extremely frankly in the act of killing, and they admitted frankly how they really felt about the whole process. Yes, of course, they admitted, it's very unpleasant, and if we didn't have to do it in order to create a way of life that we want for ourselves, we would never be involved in killing at all. But since we have to do it, why not be truthful about it, and why not admit that yes, yes, there's something inside us that likes to kill. Some part of us. There's something inside us that likes to do it. Why shouldn't that be so?* (81–82)

And she goes on using the first person plural without continuing reference to the Nazis, so that this passage, in fact, has the rhetorical force of demonstrating that the Nazis *are* indistinguishable from anyone else, except in the refreshing frankness with which they faced the need to kill.

Lemon has learned honesty from Aunt Dan, and so she, too, can take interest in the basic truths about killing and self-interest, however faulty and transgressive they might seem to most people. She will go on to argue that animal nature "enjoys" killing, hence human nature, too, on some level, since it is "derived" from animal nature, must feel that enjoyment. The doubtfulness of her assumptions here, and the shaky logic of the argument, are overcome by a still more accelerated and rhythmic mode of speech. In the following four climactic sentences, the hypnotizing repetitions initially build to a peak and then, after a series of protracting phrases that increase the tension to a maximum, release into the conclusion that has perhaps impelled the whole speech, if not the whole play:

➥ *In polite society, people don't discuss it, but the fact is that it's enjoyable — it's enjoyable — to make plans for killing, and it's enjoyable to learn about killing that is done by other people, and it's enjoyable to think about killing, and it's enjoyable to read about killing, and it's even enjoyable actually to kill, although when we ourselves are actually killing, an element of unpleasantness always comes in. That unpleasant feeling starts to come in. But even there, one has to say, even though there's an unpleasant side at first to watching people die, we have to admit that after watching for a while — maybe after watching for a day or maybe for a week or a year — it's still in a way unpleasant to watch, but on the other hand we have to admit that after we've watched it for all that time — well, we don't really actually care any more. We have to admit that we don't really care.* (82–83)

Here she turns explicitly to one of the "things I was told" as a child, a memory that surely impels the emotional surcharge laid upon this abandonment of care: "I remember my mother screaming all the time, 'Compassion! Compassion! You have to have compassion for other people! You have to have compassion for other human beings'" (83). It is the word "screaming" that points to the emotional double-bind she had known as a child. Dan had taught her, as she later says, "a kind of honesty" (84) that enabled her to face the absence of compassion as an experience within her life. This is a lesson Lemon had learned and that she now seeks to pass on to the audience. In the opening words of the play, she addresses the audience as "little children," reminding one of Oedipus's opening words to the citizens of Thebes. But opposite to Oedipus, whose discovery of the truth about his infancy in the course of the tragedy undercuts his use of the parental voice, Lemon discovers the (a)moral authority at her command despite the fact that she has not matured, has not grown up.

Ultimately, of course, Aunt Dan, like Lemon's mother and father, had proven herself part of the world that must be rejected because in the end she had spoken feelingly of the woman who cared for her, while Lemon had found herself quite unable to face the "unpleasantness" of the death that was occurring, slowly, before her. Lemon recalls: "And plenty of people have cried in my presence or seemed

the audience. The giving of applause is a sort of compensation offered for the work. Here, though, in this inverted sort of play that does not trade on an exchange of sympathy for suffering, with the assumption that such an exchange affirms the humanity and moral elevation and aesthetic sensibility of the audience, the call for applause works as something else. First of all, the character who makes this call, Lemon, requests no thanks for her own role. Instead, she calls for the audience to thank those others, unnamed, who kill. Those are the true actors, since they are the ones whose actions preserve the "certain way of life"—the way of life in which people can amuse themselves as they wish, including going to the theater. Lemon is grateful because within this comfortable way of life she can quietly follow her personal interest in Nazi death camps.

Lemon has a passive but frank attitude toward this situation, and the audience must question the extent to which their passivity (while "enjoying a certain way of life") makes them *complicit* with Lemon and thus forthcoming with the "tiny, fractional crumb of thanks" for such killers as the Nazis were once and someone else is now. Exactly how do we distinguish Lemon's interest in the Nazis from our interest in Lemon and Aunt Dan and all the other characters who exist in a world that subsists on killers? In a world where grass has grown on the death camps, just where is the place where one discerns that the Holocaust still exists, not as a memory but as an immanent condition? Claude Lanzmann takes the viewer repeatedly down the track (the very same track!) and through the gate into what was Auschwitz. One listens for the "click," the demarcation into strangeness and atrocity, but instead hears nothing. In listening to Lemon's final speech, one listens also for the "click" that signifies she has become a monster, an incarnation of evil, a dismissible wrongness that would allow for quick and sure rejection of her point of view. Shawn has described the process by which a Lemon is made in an essay, "On the Context of the Play," that is published along with the script: "A perfectly decent person can turn into a monster perfectly easily. And there's no reason why he would feel any different. Because the difference between a perfectly decent person and a monster is just a few thoughts. The perfectly decent person who follows a certain chain of reasoning, ever so slightly and subtly incorrect, becomes a perfect monster at the end of the chain" (99).

Certainly there are moments when Lemon's reasoning by analogy (from animal to human, human to animal) becomes questionable. Then, too, she seems to speak from an idealized understanding rather than a practical sense of just what it is she is condoning. There are other moments when bitter personal feelings stemming from her past seem to give fire and direction to her rhetoric. But compare, for a moment, Sonya's long speech at the end of *Uncle Vanya* in which she attempts to soothe Vanya (and herself) with a hopeful vision of future peace to follow a life of work and self-sacrifice. Sonya's vision might well strike an audience as a dream, an ideal, with little possibility of realization. Her consolatory words, offered for the audience's benefit as well, might encourage a resignation to the degraded conditions that exist rather than a will to change them. Lemon's speech, in many ways diametrically opposite, also offers a sort of comfort to the audience, through acceptance of the circumstances that support a comfortable life, asking only a crumb of thanks in return. Both characters speak idealistically, arguably even falsely. Both come to these strong concluding words through the somewhat unlucky circumstances and turns of their pasts and families. If Sonya might be excused, in the moment, for her resort to euphoric idealism, considering the recent failure of her hopes for Astrov and the obvious despair of Vanya, then should not the same audience find a way to excuse Lemon for the withering of her belief in love and compassion, given her experiences with her parents and Aunt Dan?

Lemon has embraced the position of those who choose the "certain way of life," whatever "unpleasantness" that might involve, while Sonya has embraced the religious vision that foresees a fulfilled life after death. Within the dramatic context of these plays, their final positions can be interpreted, understood, even accepted as valid for the characters. But when, as necessarily happens at the terminus, these final speeches become detached from the play and "speak to" the audience, a shift occurs. Is Chekhov "promoting" a faith in the redeemed afterlife? Excepting this final speech, it is hard to find much in the play that could be construed as such. Is Shawn "promoting" a rejection of compassion or an appreciation of the Nazis? The play that he has written could hardly be seen as an effective instrument for those purposes. And so here, as in the Chekhov play, the ending with (or out of) the long final speech involves a subtle and deceptive transition. But Shawn's play puts the audience on very dangerous ground at the end, because the very process of showing appreciation for the play, through applause or otherwise, is implicated into the structure of Lemon's argument. Shawn has put a "click" into this ordinarily smooth transition, in which the play on some level routinely confirms the beliefs of the audience, and the audience in turn confirms its belief in the play, or at least in the cultural enterprise of which the play is a part, the theater. This play ends with the click that marks the transition to real life as a transition into monstrosity, immorality, atrocity, unless a reply can be assembled at once. The audience must respond or this play fails disastrously. What, they must ask, is wrong with Lemon's argument? and what is wrong with the world in which she lives?

Lemon asks for a little honest gratitude. Shawn asks for something more, which is a turning away from the gratifying illusions supplied by the theater, even if that means a rejection of the theater itself. This last step is not one that Shawn seems to find unacceptable, at least in the United States, where the theater has never had quite the central communicative function that it has in other countries. *Aunt Dan and Lemon* aims at a transcendence or rejection of a theater that diverts, soothes, entertains "common humanity." The "certain chain of reasoning" leads inexorably by bonds of trust from the origins of theater in perfect innocence, in the garden, through the mythic tradition, from Mindy to Dan, from Dan to Lemon, from Lemon to the audience, a chain of corruptions that might result in a perfectly complicit, perfectly monstrous audience, giving thanks at the end, unless those bonds of trust are broken and the theater becomes a space of debate and confrontation with reality. Ahead of its time, *Aunt Dan and Lemon* is a child who demands a divorce from its parents, the theater, and all the Aunt Dans and Lemons who fill its seats. *Aunt Dan and Lemon* aims at the words that have been and are still to be written beyond itself.

Of course, it is not unusual that a play should represent and even feature a political attitude that might differ from that of its audience. What is strange is that this play has not subjected that attitude to a debate, so that the merits of the case could be weighed, so that sides could be chosen. Instead, a vaguely faulty argument about a moral ambiguity is advanced at the conclusion of a peculiarly disengaging play, and no counter-argument effectively answers it. Rarely is the audience drawn so directly into a play's dialectic. In its historical moment, those who saw the play contextualized it as either an expression of or an attack on the state of self-interested amorality of the Reagan years. When asked in an interview why no articulate liberal response had been included in the play, Shawn was direct:

➡ *For two reasons. One is that I'm trying to hold the mirror up to nature. What you might call the liberal voice is not the dominant one in America right now. People like myself have been reduced to a gaping, open-mouthed silence in this particular period; and the response to Reagan by those who oppose him hasn't been as inspired as one might hope. But the second point is that I'm trying to provoke a response in the many hundreds who I hope will see the play. I think it's more interesting not to put my own attitudes into the play, which would allow the audience to go home satisfied. The audience has to react to this play, otherwise it's a disaster. If they sit there like a piece of cheese, it would be a horrible experience.*[9]

In an effort to insure that the audience will not turn into cheese, Shawn has attempted to fill in some of that context, some of that blank space at the conclusion of the play where a reply must be formulated, in "On the Context of the Play." This essay appeared in the souvenir program of the first production and appears also in the "acting edition" (where the blank space at the beginning of the play is also filled in with an even more directive preface called "Notes in Justification of Putting the Audience through a Difficult Evening").[10] In the first person, Shawn recounts his own experience of being trained in moral responsibility and then, in recent years, witnessing some of his friends "throwing away their moral chains and learning to enjoy their true situation." They accept the good fortune of nice homes, gardens, food, toys for the children, even at the cost of becoming very hard-nosed about those who would threaten their prosperity. They take a lively, dispassionate interest in the brutal ways of gangsters. They learn to manipulate and deceive. They arm themselves. With simple, small decisions they move along the moral scale. Shawn writes:

•• *There are a million possible degrees of obedience [to morality], and the person who obeys morality to a higher degree is more admirable than the person who obeys it less, and the person who doesn't struggle to obey it at all is not admirable at all. Of course, almost everyone describes himself as a servant of morality, and even the most outrageous criminals will make such claims, not just publicly but even to themselves, and undoubtedly Hitler himself was no exception.* (105)

As one moves along this scale, where exactly does one hear the click that signifies a crossing into something atrocious, approaching even Hitler himself?

This is the test *Aunt Dan and Lemon* poses for its audience, the dilemma of passively following a faulty chain of reasoning (Lemon's) to its end, or of actively constructing a new bridge to morality, however uncertain of definition that might prove. How simple the one, how nearly impossible the other. When this test was put to audiences in 1985 in London and New York, and since then in other cities, it provoked a remarkable range of critical responses. In an interview, Shawn had praise for the part that critics (most of them) played in taking a "leadership role" in interpreting this admittedly difficult play and sending the audiences into the theater "in the right frame of mind."[11] Frank Rich, for example, in the *New York Times,* gave this summary:

•• *[T]here's a whiff of Shaw in Wallace Shawn's* Aunt Dan and Lemon, *a perversely funny play in which the most genteel characters say the most monstrously fascist things in lengthy, oddly shaped monologues. "Aunt Dan" can drive theatergoers of all knee-jerk ideological persuasions wild by refusing to tell them what to think. The audience must instead muster its own counter-arguments to the characters' seductive rationalizations for governmental immorality.*[12]

In general, the critics worked out and admired the twisted dialectic of this play and had then the task of selling an evening that might prove important but not especially delightful. John Peter, for the *Sunday Times* of London, successfully captured this paradox, calling the play "an astringent and uncomfortable experience, both demoralizing and invigorating: like a breath of black, fresh air."[13]

Sylviane Gold, however, in a review in the *Wall Street Journal,* under the headline "Unopposed Neo-Nazism Is Irresponsible," took quite an opposite point of view. Referring to Lemon's final speech, she writes:

•• *Whether you see this line of reasoning as a defense of the Nazis or as an indictment of everyone else, it's unacceptable. And it's especially unacceptable in the theater. It's one thing to read Hobbes or Nietzsche alone at home, cozy in an armchair with a good, non-glary reading lamp nearby, and to say, "Yes, this is really the way we are, and life outside really is nasty, brutish and short." But when we go to a play, we are outside, surrounded by strangers among whom we will let down our guard and be touched or amused or chagrined by what is happening on the stage. Going to the theater is itself an act of trust, an affirmation of our common humanity, and for a playwright to tell us that we are all killers is to subvert the very meaning of theater.*

The plays of Aeschylus, Shakespeare, and O'Neill tell "unpleasant truths," she writes, but "leave us with a shred of hope, or . . . feeling the terror and pity of tragedy," or at least "with our humanity intact." Dismissing the "sophisticated dramatic ploy" that asks the audience to disagree with "what his play actually says," she relentlessly pursues this theme of betrayal of the theater. In doing so, she portrays the audience for this play in terms disturbingly familiar to Shawn's essay "On the Context of the Play":

➥ New Yorkers are going to go to this play because they've been told it's important, because they'll want to have their say when it comes up at the next dinner party. And besides, it's not cool to be revolted by something we've seen. It's even faintly embarrassing to bring up old-fashioned notions such as moral responsibility in talking about the theater. Yet it occurs to me that Mr. Shawn has failed to consider not only what theatergoing is all about, but also that there may be some people in his audience who will buy Dan's and Lemon's arguments, who will see the logic and not the horror.[14]

In summary, Gold sees this play as an occasion for the gathering of a new sort of audience, chic, smug, too cool, morally anesthetized. This play helps them sustain their "certain way of life" by giving them the opportunity to "have their say," and despite the fact that it says "we're all killers." They know enough to discredit its ideas as all part of a terribly sophisticated ploy, a ploy to leave the unsophisticated audience still more in the dark. (Shawn recalls with pain the experience of watching a small segment of the audience each night so totally misread the play as to think it a return of Hitlerism.)[15] This betrayal of "common humanity" derives from Shawn's basic abuse of traditional theater. Of course, the fact that Gold sees through the sophisticated ploy does not signify that she is detached from common humanity, because she (like Shawn, in his essay) is able to overcome the embarrassment of bringing up "old-fashioned notions such as moral responsibility in talking about the theater." It appears that what she objects to is that the play will become the substance of dinner party conversations, rather than being left quietly behind in the sacred precinct of the theater, and yet she, too, perpetuates discussion of it in her contentious review. Frank Rich observed: "The absence of ideological or moral closure is why even the play's detractors can't stop talking about it."[16]

Gold's argument is finally contradictory, but it raises an important issue: Shawn's self-conscious abuse of the theater. Here is another "chain of reasoning" that Shawn has pursued to its end. Aunt Dan has exposed Lemon to a series of scenes from a mythic tradition (legends of demonic women) and unopposed speeches, and in this way has exploited the sensationalizing capacity of a certain sort of drama in order to abuse its instructional function. Lemon passes on that abuse to the audience of the play by using the occasion of its gathering to relay the same images and more from her own past, with again a series of unopposed speeches. Even the element of Dan's corruption of a minor is passed on, as Lemon addresses the audience as "little children," in the opening speech. Indeed, the play's title might be taken for that of a children's play or story. Lemon exclaims at the innocence of the audience and then invites them into her flat. Of course, children should never go into the house of a stranger, especially one who knows too much about the Nazis (see Stephen King's novella, *An Apt Pupil*). Lemon draws this innocent audience along her "certain chain of reasoning" to the point where perfect monstrosity is within reach. Lemon was drawn passively along a similar (but not identical) chain of reasoning by Dan, and Lemon might have finally reached her hand out to touch. At the end of the play, Lemon invites the audience to reach out from their passivity and give "a tiny, fractional crumb of thanks." Even applause, using the hands in the traditional manner to express thanks for the play (and for Lemon's instruction), becomes defined as giving thanks to the killers.

Indeed, this is a corruption of the theater and an entrapment of the audience. The very quality of "trust" that Gold values so highly in the traditional theater here becomes redefined as complicity with a deceptive mechanism, the theater itself. The traditional theater, in perpetuating the notion that those who enjoy the comfort of "a certain way of life" are equivalent to "common humanity," participates in the killing mechanism that eliminates from view all those who lack that comfort and who would therefore threaten that way of life. Lemon's "honesty" at the end of the play coincides with Shawn's to the extent that both think it wrong that people should go away thinking that the exercise of something they call compassion, at a distance, in a theater, somehow qualifies them as part of a better world, discontinuous from the world where killing takes place.

"A Piece—Of a Human Brain"

The Fever

•◦ *"what an hour of my labor would probably be worth"*
—Wallace Shawn, *The Fever*

At one point in *My Dinner with André,* André recalls an impulse he had when directing the *Bacchae* at Yale in 1969. What he wanted to do was get a real head from a corpse at the New Haven morgue, so that when Agaue enters toward the end of the tragedy with the head of Pentheus she could pass it around the audience to make people realize "that this stuff was real, see." The actress refused to consider the idea. Years later, after his long quest for something to reanimate his impulse toward making theater "real," André doubts that he would again propose such a solution, but, he acknowledges, "I still think it would be wonderful if the perceptions of the audience could be brought to life, if the senses of the audience could be brought to life."[1]

Bring death itself or its intimation into the theater, the thinking goes, to waken the sleeping—or dead—sensibilities at a primal level. On the other hand, in the same context André wonders whether "serious contemporary plays" by writers like Wally might be inappropriate vehicles for a reawakening; perhaps "those works which once were outcries *against* the darkness can now only contribute to the deadening process." This leads to the most reflexive moment of the film, the moment that is about why neither one of them, at that moment, is engaged in making theater, instead they are talking, head to head, in a restaurant, in a film. This moment is about the death of theater and must, therefore, frame the dialectic of the film and frame also the subsequent "serious contemporary plays" by Wallace Shawn:

➡ *Well, Wally, how do you think it affects an audience to put on one of these plays in which you show that people are totally isolated now, and they can't reach each other, and their lives are obsessive and driven and desperate? Or how does it affect them to see a play that shows that our world is full of nothing but shocking sexual events and violence and terror? Does that help to wake up a sleeping audience? You see, I don't think so, because I think it's very likely that the picture of the world that you're showing them in a play like that is exactly the picture of the world that they already have. . . . So the play simply tells them that their impression of the world is correct, and there's absolutely no way out, there's nothing they can do. They end up feeling passive and impotent. And so the experience has helped to deaden them. They're more asleep than when they went into the theater.*[2]

The Fever, which is serious and contemporary, though probably not a play, tests André's suspicions about plays that show people in "total isolation." Through approximately two hours of monologue, Shawn's solitary, unnamed character (played initially by Shawn himself) frankly confronts his feelings of passivity and impotence in the face of a world gone mad with violence and terror, in the face of death. The storytelling is triggered by the onset of sickness in a Third World hotel bathroom. He speaks of his privileged childhood, his adult life in the elite culture, the crisis of coming to face the reality of poverty in the world, and the existence of a revolutionary impulse directed toward his class of society. He resolves nothing but shapes a fully dimensional image of his guilt.

The piece has the effect of picking up in an abstract way André's suggestion for the *Bacchae.* Here, however, the object to be passed around the audience is the news that theater as it is known and expected is dead (or, more specifically, and in keeping with Euripides, that tragedy is dead). The work challenges the deep assumptions about what it is to have a life in the theater by juxtaposing reflections about what it is to have death in life.

Suppose we in André's deadened "audience" suddenly wake up now, but wake in a terrible fever. Who would be the doctor to tell us the feverish awakening is better than sleep and oblivion? Shawn takes on that task and reminds us forcibly of the traditional and now suspect function and purpose of catharsis. Purgation of the tragic emotions, pity and fear, through vicarious participation in enacted myth, myths of downfall—this is the effect that the earliest audiences are said to have sought from the form of theater itself. It is the effect that initially separated actor from chorus member in the dithyrambic chorus, so the theory goes. And that separation—of the one who represents suffering from the one who empathizes—mirrors the separation of performer from spectator. Separation—scapegoating—is what the theater, the "seeing place," was born for. Someone would enact that scene of suffering so that others could watch.

However, *The Fever* is a play of sorts that invites us to awaken not in the theater. Shawn's note to the work tells us the piece was "originally written with the idea in mind that it could be performed in homes and apartments, for groups of ten or twelve."[3] In fact, "piece" is the term Shawn seems to prefer for it, and in the "Note on Performance," included in the acting edition, he explains why:

➥ *One way to think about one of the problems of doing the piece is that you want people to listen to you and to understand what you're saying, but what you're actually saying is something that 99 percent of your audience will not want to hear. You yourself probably don't really want to hear it. So if people say to you afterwards, "I really enjoyed the show," you will feel that you failed, because the piece, while it is after all, in a way, a play (about a particular character going through a particular experience) is also at the same time something else which is not a play, some kind of human exhortation which is meant to arouse thought and action, not appreciation or enjoyment. So if too many people say, "I enjoyed the show," the temptation is then to do the piece more militantly or with more passion so as to underline the non-play aspect of the play. The danger, though, is that if you perform it too forcefully, many audience members may be unable to listen to you. Also, a forceful performance may not be appropriate, in the sense that the drama of the event should really occur in the spectator's mind, not in the performance.*[4]

And so it's a fever in our life we awaken to, and the writer could be right here, in our midst, in our *living* room. Shawn is the writer, and Shawn has been its performer, in homes and apartments, and in several theaters as well, in New York, London, Los Angeles, and elsewhere, addressing audiences as small as three and as large as eight hundred. The production traveled easily, requiring only Shawn, who usually performed the whole thing sitting in a chair, without so much as a blackout to frame the piece as theater. Indeed, Shawn discovered a fascinating paradox about the piece's representational dynamics, a functional absence within its presence:

➻ *I often felt, as I performed the piece, that there was an almost mathematical relationship between my own involvement in a given line on a given night—the vividness of my perception of the images, the intensity of my feeling about what I was saying—and the interest, involvement, and concentration of the audience: The more involved I was, the less involved they were. The longer I performed the piece, the more I learned that I could almost withdraw myself entirely from certain passages, so that it seemed to me almost as if I were reading from a book, or as if the audience members were reading the book, and the whole issue of how I "felt" about what was being said just dropped away.*[5]

How *I* "felt" about what was being said provided the occasion for this chapter, indeed this book, which began with this essay (not a review), since I write in Santa Barbara, a place where theater of national importance, by and large, is not. Wallace Shawn had not been here when I first read and wrote about *The Fever,* at least not so far as I know, although André Gregory had just moved to a ranch in the valley above. But conceivably the work *might* be here, in the overpriced homes and apartments, among groups of ten or twelve. It would be hard to imagine finer living rooms in which a skull might be passed around, or in which a Harvard aristocrat might dwell on the fact that he no longer felt at home. Many, many a living room in Santa Barbara might have been opened for the after-dinner visit of the entertainer *manqué,* the undertaker on a ludic bent—the theater in exile. Perhaps *The Fever* means to say that it is only in the homes and apartments of those who entertain the concept of theater and of tragedy that the theater can address the waking or resurrected senses of those people. In an interview, Shawn spoke of his intention for among the privileged and the parallel effects of giving and receiving presence in a theater were what drove Shawn to the unnamed, underprivileged foreign country where, with vomiting, Shawn's story begins, or begins over again. In the "present" of the narration, he is away from the theater, very sick, purging himself horribly, and in the "present" of the (imagined) performance in my home or apartment for a group of ten or twelve he is also away from the theater, purging himself of accumulated guilt about the idle satisfactions of his life, including his life in and around the theater. *The Fever* represents a self-imposed exile from the theater, including what André called "serious contemporary plays," to a place where the conditions of presentation (giving presents) might be more favorable.[8]

Euripides, the latest and bitterest of the three extant Attic tragedians, who seems to have come to great acclaim only after he died at nearly eighty years of age, made a strong gesture toward immortality with the play that was perhaps his last, first produced a year or so after his death, the *Bacchae*. This tragedy is well known for its apparent return, at the end of the tragic epoch, to the origin of the form in the ritual celebrations of the cult of Dionysus. Dionysus speaks first in the play, announcing his return home to Thebes after a long sojourn in foreign countries to the east. Dionysus had been largely absent all those years from the dramatic form he had given birth to—perhaps laid low in a foreign hotel—but he has returned to tragedy, and he is now masked. His kinsmen do not acknowledge or recognize his godly power, do not serve his image, and so he has struck some of them mad, and others, including his "cousin," the royal Pentheus, he entices into theatrical self-representation—cross-dressing, no less—which gets Pentheus slaughtered as a beast. All of this results, sequentially, in a recognition of the bliss of the Dionysian and the catastrophic horror of the same. The entertainments of theater are ever entwined with the bloody entrails. Dionysus, the purveyor of ecstasy, returns to the "living room" of prosperous Athens in this play (by way of the spectacle of Dionysus the god returning to prosperous Thebes), and he serves up a meal worthy of Tantalus. The piece he offers is meat that cannot be digested, a tragedy that is a horrifying mockery of tragedy—a grinning skull. He leaves the Athenian spectators in a situation like Agaue's, holding the bloody head of her son, whom she has mistaken for a lion. Dionysus has brought madness—the fever—home with him.

At a certain point, the lore goes, Euripides, within a few years of his death, perceiving unmistakable signs of the demise of Athenian civilization, and never having had great success in the competitions against Sophocles and others, turned his back on Athens and the Theater of Dionysus and exiled himself to Macedon to live out his days in disgruntled isolation in a cave. He left the theater behind. And he wrote the *Bacchae,* which was enough to make a decent Athenian choke on his catharsis, even more so than the same author's utterly cynical *Orestes* (his *Aunt Dan and Lemon,* with the god who is no god speaking at the end) of a couple years before.

Euripides sent the swan song off to Athens and posterity, where it has been largely misinterpreted ever since. Its most obvious message—Don't count on the theater for the exaltation of your pathetic life—has eluded a surprising number of interpreters. Nietzsche, however, called it the death of tragedy. He said Euripides had brought the spectator, the average theatergoer, which is to say the privileged child, onto the stage, there to inspire distrust of tragic illusion and its emotional release and to replace them with the Socratic dialectic. Plato's dialogues, one recalls, also take place in homes and apartments for groups of as many as ten or twelve.

It's Christian of him—Shawn, Dionysus—to come among us and to allow us to come unto him. Where two or three are gathered, there something other than and in replacement of the theater, the tragedy, the passion, can be. It is a different sort of cult, not like the one that made followers of the theater out of followers of Dionysus or Christ. Instead, we find what Shawn discovered in a "follower of Marx," an armed guerilla named Juana, for whom Marx was wonderful because he "had made the strange gesture of throwing his life at the feet of the poor. In other words, *Marx* was a follower of *theirs*" (25).

In this Euripidean cadenza on the *Bacchae,* Shawn has returned home after a series of journeys to poor countries where his language isn't spoken, having discovered the extreme detachment from life that his upbringing and his chosen career in the theater have allowed him. A kind of ecstasy—removal from oneself—has been available to him in pretensions to superiority or godhood, all of which the theater offers to its followers. But that ecstasy has also afforded the Dionysian followers the opportunity to mask the true tragedies of the world, the scenes of rending or *pathos,* the victimization or scapegoating, that exist as a necessary precondition to tragic representation.

Dionysus returns home to test his people, especially his mother's sister, Agaue, and her son, Pentheus. Both have denied the fact of his godhood and his powers. Pentheus he manipulates into assuming the guise of a cult follower in order that he might watch the rites as an audience member. Agaue he inspires with the ecstasy of his cult, then deludes with madness to the point that she mistakes her son for a mountain lion and kills him. Both are made to experience the creative and destructive forces inherent in the theatrical form, the pleasures and the dangers. How bitter this pill must have seemed to the Athenian audience in 405–6 B.C., at the point of utter defeat in the Peloponnesian Wars and with the last vestiges of democracy being rudely swept away.

Shawn, too, returns home in this piece to test his people, in this case by decentering the dramatic from the theatrical. Into our homes and apartments comes Shawn or his $8.95 paperback, and there we are challenged to accept this desperate apology (arguably also a variation on Socrates's) as a play. If we do so, though, if we put it on an imaginary stage and take from it the occasion for our personal catharsis or release, then we are likely to feel, like Pentheus, wounded where we had sought satisfaction. Because it offers no redemption, no godhood, it flatters no vanity—in place of wine it gives vomit. As the speaker says: "And it's as if a voice like vomit is coming up slowly from my throat. Stop!" (54).

So removed is this primary gesture from the usual gesture of the theater that the piece must end by begging forgiveness. The speaker concludes with an anticipation of the moment of his return home, when he will bring this terrible wisdom along and give it to his friends, his producers, his followers ("Everyone has always been so good to me" [54]). And in this moment comes an anticipation of the fragmented body, the death's head, that he will then bring back to pass among the audience:

⊷ *Next week, home.*
What will be home? My own bed. My night table. And on the table—
what? On the table—what?—blood—death—a fragment of bone—a
fragment—a piece—*of a human brain—a severed hand.—Let every-*
thing filthy, everything vile, sit by my bed, where once I had my lamp and
clock, books, letters, presents for my birthday, and left over from the present,
bright-colored ribbons. Forgive me. Forgive me. I know you forgive me.
I'm still falling. (68; emphasis added)

He gives us this *piece* to take home, unless we happen to be there
already.

Theater permits the seemly catharsis, a cleansing of the inner life
behind the mask. The spectator remains safely at a distance from
the wounding. The Greek theater is a tripartite structure that provides clear division, if not separation, between the place of the audience (*theatron*) and the place of the chorus (*orchestra*) and the
place of the actor (*skene*). These are three distinct architectural en-
tities, and it is only the performance that brings them into relation. A participant in the ritual form, and by extension the actor
in the tragic form, feels the Dionysian release from individuality,
and the spectator, by an inner communion with the rite feels the
release, as well, but without having to discompose himself. However, argues Nietzsche, to become legible to the spectator and allow that inner communion, the tragedy must take on Apollonian
form or clear image.

Shawn approaches the theater from a background that values the
inner communion above all. André Gregory's exploration of the
Dionysian in productions like the *Bacchae* and *Alice in Wonderland*
and *Our Late Night* formed just part of this background. Experience
with the plays of Chekhov and O'Neill did as much to found his expectations. But he finds himself suddenly out of touch with his history, as in this incident reported in *The Fever*:

⊷ *I went to a play with a group of friends—a legendary actress in a great*
role. We stared at the stage. Moment after moment the character's down-
fall crept closer. Her childhood home would at last be sold, her beloved

cherry trees chopped down. Under the bright lights, the actress showed anger, bravado, the stage rang with her youthful laughter, which expressed self-deception. She would be forced to live in an apartment in Paris, not on the estate she'd formerly owned. Her former serf would buy the estate. It was her old brother's sympathetic grief that finally coaxed tears from the large man in the heavy coat who sat beside me. But my problem was that somehow, suddenly, I was not myself. I was disconcerted. Why, exactly, were we supposed to be weeping? This person would no longer own the estate she'd once owned. . . . She would have to live in an apartment instead. . . . I couldn't remember why I was supposed to be weeping. (26–27)

One is supposed to weep in this situation as a reflexive response to the represented sufferings. Sympathy is supposed to bring one to a catharsis of the tragic emotions. Chekhov relies on the audience for that.

In his fever, though, Shawn confronts the fact of his composed and unreflected spectatorship through all that empathetic participation: "The incredible history of my feelings and my thoughts could fill up a dozen leather-bound books. But the story of my life—my behavior, my actions—that's a slim volume, and I've never read it" (7). What he faces is the Apollonian aspect of spectatorship, the forms of life that are traced out upon the composure of a people used to looking on passively: "Something—a part of myself—has been hidden from me, and I think it's the part that's there on the surface, what anyone in the world could see about me if they saw me out the window of a passing train" (7). The old forms do nothing to address directly this hidden dimension, the surface of one's role in life, and so "new forms must be invented," as Chekhov's Konstantin declares. For Shawn, in recent years, this has been a regular practice, as he admits in an interview: "I'm driven to write plays but I don't have the skills ordinarily required. So I come up with new structures, new ways of organizing the form that will draw the audience along."[9] In the case of *The Fever,* his new form turns the theater onto the spectator and turns the speaking subject inside out, outside in. A new catharsis.

Is *The Fever* worth the agony? Many theater reviewers have thought not, calling it mere self-flagellation, or worse. But then, they write of its incarnation in a theater, where it was not intended to be seen, and as a play, which it refuses to become.[10] Shawn's arrangement with the presenting theaters was to do the piece at a ticket price of about ten dollars.[11] That was his way of honorably reaching a larger audience when he realized, "I'm not making a dent in all these apartments."[12] There is a commendable generosity behind this decision; as Shawn says in the piece: "I'm doing whatever I possibly can. I try to be nice" (47).

But there is also something awkward and inappropriate about this work seeming to invite universal acceptance. This is a problem often encountered in multicultural studies, when a work that is aimed at a very specific community is criticized as if it sought universality. The concept of universality in meaning and the use of it as a standard for artistic value are outgrowths of the dominant traditions in Western culture, so it is not uncommon to see the works of minority artists dismissed as parochial or valued for qualities that were secondary to the artist's intention. It is far rarer, however, to see a work of a member of the ruling class self-consciously addressing that class as a parochial entity and without pretensions to universality. The circumstances of an empowered life such as his are all too well known by the rest of the world. As he realized, the discoveries he is making here are to some extent about "what anyone in the world could see about me if they saw me out the window of a passing train" (7). Only from the point of view of a particular ignorance can such revelations bear great significance, while in a crowd of ten-dollar ticket holders and ink-stained critics in a nonprofit theater the same revelations come across as "the sound of one head swimming."[13]

At one point, while consumed with guilt in a nightmarish fantasy about being brutally punished for his privileged status, the speaker thinks, "Yes, it could have been predicted, from knowing these things—where I was born, how I was raised—what an hour of my labor would probably be worth—even though, to me, from the inside, my life always felt like a story that was just unfolding,

Epilogue I

"A Genuine Family Drama":
Vanya on 42nd Street

One hundred years. By the time anyone is likely to read these words it will be 1997 and one hundred years from the time when Chekhov published *Uncle Vanya* in 1897. "It takes one hundred years to make an antique, but you can lose it in a day" said my grandmother, an appreciative observer, not owner, of antiques. Antiquity entails risk but sometimes confers value—classic status. But within the life of a person, an old chair—not yet a classic—might also break down. The wonder of an object's preservation comes into tension with inevitable decay, neglect. Preservation resists entropy. Life gives way, and the old chairs go their separate ways and reveal at last the flaws that doom them to dust. Perhaps this is why my grandmother, now dead, preferred things brand new. From within *Uncle Vanya* comes the voice of the doctor, Astrov, a visionary all too aware of flaws but committed to planting the forests of the future, recalling a patient who had died on his operating table: "I sat down and I closed my eyes and thought: One hundred years from now. One hundred years from now: those who come after us. For whom our lives are showing the way. Will they think kindly of us? Will they remember us with a kind word, and, nurse, I wish to God that I could think so."[1]

In 1989, André Gregory, then approaching sixty, made a decision of uncanny rightness. He decided his new work should be to direct Chekhov's nearly antique and not at all forgotten play. This was actually the first play Gregory would direct since about 1975—*Our Late Night* was among the very last plays he directed before his famous hiatus. Ironically, *My Dinner with André* registered André as one of the more famous American directors just at the point when he would not, probably under any circumstances, direct. The theater was, to him, shockingly something that was indisputably dead, and to love something dead, in the way that he had loved the theater, was revolting. Death and death and death. All the youthful exuberance one brings to the theater faces that inexorable final curtain, the temporizing but terminal period of a show, dying on the table.

Gregory had David Mamet's recent adaptation of *Uncle Vanya* to work with, a version that does nothing to update or recontextualize Chekhov's play, but which somehow connects Chekhov's language with the rhythms of American speech. To it, he brought a fresh (and jaded) cast of performers, in a way reminiscent of the request he made of Grotowski when he agreed to do a workshop in Poland in the late 1970s: "If you could give me forty Jewish women who speak neither English nor French, *either women who have been in the theater for a long time and want to leave it but don't know why, or young women who love the theater but have never seen a theater they could love,* and if these women could play the trumpet or the harp, and if I could work in a forest, I'd come" (emphasis added).[2] The company consisted of some of the members of the Manhattan Project, such as Larry Pine (Astrov) and Jerry Mayer (Waffles). George Gaynes, who began working with André even before that, with the Theatre of Living Arts in Philadelphia and later at the Inner City Repertory Company in Los Angeles, from which he turned to some generic film and television roles (e.g., in *Police Academy* and *Punky Brewster*), would play Professor Serebryakov. Ruth Nelson, whose career as an actress began with the Group Theatre in the 1930s, took the role of Marina, and after her death in 1992, Phoebe Brand, who also had acted with the Group Theatre, played the part. Lynn Cohen, a veteran of New York and regional theater, played Vanya's mother. And then there was Shawn as Vanya. These were people who had worked in or around the theater for a long time. Brooke Smith and Julianne Moore, whose performing careers were just getting underway, played Sonya and Yelena, and indeed both got notable film roles (in *Silence of the Lambs* and *Short Cuts,* respectively) during these years that established their industry credentials. All of these people were working for free, initially. As Shawn put it, "André Gregory, our director, an unusual person, had the idea that we should just work on the play."[3]

In 1990, during the first year of rehearsals, Shawn became forty-seven, just the age of Vanya. Since the early 1970s, when Shawn had seen Gregory's *Alice* and had begun working with him on *Our Late Night,* they had, as Florence A. Falk has written, "revolved and circled one another like two satellites, exchanging place, perspective, and vision as if by some deterministic design."[4] Gregory himself marvels at how they form "bizarre reflections of each other."[5] Since *My Dinner with André* they had undergone almost a total reversal—"Wally has become André, and I have become Wally," says Gregory[6]—so that Shawn seems to be nearly crazed with self-doubt and *Fever* and seeking desperately in places like Nicaragua some replacement for the theater that had seemed to die before his eyes. Gregory meanwhile had become relatively content with the life he managed to live amid the insanity. Indeed, Gregory during the 1980s was devoting at least as much energy to the world of New Age thinking as he was to the world of the arts. The only solace he could offer his despairing, mid-life friend, Shawn, was a transplant from the most vital theater of the past into the core of the dying theater of the present, exactly at the site of its most cancerous self-doubt. Translate Chekhov into Shawn.

This transplant was executed under ideal surgical conditions, in confidence, intimately, with no expectation that the play would be performed for the public. Indeed, Gregory has said that the group "literally made love together" in these extended rehearsals, establishing bonds of such closeness that they became more a family than a company: "This *Vanya* is definitely not theatre. It is a sort of spiritual community in which people search not only for the darkest in themselves but also for the lightest."[7] The first summer they spent "improvising." Then, they would meet in a loft and rehearse for a few weeks, then several months later gather again for three days, later a couple of weeks or a day, and so on. After a year and a half of this, they moved their rehearsals to the Victory Theatre, an abandoned and decaying cinema off Times Square where they began to invite as an audience small groups of friends, initially just ten or twelve, later about thirty. This audience would be shifted from one place to another in each of the play's four acts, and they were always close to the performers—in one act, literally across a dinner table from them. Gregory confirms the notion that the production was more like a movie than a play, saying, "The audience became the camera in close-up."[8]

The film they made in 1994 is already, justly, famous. It does nothing more and nothing less than bring an audience in from the urban nightmare of 42nd Street to a space, disastrously ruined, yet reminiscent of the not-quite-innocent enthusiasms of the past, where they can watch Chekhov's antique play unfold in a way that is utterly immediate. Chekhov's "forest," now fully grown, sustains an impressive cross-section of life. It shades. Virtually everyone who saw this film *got* that this was Chekhov, that here was acting of remarkable honesty, that the present was in sudden, astonishing contact with the past. Chekhov, whose life ended at the dawn of this century and at the advent of film, was finally fully served by the now antique artistic medium, which would, at last, fully serve the play to an audience that was at long last as close as two human beings can get.

The critics have acclaimed just about every aspect of this film—Malle for his revealing but unobtrusive scenography, and Gregory for what Janet Maslin called "a psychodrama that has been coaxed forth here with illusory ease."[9] The cast members have been congratulated for their fully realized characterizations. The one who has been singled out for special comment and some criticism is Shawn. His performance and the comments he has provoked, in some strange way, seem to form an addendum to his career as a writer. Shawn is not just acting in this film, but in a sense resigning himself to it, even as he is reinscribing it.

"Personally, I don't know anything about what was going on in Russia in the years the play covers," said Shawn during the shooting of the film; "I have no interest in that aspect of theater, and I have no talent for it. This could be considered an unpleasant thing to say. But I still did become involved. I'm not interested in trying to recapture that past aspect of history in my performance. I wouldn't know if the play is relevant to our world today. I draw a complete blank and don't know what to say."[10] *Vanya on 42nd Street*, then, gives us, among other things, the spectacle of the writer, Shawn, mute and submerged, as he should be, in the words of Chekhov, who is his dramatic father. Person B subsides into Person A. The man with *The Fever* returns home, not to sleep as he had hoped, but to a house where there is no sleep. As I noted in the preceding chapter, the speaker in *The Fever* recalls going with friends to see a famous actress in *The Cherry Orchard* and discovering an unexpected effect: "My problem was that somehow, suddenly, I was not myself. I was disconcerted. Why, exactly, were we supposed to be weeping? This person would no longer own the estate she'd once owned. . . . She would have to live in an apartment instead. . . . I couldn't remember why I was supposed to be weeping."[11] By the extreme act of empathy, taking on Chekhov's words, Shawn becomes Vanya, and, as it were, comes home to the reason for weeping. Vanya is a character whose entire routine—of service to the intelligentsia, of self-sacrifice to a collapsing, exploitative economy, of the aspiration to love—comes to a sad end just at the beginning of the twentieth century. At the end of the twentieth century, just at the point when his real father was being removed from his editorship of the *New Yorker* (in 1987) after fifty-four years of service to the intelligentsia (and the elite appetites), and through the time when his father died of a heart attack at eighty-five (in 1992), Shawn's other father figure—André Gregory—found a new role for him, somewhere between Persons A and B.

It is a role into which he does not fit, as several have pointed out, but some have gone on to declare that this misfit is somehow fitting, or even essential, to the work. After quoting Shawn in the words above, stating that he does not know what to say about the relevance of the play to our world today, Amy Taubin observes:

➥ *Does Shawn protest too much? In any case, it's his performance that gives this* Vanya *its* raison d'être. *Everyone else in the company—even Moore, her carrot-colored hair slicked down 40s style and her mouth a crimson slash across opalescent skin—has the actor's chameleonlike ability to blend into the woodwork of any period. Only Shawn, with his herky-jerky gestures, his Ping-Pong eyeballs, his patented squinting before he leaps, his bullish strategy of transforming self-consciousness into public spectacle, seems not to fit in. But the way in which he's a misfit in this putative nineteenth century is not unlike the way he's an oddity in the twentieth. Like Vanya, Shawn has had eccentricity thrust upon him. If he glories in it, it's only because he can't wish it away. In making the connection between Shawn, the persona, and Vanya, the character, we're forced to confront the parallel notions of normality in Chekhov's Russia and our America. And if there's anything that defines middle class across centuries and continents, it's the obsession with what's normal and what's not.*[12]

Vanya/Shawn is not normal because he does not sit within his time (nineteenth or twentieth century), or within the house that is his home (the Russian estate, the decayed theater in New York City), but restlessly dislocates himself, into the other's time.

Jack Kroll writes: "Shawn is hardly classic casting, but his natural style, a fusion of farce and pathos, is perfect for the anguished clown that is Vanya."[13] Terrence Rafferty also helps define this cyclical flow between what is natural or normal and what is original, by which the unnatural is made perfect: "What makes Shawn's performance so original, and so electrifying, is that he represents Vanya's pain as something vivid, immediate, and omnipresent—as the sort of chronic pain that turns not to dull apathy but to unremitting, futile anger."[14] Shawn is the originator whose extraordinariness (and deformity) becomes suddenly right and immediate only when it is removed in time and space and detached from his usual means of self-expression.

The effect of this is that somehow, in the hands of Gregory, *Uncle Vanya* comes to an unforeseen conclusion, where, indeed, the often hopeless ending does have hope, just as the ending of *The Fever* does have hope. Before I ever saw the film, I heard Gregory talk about this ending which, he kept saying, does have hope, for Vanya and Sonya and for us all, but in particular, he said, for Vanya, for Shawn.[15] I had my doubts about this. I suspected this was just his way of affirming the connection he was trying to make between this film and *My Dinner with André*. Their dinner had ended with André asking Wally, "Where's that son?" The suggestion was strong that Wally had come to realize that that son was right here and right now, caught in the act of making this film. As Sonya suggests, at the end of *Vanya,* they will work. And Gregory, the elder who helps identify the son's work, later could define with some precision just what that work was: "To sense, more and more closely what life actually feels like as it passes, and to see the unfolding of the human being in all its ambiguity."[16] And so, *Vanya,* which so clearly addresses exactly this type of work, could be seen as a fulfillment of the quest in *My Dinner* if only that ending, which *is* the feeling of life passing, might be construed as hopeful. But how? Chekhov provides no line or stage direction to indicate how Vanya receives Sonya's words, except to imply that there are tears in his eyes.

But it's true, the ending is hopeful, because one senses the many layers of family love that have been found in that moment. Gregory recalls the family feeling among the company members: "It was real love, not that movie-set love where you say you love somebody and then you don't recognize them when you see them on the street. Generally, in movies about families, or in movies about love affairs, the actors pretend they're in love, which is like telephone sex, but they are not really in love. And I think that this love that developed between the people over the four years really transmits in the movie, and it illuminates what is a genuine family drama. Generally, when we see movies about family, we get the anger, the frustration, but we don't feel the love which that frustration and anger have grown out of."[17] There is solitude at the end of every one of Shawn's plays except, ironically, *The Hospital Play,* Shawn's most hopeless work, and *My Dinner with André,* which brings him home to Debby. But Debby—or the family—is also there, just beyond reach, in every one of those solitary endings. Sonya is there. The theater has that effect of placing even the starkest loneliness in the midst of a community of relations. It could be said that one of the effects of Shawn's entire career as a writer has been to evoke the words of all the various contemporary Sonyas, the voices that would urge Shawn and the audience to go on.

Epilogue II

"I can't . . . just . . . I can't . . . totally":
The Designated Mourner

MESSAGE MACHINE: *"Message 1. 3:33 p.m. Tuesday."*

WALLACE SHAWN: *"Uh, Dave, are you there? It's . . . Wally Shawn, . . . a character you've created. . . . Well . . . I've been away for a while. I came back . . . and, uh, . . . well, uh, . . . I don't want to confuse you, . . . but I've written a new piece, I'm afraid, . . . so, uh . . . That might be an* incredible *pain in the ass for you. On the other hand, it doesn't seem fair not to mention it. . . . What if you put in your book that 'The one thing Shawn will never do is write a play about cats because he's so allergic to them,' and then it turns out that this—"* (beep)

MESSAGE MACHINE: *"Message 2. 3:35 p.m. Tuesday."*

WALLACE SHAWN: *"So, I think your machine cut me off—or maybe not . . . But I'm at — —. So . . . what should we do about it, Dave? Do you want to read the play? Do you want to just forget about it? You kindly in your letter . . . express hope that I will write more, but I realize it could be . . . sort of . . . not the greatest moment for you, but what can I do? I can't . . . just . . . I can't . . . totally . . . twist. . . . I mean, I can't control the pace of my writing out of consideration for the possibility that it might just bother you . . . uh . . . . . . so, uh—"* (beep)

—Phone messages, August 1995

And so, with Sonya's "We shall rest," it might have ended, fixed in the present but with a hopeful look to the future, but then came *The Designated Mourner* in the summer of 1995, which passed right into that future, only a future much worse than Sonya imagined. The play is set in that moment, both familiar and strange, when the disaster that is incipient in our own society is just breaking out. It is the future of a certain sort of (political) science fiction—Walker Percy's *Love in the Ruins* and LeRoi Jones's *The Slave* might be models.[1] As in those works, the revolution that has come is not what the activists had anticipated.

This future begins with the death of something that came before, and Jack is the designated mourner who feels he has been assigned "to grieve, to wail, and light the public ritual fire," because, as he tells us at the very beginning of the play, "a very special little world has died."[2] Jack is not precisely a survivor of that special little world, because, as we will hear, he has gradually detached himself from it, or slipped away, which explains why he survives. But his ties to that world are strong enough that he is the one assigned to mourn ("Someone is assigned when there's no one else," says Jack). Jack's connection to that special little world is through his former wife, Judy, and her father, Howard, who both are finally punished for association with that world. Howard is a literary lion, a writer who knows his Donne, not from a pedantic standpoint, but in the way that fuses literary tradition with the exigencies of the present moment—like Donne. Howard began as a writer of daring prose, notably an essay on the allure of "the enemy" (communists, of a sort, presumably), showing him to be an independent, perhaps even iconoclastic writer who was willing to challenge the foundations of the culture and society into which he was born (i.e., the elite). Later, he transformed himself into a poet and an activist on the radical fringe, a champion of the "dirt-eaters" and their leaders against the "rats" in power. From Jack's point of view, Howard's career is trend-driven, not in the sense of his following trends, but in the sense that his reflex has always been to set himself in contemptuous opposition to trends, to excoriate the liberals and moralists for their pretensions, without necessarily holding any deep beliefs or commitments of his own. To some extent, the "dirt-eaters" are, to Howard, a club with which he can beat the intelligentsia.

Judy, his daughter, has taken up with Jack as an exercise of her own independence in a relationship of determined, second-generation torch-bearers—the little literati. They married and for a time lived away from Howard, but she has remained within the sphere of influence of her father, and ultimately Jack cannot match that influence.

Jack describes himself with morbid delight as "a former student of English literature who—who—who went downhill from there!" (4). Jack was impressed by the sheer power of Howard's withering "contempt" for all the hypocritical claims to "morality" made by other luminaries. Caustic Howard drew him along, but more particularly caustic Howard's daughter captured his attention, and briefly, during their marriage, Jack, whom Howard regarded as "vague," drew Judy away from her father, but, as he says, he "went downhill from there." Jack can account for his decline in great detail. Indeed, such an accounting seems to be the general purpose of the play, which is largely narrated by Jack from a time after the deaths of Judy and Howard, looking back over the whole time he has known them.

The subject of the play is the evolution of Jack into a familiar monster within postmodern bourgeois liberalism—that is, an insulated and indulgent man of outmoded sensibility and paralyzing timidity. In his detachment from the world and from close attention to the question of his own morality, he resembles Lemon. In his habit of shifting among the shards of his aesthetic experience for some relic of what had once seemed so valuable, he resembles the speaker of *The Fever*. Dramatically, the piece works by juxtaposing the narrative of Jack against the ironizing voices of the others, and those others are at least as substantial as Aunt Dan is to Lemon. But one is aware, from early on, that those other voices are, like Dan's, now gone. Jack's experience lies temporally beyond the wasted present of Lemon and beyond even the return home to an uncertain future of the speaker in *The Fever*. What he recounts is his own slow death in a postulated future, a gradual giving way to the disease of a process of history, so that, in the end, his self is nonexistent. The world he is living in is going to hell—apocalyptically now—in an armed uprising of "the enemy," but the more insidious threat is that a person could come to the point where he does not care. The future does not look good, even though the play ends with Jack, in a state of perfect complacence—literally without a care—on a park bench, thrilled by the caress of an evening breeze. The future lacks a soul.

From the beginning, Jack is utterly clear about the fact that he is no hero, that he is, more precisely, an "asshole." He knows for certain that he is also what is called a "high brow," a term he takes pains to define as the relatively rare sort of person who does not succumb to popular ideology. Judy seems also to understand that Jack's contra-distinction of himself from the popular is merely another form of false consciousness, but she, too, has inherited an elite sensibility and not a little of her father's contempt. For instance, she remarks the "new herd of swine" who have assumed power in the city, "the new generation, who dressed in new colors—those chalky colours, yellow and pink and various greens—and lived in new neighbourhoods, and even ate in new restaurants with new styles of cooking" (20–21). At the same time, protests and other signs of disturbance begin to be heard: "People kept asking, well, were these demonstrations the usual fakes, or were they real this time? For some reason, it was awfully hard to say. The customary markers were not in place" (21). An unforeseen consequence of the dying of the special little world was that the elite would lose even their ability to read (cultural markers) and to determine the appropriate colors.

Judy, like Lemon, interprets evasive behavior, like Jack's, as no more and no less than a function of human instinct, which means clear (if brutal) impulses by which all people tend to live:

➡ *There are ideas that are almost like formalized greetings. Everyone agrees with them, but we keep repeating them anyway, all day long. Everyone keeps saying, for example, 'Human motivation is very complex.' But if you stop and think about it, you have to admit that human motivation is* not *complex, or it's complex only in the same sense that the motivation of a fly is complex. In other words, if you try to swat a fly, it moves out of the way. And humans are the same. They step aside when they sense something coming about to hit them in the face. Of course you do see the occasional exception—the person who just stands there and waits for the blow.* (2–3)

It turns out Jack is no exception.[3] Jack has stepped aside and escaped the blow. Judy finds herself in a more difficult spot beneath the swatter: "I love silence, the beauty of silence. The shadows of trees. Japanese monasteries buried in snow, surrounded by forest. Loneliness, death, in the dark forest. But my life was different, a different way: A city. People. Concerts. Poetry" (3).[4] She also loves her father and shares his sense of mission; the combination of refined taste and radical zeal is what unites them. She loves Jack, too, for a time, but the basis for her love for him is unclear.

Jack confesses himself a bad lover and disloyal. Then, too, in his decline he loses grip on his self-definition as a free-thinking liberal. Maybe it is his basic unhappiness, which she mistakes for the feeling that inspires her father's famous contempt. In any case, under pressure from Judy and Howard, Jack breaks down. He recounts the experience of a night he impulsively spent away from the house, alone, in a hotel room outside of town. Lying in bed, reading poetry, he suddenly heard a couple in the next room, laughing, teasing, then kissing and making love. He recognized at once the decision he had to make, whether to use earplugs and continue reading or listen, "maybe with one of my hands sort of accidentally falling onto my dick" (18). Even after the couple finished making love, rather than continue with his poetry, he picked up the magazine he had bought in the lobby, "the one with all the stories about healthy, well-exercised, rather young actresses" (18). Soon, the television captures an hour of his attention, at which point he is thinking:

➡️ *Well, at some point we have to draw some distinctions—don't we? I mean, pardon me, but shouldn't there be some distinction drawn between the things we say, the lies, the 'I like poetry,' 'I like Rembrandt,' on the one hand—and I mean, of course it's important to say those things, because after all if you don't say them then you really become simply a zoo animal, you become an empty thing, you're nothing more then really than a large balloon with a mouth, genitals, paws, and an ass-hole, a nice great big one—but still they're lies, they are lies—and then on the other hand things that are true, like 'I'm watching this very nice screen right now, I'm watching it, and I'm enjoying it'?* (18–19)

A life freed from the constraints of "good taste" and the constrictions implied by a sense of "morality" has tremendous seductive power for Jack.

At the same time, the ferocity with which he attacks his own self-indulgence comes to a climax with his listening to his own dramatic monologue, that highly prized stream of consciousness that is the aria of modernity:

⟶ *And then I asked myself, well, what about that noise I always hear, that intolerable noise which comes from somewhere inside my head? And I realized consciously for the first time that, rather like a singer who accompanies his own singing on the piano or guitar, I accompanied my life with a sort of endless inner tinkling, an endless noodling or murmuring—a sort of awful inner murmuring of reportage and opinions, idiotic arpeggios of self-approbation—'Yes, this is what I'm doing, this is what I'm doing, and this is the right thing to be doing now, because murmur murmur murmur, and* this *is right because murmur murmur murmur, and* this *is right because murmur murmur murmur—' I thought about all the sincere consideration which I gave to the future, to my plans, you know, and all the solemn concern I lavished each day on the events of my past—my "memories", as we call them, wiping away a few tears—and I wondered: was all this really tremendously valuable? Or was it perhaps just a bit unnecessary, when you consider the fact—rather often overlooked—that the past and the future don't actually exist?* (19–20)

When Howard finally sickens, just at the time when the "dirt-eaters" (or whoever) are executing their revolution and suddenly demanding of Howard more than he ever had the strength or perhaps the will to supply, Judy leaves Jack in order to support her father, but their leaving of each other was a foregone conclusion in any case. They were, in fact, doomed by history.

Similarly, the future of Vanya and his like would not, in fact, have given them the opportunity for "rest" or "peace" or however you like to translate Sonya's words. The future would be revolution and work and perhaps a righting of old wrongs but not for the members of Vanya's or Sonya's "special little world"—the complacent intelligentsia. Vanya attempted unsuccessfully his own small revolution, against the professor, but he and the professor would soon take the brunt of the people's revolution against the estate holders. Jack is a modern-day equivalent of Vanya, in that he is engaged in conflict with Howard and later also with Judy. The result is their separation. Meanwhile, during the course of the play, which is mostly narrated by these three characters, an armed overthrow does occur, and in the reign of terror, Howard and Judy are killed. Jack is detached from these dangerous political shifts, which gives him the freedom or luxury to examine the multiple levels of causality in this revolution and in his divorce. Jack loses Judy because (a) an armed revolution brings her for her beliefs to a prison sentence and later to execution, (b) because Judy finally remains most loyal to her father and succumbs to the historical force that overtakes him, (c) because she proves to be the person who can reveal Jack for the fraud he is, (d) because he cannot tolerate the fact that her loyalty to him is divided, and (e) because he is a weak and unprincipled person, a selfish worm. Similarly, Vanya could not win Yelena (a) because she did love the professor, (b) because her sense of duty outweighed her passion, (c) because she was too conventional to risk adultery, (d) because her head had been turned by the appearance of Astrov, and (e) because Vanya finally is a loser, with low income, little power, and, not least, he does not turn her on. All of these statements are probably true, concerning both plays, but they are all also probably false to some degree. Indeed, Jack, like Vanya, has a considerable sense of the structural ambiguities of selfhood and sees just why one must treat principles and moral imperatives with caution. Impending crisis has brought him to the point of questioning all inherited guidelines, especially those associated with the intelligentsia. Jack has cut himself loose from a tradition, and from a marriage, and the play offers an occasion for considering the question of just how those two mooring points—relationship and inheritance—compare.

The future of this modern-day Vanya is truly excruciating. He comes to stand at such a distance from his formerly pampered self that he finally sees it as a figure standing by the window in fading light—"that ludicrous figure whom I'd approached till now with such ostentatious displays of respect—such fervour, grovelling, hand-kissing and tears . . . the unpleasant little self" (49). He now sees it as an enemy and beats it to death. Whereas before he had taken such pleasure in books, he now finds that reading, even the newspaper, is "sort of like spooning food into the mouth of someone you happen to notice has suddenly died" (50). One evening, on a sudden impulse, he delights in placing a book of poetry into the bathtub and pissing on it, later also shitting on it. These are among his "Experiments in Privacy," which is the title of his diary (50). The story of his life becomes a record of efforts made to cut himself away from that "special little world." Sex magazines take the place of the books he once had cherished, and they serve to channel his desire for otherness, until even models hold little interest for him any longer, pretty and forthcoming though they seemed to be.

All ties to the world, all contact with other people, all responsibilities and duties and expectations made of him come to seem unbearable burdens that must be discarded at once. Early in the second part of the play, Jack speaks words that might easily (in a far more pessimistic version than *Vanya on 42nd Street*) have been Vanya's—his silent resolve made while Sonya projects a future of work and then rest. Here Jack imagines a future of utter detachment, of selfless solitude, existence reduced to mere sensation:

➤ *After a while I just concluded there wasn't any hope—an important insight. There'd be no happiness in my own life, nor would peace be won in the world at large. Was there anything, then, that I could expect to achieve in the coming years? Well, perhaps I could somehow train my mind to focus less compulsively on terrifying images of death and disease. Perhaps I could learn how to pass more easily from one moment to the next, the way the monkey, our ancestor, shifts so easily along from branch to branch as he follows the high road through the forest at night. Let me learn how to repose in the quiet shade of a nice square of chocolate, a nice slice of cake. A delicious cup of tea isn't, perhaps, that hard to come by; the trick to be learned is just not to think of other things while you drink it.* (40)

The metamorphosis of Jack is nearly complete when he comes to Judy after her father has been murdered and discovers that every trace of his love for her has vanished. And then one day, he happens to see on television one of the group executions which the new

regime broadcasts in its "perennial parallel campaign for the better-
ment of humanity," and there is Judy, dying, along with a couple of
the old-school moralists whom Howard had always "found so boring" (52). A final flailing of his old self drives him to seek any sign
that a more compassionate world might be possible, but he has no
better place to turn for such a sign than to the smiles of the models
in the sex magazines. A small advertisement catches his eye: "Have
you ever ridden on the train which carries the bodies of the dead? . . .
I have, and I was given a berth right next to theirs" (53). The whole
course of Jack's life rides on the tracks of that train. He walks to the
park, where the leaves have turned color and are falling, and it suddenly occurs to him "that everyone on earth who could read John
Donne was now dead" (53). Alongside sex, alongside death (both of
which Donne had experienced so fully), Jack's life, such as it was, had
left him in the strange situation of realizing that he "was the only one
left who would even be aware of the passing of this peculiar group,
this group which was so special, at least in their own eyes" (53).

He resolves to be the designated mourner and performs an absurd
little ceremony, burning the paper from underneath a sticky dessert
pastry. In a final flickering of nostalgia, simultaneously revolting and
deeply affecting, Jack thinks: "I thought I heard John Donne crying
into a handkerchief as he fell through the floor—plummeting fast
through the earth on his way to Hell. His name, once said by so
many to be 'immortal', would not be remembered it turned out. The
rememberers were gone, except for me, and I was forgetting: forgetting his name, forgetting him, and forgetting all the ones who remembered him" (54). This ceremony, once performed, leaves him
free, perfectly free to enjoy "the sweet ever-changing caress of an
early-evening breeze" (55). So, the play ends, on a note reminiscent
of Lemon's call for the audience to give thanks to the killers, but in
this case, in our future, expecting only the utter passivity of an audience already drifting along.[5]

Drifting along gives you certain roles, roles which you do not demand, though they might sustain your life. Shawn sometimes occupies those roles, the roles of those who do not write their own con-
tracts—character parts, parts of the hero's whole, service to the mass

market, Person A. He has written in *The Designated Mourner* Person B's reflection on his reciprocal self, and the portrayal is imbued with a sense of the mortality of personhood itself. *The Designated Mourner* is something like a deeply ironic Nō play, in which a man who is a ghost (of his former self) returns in narrative to the troubling events and the worldly attachments that he must overcome to attain enlightenment. What he attains instead, at the culmination of the play, is a thorough unawareness, an unconsciousness of the slightest otherness. In place of the vicious circle of self-hatred, self-love, which had contorted him for so long, comes a stasis, a perfect complacency. He is, at the end, the perfect medium, altering nothing of the substance of what he touches—a voice without a voice. He is thus, in a sense, a nightmarish version of a performer who is perfectly complicit with the media, an actor without agency. In this way, the play can be read as Shawn's revisiting (as a ghost) the world that he left (in *The Fever*). In the play, he returns to many of the scenes and images of his earlier plays: the breakfast and hotel rooms, the pigs and pornography, the poetry no longer read. The world he reflects upon is a horrible one, a world without grace or compassion, very much the world of Shawn's earlier plays. The frightening logic that leads a person to become complicit with brutality ought to leave a person like Jack in a state of horror, but instead the play shows him (like Lemon) giving way, bending.

Zeami writes in one of his treatises on the Nō drama: "Therefore, an actor who has truly identified one aspect of the Flower, even though he has not mastered every form of Role Playing, may be able to grasp the beauty of Bending. Indeed, this quality can be said to exist at a stage even higher than that of the Flower. Without the Flower, Bending has no meaning. Without the Flower, the effect of Bending is merely gloomy and grey."[6] Gloomy and grey it is for the unenlightened subject who revisits the world that occupied his attention, the world in which he had his part, yet *The Designated Mourner* leaves the audience contemplating the future, when other fates are possible. *Aunt Dan and Lemon* called for the audience to be heroic, to lash out with all due ferocity. *The Designated Mourner* seems to have a more modest expectation of what the audience is capable, something closer to Bending, an active and open-eyed submersion in the role. Bending is not mere compliance, not inaction, but a project that aims always at transformation. In the same treatise as quoted above, Zeami writes: "One who wishes to follow the path of the Nō must engage himself in no other art. There is one exception: the art of poetry deserves study, for it is a means to open the actor to the profound beauties of nature and enrich his life."[7] What poetry is it that Jack should read, or Person A or Person B—daffodils or the flowers (of evil) or *flores para los muertos*? Where to begin to touch the profound beauties?

In one of his more difficult and some would say grotesque poems, Donne himself took on the role of designated mourner, writing on the anniversary of the death of a fifteen-year-old girl, "An Anatomie of the World . . . Wherein, . . . the Frailty and the Decay of this Whole World Is Represented."[8] The conceit of this long poem is that the world itself has, in a sense, died in the loss of so beautiful and innocent a person:

> *Shee, shee is dead; shee's dead: when thou knowest this,*
> *And learn'st thus much by our Anatomy,*
> *That this world's generall sicknesse doth not lie*
> *In any humour, or one certain part;*
> *But as thou sawest it rotten at the heart,*
> *Thou seest a Hectique feaver hath got hold*
> *Of the whole substance, not to be contrould,*
> *And that thou hast but one way, not t'admit*
> *The worlds infection, to be none of it.*[9]

It is a pervasive—physical and metaphysical—death of the world that Donne anatomizes, all to emphasize, by way of contrast, the splendor of the life that passed with the death of this girl. In a sudden, striking contact with modernity every bit as marvelous as Shawn's (or Jack's) sudden, striking contact with tradition, Donne suddenly, strikingly foresees the attitude of Jack (or Shawn):

> *And new Philosophy calls all in doubt,*
> *The Element of fire is quite put out;*
> *The Sun is lost, and th'earth, and no man's wit*

Can well direct him where to look for it.
And freely men confesse that this world's spent,
When in the Planets, and the Firmament
They seek so many new; then see that this
Is crumbled out againe to his Atomies.
'Tis all in peeces, all cohaerence gone;
All just supply, and all Relation:
Prince, Subject, Father, Son, are things forgot.[10]

This is the worldview expressed exhaustively in Donne's poem, in full recognition that the poem itself is no remedy for any part of the modern crisis except the forgetting. What Shawn offers in *The Designated Mourner* is no simple ceremony, no decorous disposal of the past. Shawn writes at the death of the world and at the death of that which was beautiful or admirable in it, including the theater. Shawn does not accept what the theater has always done with its final curtain, when it arranges perfect tableaux of death, worthy of applause, exactly suiting the self-pity and self-love of the audience. Instead, he stages a different sort of wake for those long evening hours before sleep—a wake neither so hopeful as Sonya's "We shall rest," nor so hopeless as Eliot's "human voices wake us, and we drown." Something remains behind in the wake of Wallace Shawn—a "Hectique feaver," a stubborn object, an upset waiting to be righted.

Appendix

The Man behind the Voice:
Interview of Wallace Shawn

by Mark Strand

I met Wallace Shawn a year ago in Salt Lake City. Deborah Eisenberg, author of a brilliant collection of short fiction, Transactions in a Foreign Currency, *had come to give a reading at the University of Utah, and Wally, who lives with her, came along, too. They spent three days in Salt Lake, most of the time with me and my wife. It was cold, and Wally must have been wearing five layers of clothing to stay warm. And I remember how good he was about keeping me company while I drove around doing errands, how graciously he suffered the stares and hellos of people who had seen him in his various films, how effortlessly, in fact, he would engage his fans in conversation. At any rate, that's when I met Wally and began a dialogue that has been ongoing, about what to do with the rest of our lives. Now, when I go to New York, we see each other, and there are plans to meet in other places. Perhaps meeting in other places is what we'll be doing for the rest of our lives, or at least planning to.*

We talked in New York early one Saturday morning over cappuccinos.

MARK STRAND: *As a child were you encouraged to write plays and excel in school?*

WALLACE SHAWN: I would say that I am virtually an experiment in receiving the most encouraging upbringing possible. I would say I was encouraged to think that the world was a wonderful place and that the job of each person was simply to choose what he wanted to do in life, what would be the most rewarding and satisfying. The schools that I went to encouraged all of the students almost to the point where you could say that they were paid

Originally published in **INTERVIEW,** Brant Publications, Inc., March 1989.

to provide a flattering environment for them. Although, of course, the individual teachers didn't see it that way. And the individual teachers weren't paid that much. But the relationship of the school to the student was not unlike that of a therapist to a patient in the sense that the therapist is paid by the patient to feel interested in the patient's struggles and perhaps to encourage the patient to feel that he's a better fellow than he might have feared. So the schools encouraged and encouraged, and when you did a painting, a little drawing, teachers would think it was just marvelous. We were not told: "No, you made a mistake. A foot doesn't grow out of the leg that way. It grows out the other way."

MARK STRAND: *Did you ever feel discouraged? Did you ever feel when you were a student at school that your teachers may have been pulling the wool over your eyes?*

WALLACE SHAWN: Well, there were one, two, or three brilliant teachers, who were particularly satisfying—those were the ones I liked the most, I suppose—who understood how to criticize. But independently I don't think I ever criticized myself or had any doubts about myself on the intellectual level until about five years ago. From the age of four to forty I would say I just didn't have any doubts.

MARK STRAND: *But there must have been different kinds of encouragement in that time and different kinds of discouragement. In other words, your sense of failure is measured by an altogether different standard when you're thirty than, say, when you're fifteen.*

WALLACE SHAWN: But by the time I was a teenager I'd had so much encouragement that nothing could shake my confidence in myself. It didn't occur to me at the time that this was simply a formula that was applied to all students.

MARK STRAND: *But you've had a lot of success: your plays have been produced; you've been in movies.*

WALLACE SHAWN: When I started writing, most people that I knew, including my friends, thought that my writing didn't have much value. There were really only two people who admired my plays and nobody else particularly.

MARK STRAND: *Had anyone else seen them?*

WALLACE SHAWN: I showed them to a lot of people, and I submitted them to many theaters in the hope that they would be
produced. I showed them to anyone I could get to look at them,
really.

MARK STRAND: *You weren't discouraged by the fact that only two of
your friends thought well of them?*

WALLACE SHAWN: I was not discouraged because I still felt that
almost maniacal confidence.

MARK STRAND: *Dalton had done its work.*

WALLACE SHAWN: I believed that everybody else in the whole
world was wrong. Also, the two people who liked my earliest
plays were people I respected. They both worked for my father,
but I didn't at that time take a Marxist view of it and say, you
know, for that reason I have to totally discount their opinion. Although I did sort of think, Well, obviously the mere curiosity of
the fact that their boss's son was writing anything at all would encourage them to direct extra attention to what I wrote and to at
least consider the possibility that it was good.

MARK STRAND: *What's happened to those plays?*

WALLACE SHAWN: Well, one of them was actually performed. It
was a play called *The Hotel Play* because when I wrote it I was living in a hotel in the West Indies where I'd gone with money that
I'd saved. Most of the time I was the only guest in the hotel. I
imagined this hotel with a lot of guests, and I wrote a play that
had eighty characters in it. Of course, none of my plays were being performed anyway, so it didn't matter. But this one was put
on at La Mama about six years ago.

MARK STRAND: *What did you think of it?*

WALLACE SHAWN: Well, I actually thought that it was quite good.
I was very pleased about it.

MARK STRAND: *When did you write* A Thought in Three Parts?

WALLACE SHAWN: I wrote it in 1975. It was done in New York in
the form of a workshop. And it wasn't really open to the general
public; it was just for those who were subscribers to Joe Papp's
theater.

MARK STRAND: *What did they think?*

WALLACE SHAWN: Oh, it was a disaster. It was unspeakable how much they didn't like it.

MARK STRAND: *That didn't give you any doubts? You just went on and wrote more, still convinced?*

WALLACE SHAWN: Right. The idea was that the mere fact of being me was so marvelous and extraordinary that anything I would do would have to be marvelous and extraordinary. Of course I think I always felt that I was also terribly special because people paid a certain attention to me because of my father. There was always this sense, Well, he's special. Not even just, He's another kid who's going to this school where everyone is marvelous. But, He's even more marvelous.

MARK STRAND: *So you had this horrible response to* A Thought in Three Parts *and went on nonetheless writing more plays. What happened?*

WALLACE SHAWN: Well, in England the response was much, much more positive. For one thing, the play was actually performed for the public. The English were overjoyed to have the opportunity to put on this play.

MARK STRAND: *Was it the sex that got the Americans in trouble?*

WALLACE SHAWN: There was a lot of explicit sex in plays in the sixties but not usually in written plays that were being performed in the regular theater. Those explicit plays were done by far-out groups who had a far-out audience, whereas this play was being done in a regular theater with a regular middle-class audience.

MARK STRAND: *Has it ever been done here again?*

WALLACE SHAWN: No. It was just never done again.

MARK STRAND: *It's so frenetic and so lively. The sex is so peculiar. People barely see each other and they're ready to go to bed just because they have nothing to say, so it has a kind of urgency but no passion, a kind of ongoingness but no purpose. And you're never sure if your characters are responding to some other prompting. Sometimes they seem to answer each other, but sometimes they seem to be completing some rhetorical obligation to speak at that moment, a need to manifest a sound or a gesture right then, to punctuate what the other person has said but not quite answer them. It's startling and different.*

WALLACE SHAWN: I'm a little thrown to hear you say these things because I've sort of been coming around more and more to assuming that I am really just a kind of joke about a progressive upbringing. At least, that all of my early writing is utterly without value, that it simply expressed maniacal overconfidence and that's all it expressed. Of course the theater is such a peculiar field for me anyway, because what you do is never looked at as writing. Yet if there's any point to these plays it has to do with what they are as writing. And another of the odd things about theater is that it's a field that doesn't have any real standards. So you don't ask, Is it good? very often. You do notice that some things survive and others die. *Aunt Dan and Lemon* got a good review in the *New York Times,* so it has been done in several other places, and the book has sold a certain number of copies. My other plays didn't get good reviews in the *New York Times,* so they really have never been mentioned again and made absolutely no dent in the world in any way. E. H. Carr says that there are certain facts that are facts of history, and there are other facts that are just facts and they're not facts of history. And the fact that someone walked out of his house one day and on the way to Balducci's he slipped on the street, and then he picked himself up and continued his walk to Balducci's, that is not a fact of history. And that's what my plays have been really, except for *Aunt Dan and Lemon.* You know, they just sort of happened. A few people saw them—many of them were personal friends of mine whom I invited—and a few other people wandered in, saw something that they found awful or boring, and then left. And one comes to feel that if something didn't make any impact it must have just been a mistake.

MARK STRAND: *Isn't there anything like delayed impact? Isn't it conceivable that in five years one of your earlier plays will be put on and perceived differently?*

WALLACE SHAWN: Yes. That could happen, and I occasionally think, Jesus Christ, maybe I did know what I was doing all of that time and that will actually be established. About three years ago I read a long article about myself that describes me as a fraud. And it was not about my old plays (I don't think the person who wrote the article had ever heard of them), but it was about me in general.

It was about *Aunt Dan and Lemon,* the little essay in the back of the published version of the play, and then it was just about me in general and why people had ever paid any attention to me one way or the other. And I did think, there's a good possibility that this is absolutely true. Because if I were a complete fraud I would probably be slower than most people to recognize it.

MARK STRAND: *When you said you'd come to doubt yourself, was it because of this article?*

WALLACE SHAWN: Oh, no. The article was just one little confirmation from the outside.

MARK STRAND: *Was it after* Aunt Dan and Lemon *that you started to have doubts about yourself?*

WALLACE SHAWN: Yes, I would say so. Before that I was so obsessed with myself and with trying to foist myself on the world that I didn't notice anything except myself.

MARK STRAND: *Has it made it impossible to work?*

WALLACE SHAWN: Oh, no. And I just am not as interested in myself as I used to be, so even if I were a fraud it just wouldn't bother me half as much as it would have ten years ago. I did get very concerned about myself when I was doing *Aunt Dan and Lemon* when we were rehearsing it. I felt that it wasn't going to work, and that really terrified me. I mean, a play is either boring, so that people wish they weren't there anymore and fall asleep, or not boring. And it's really hard to write one that's not boring.

MARK STRAND: *Were you worried about the audience's response to what was said about Kissinger or the Nazis?*

WALLACE SHAWN: No, no. Just that it might not work as a play, that it might be boring.

MARK STRAND: *But there's a way in which* Aunt Dan and Lemon *ceases to be a play during those monologues when an appeal is made to reason, when logical arguments are given in support of unreasonable behavior, when compassion and insensitivity become sadly inextricable. I'm sure a large portion of the audience felt put on the spot. Here they are, the very people that Lemon was describing, who live private lives without major responsibilities. They complain about the lack of righteousness of those who protect their right to complain, who assume re-*

sponsibilities that demand a certain ruthlessness. Here is a situation in which the audience saw itself as part of an argument, not necessarily as a character in the play. In those monologues, they figure in. Their ideas, their passivity are exposed.

WALLACE SHAWN: Well, that's the trick of this particular play.

MARK STRAND: *Do you ever call up friends after a play and say, "Hey, what do you think? I didn't see you after the play"?*

WALLACE SHAWN: When I first started writing, when I would show things to friends and they didn't get it or just didn't respond, I was very, very upset. But then I reached a point of thinking, Well, if I make that the criterion for friendship I won't have any friends.

MARK STRAND: *Can you be friends with somebody who doesn't like your work?*

WALLACE SHAWN: It's an interesting question. Mostly it was that some of my friends were worried about me. They sort of thought: Well, he's in trouble. There's an intelligent guy; he had a good education; he could do something. But instead he's doing this. How sad.

MARK STRAND: *Did they ever tell you what that other thing might be?*

WALLACE SHAWN: One older friend said that I would've been a good judge.

MARK STRAND: *This is predicated on what? Knowledge of you as a person?*

WALLACE SHAWN: Yes. Also, the fact that the plays were odd and in some ways obscene or not written in normal English—certain people who knew me thought: He's troubled. He's a troubled person; he's writing these unpleasant and sort of sick plays that are not successful, and it's sad.

MARK STRAND: *What about now? Now, in your period of self-doubt, are there people who are concerned and say, "It's not too late to do something else"?*

WALLACE SHAWN: No. Once you've written a couple of things that have been published or whatever, then if you ever say to anyone, "Jesus Christ, I sometimes think I shouldn't be doing this; maybe I should just move to Nicaragua and try to help to build a better world, or maybe I should just stop," then people rather complacently look at you and say, he thinks that he might change his life and do something else, but we know that that's not possible.

MARK STRAND: *Do you think you could go to Nicaragua to work for a better world?*

WALLACE SHAWN: Occasionally I experience moments of feeling that I could change my life in one way or another. My thoughts change, so sometimes I feel I myself could change.

MARK STRAND: *But changing the world is something else. I mean, you have more power right now in terms of changing the world. People go to see* Aunt Dan and Lemon *and you force them to reconsider the beliefs they have and the clichés they have about right and wrong. That's a kind of power, and it can be used for improved social ends.*

WALLACE SHAWN: Well, I'd like to think that, but I usually think that we're all like seventeenth-century French aristocrats, sitting around in our powdered wigs, and I'm the aristocrat who turns to the aristocrat next to him and says, "I say, my dear fellow, isn't it dreadful about those atrocities that the King committed last week?" And the other guy says, "Yes. Dreadful, dreadful." I don't know whether this has any impact on the atrocities. I really don't know.

MARK STRAND: *Is it something that concerns you now, that we're all living close to the brink?*

WALLACE SHAWN: Oh! That we are about to be overthrown, does that concern me?

MARK STRAND: *Or that we'll overthrow ourselves.*

WALLACE SHAWN: Well, I would say I'm just as brainwashed as the next person—although unlike people who actually work, I devote myself full time to trying not to be brainwashed. But I don't succeed. And to be brainwashed means that you're insensible, you're unaware of the disasters that are looming up under your nose, the atrocities that are happening already, and the horrible things that are about to happen. The main thing that makes me want to move out of the country is the brainwashing.

MARK STRAND: *Is it the press and TV? Is it that they don't tell you what's going on?*

WALLACE SHAWN: I think that the press and TV are the leaders in brainwashing, but basically we all do it to each other. We are all part of a conspiracy to tell each other that everything is basically O.K. We end up feeling, Well, if everybody's walking around acting so normal, things couldn't possibly be that far gone.

MARK STRAND: *So what do you do?*

WALLACE SHAWN: I don't know. I have a few minutes a month when I sort of mentally break out of this brainwashing and realize that things are really not all right. When I was in high school, for one year a group of friends and I used to get together and make tape recordings every once in a while, which we called "The Hour of Hate." We'd make a lot of strange noises and say things into the tape recorder. Once a month my brain programs "The Hour of Hate" and I sort of am aware of what's really going on in the world, and I feel the hatred and rage that are appropriate. The rest of the time I'm just an idiot who's having a nice time. But I do find that when I'm abroad I have a different perspective, so that's one reason why I enjoy traveling to other countries. I do it as much as I possibly can and would even consider leaving for good.

MARK STRAND: *You don't feel that other countries are subject to the same kind of brainwashing?*

WALLACE SHAWN: Well, they may be subject to it but—

MARK STRAND: *You as a foreigner wouldn't be.*

WALLACE SHAWN: Right. Maybe in Ireland you're subjected to constant propaganda to the effect that the Pope is infallible, but that's just not going to affect me.

MARK STRAND: *What you're saying is that when you're abroad you're spared moments of hatred as well as extended periods of delusion.*

WALLACE SHAWN: No, I do feel the hatred when I'm abroad—hatred for the world I've left behind. I treasure those moments. When I'm in other countries it has the marvelous effect of *awakening* "The Hour of Hate."

MARK STRAND: *I don't feel quite as strongly as you do. There are many things that I don't like about life in the United States. On the other hand, I feel that my sense of well-being is dependent on my being here.*

WALLACE SHAWN: Oh, I love being here. I simply adore it. It's just that because we *are* allowed to say to each other here that there are some problems, and that everything is not all right, and that there are at least six or seven things out of a hundred that are wrong, that need fixing—the fact that we can say all that—

MARK STRAND: *Not only say it but publish it.*

WALLACE SHAWN: That makes it particularly difficult to believe the truth, which is that this is a vile society, and we're going through a vile period. Our national enterprise is murder. We are out of control. Our attempt to preserve our powerful position, our standard of living, has made us into drunken murderers. And we may not know what we're doing, but the average farmer in El Salvador knows just what we're doing. And if the world is annihilated, everyone will know, for two seconds or whatever.

MARK STRAND: *In some ways the very culture that you mistrust is the one that has allowed you to be you and has given you a certain amount of success. So, I mean, maybe there's a way in which you'd like to start your relationship with the culture over again.*

WALLACE SHAWN: Yes.

MARK STRAND: *But one isn't ever sure whether one is talking to the culture or the culture is speaking through one.*

WALLACE SHAWN: Yes.

MARK STRAND: *And if the culture is speaking through you and you don't approve of the culture, then you naturally don't approve of yourself.*

WALLACE SHAWN: [Laughs.]

MARK STRAND: *But if you have an autonomous sense of self that is culture-free, which I don't think is possible, you can at least believe you're doing something.*

WALLACE SHAWN: Yes.

MARK STRAND: *I think that this is such a seductive culture. It gives you the illusion that you're doing something, but in fact you're just playing a part. Also, I think there is a period in everyone's career where they have severe doubts. It's not that they don't like what they've done, but they need to go on and do something quite different; in some ways the culture demands something different. . . . You brought up two countries, Nicaragua and Ireland. Nicaragua seems to indicate greater involvement, and Ireland seems to indicate lesser involvement.*

WALLACE SHAWN: Well, in Nicaragua I met a few Americans who actually work for the government.

MARK STRAND: *Our government?*

WALLACE SHAWN: No. They work for the Nicaraguan government.

MARK STRAND: *The Sandinistas?*

WALLACE SHAWN: Yeah. I was sort of struck by them because they were people whom I certainly admired much more than I admire myself.

MARK STRAND: *Why did you admire them?*

WALLACE SHAWN: They were not only working very hard—those Nicaraguan hours are very long—but they literally had poured their entire lives into this project of trying to build a better society, even though they could have been having much nicer dinners if they had hung around a little closer to Balducci's. And things are so desperate down there that they might just hire a person to do all sorts of interesting things. So I sort of had this picture that if I volunteered my services they might hire me.

MARK STRAND: *What vision of a better world do you have that could be accommodated by being in Nicaragua?*

WALLACE SHAWN: [Laughs.] Well, I believe in their national enterprise in general. And if you involve yourself in figuring out a way for trucks to reach a certain cooperative out in the countryside so that their produce can be collected and taken to the market—well, I don't do anything comparable to that.

MARK STRAND: *Well, the fruits of your labor are seen immediately in those situations, whereas the fruits of your labor as a playwright are not seen immediately. You don't know what happens to people after they've seen your play, so in a sense you're removed from the effects of what you did.*

WALLACE SHAWN: I would like to think that I can do what I find the most pleasurable, which is writing and leading an enjoyable life in New York City, and at the very same time, by coincidence, through the operations of the invisible hand described by Adam Smith, it will turn out to be the greatest contribution I can make to human welfare. How wonderful that would be.

MARK STRAND: *What about your career as an actor?*

WALLACE SHAWN: I have to say this: I am a ludicrous person. I consider myself an idiot. It's idiotic to be talking about all of these things without taking any action.

MARK STRAND: *Talking is an action. Don't you see that when you talk you're doing something? The effects of talk are sometimes more far-reaching than those of physical action.*

WALLACE SHAWN: Well, I agree with that. Yes, the world is fucked up partly because people don't understand things and they haven't thought things through. So there must be people who think. I'm not sure that I'm qualified to be one of them. But as far as being an actor goes, that's where I'm really participating with both feet in American culture. Unlike you, I am actually going out and destroying life on Monday, and then on Tuesday I'm talking about the need to preserve life. As soon as you get involved in Hollywood movies you're dangerously close to criminal activity.

MARK STRAND: *That bad?*

WALLACE SHAWN: [Laughs.] Movies have the function of—

MARK STRAND: *Putting people to sleep.*

WALLACE SHAWN: And brainwashing them. Of course I put on a big performance in front of myself about being very selective about what I'll be in and what I won't be in. I once heard Jimmy Swaggart on television say something along the lines of, "People ask me: 'Jimmy, can't I go to the movies at all? I don't go to the bad ones. I only go to the good ones.' And I say to them: 'There are no good ones. A bad tree cannot bring forth good fruit.'" When I heard him say that I thought, he's right. I think that the objective truth here is pretty close to what he said, even though on a day-to-day level I take great pride in kidding myself into thinking that I'm working very hard to make those distinctions between the good ones and the bad ones and not to be in the bad ones. There are some that are so incredibly evil that they're worse than just telling people that things are O.K. They take the extra step of saying, We're great, so we really should go out right now and kill everybody else.

MARK STRAND: *Let me ask you a question about that. There are some movies that tell you America is not O.K., but they do it in such simple-minded terms and they are so littered with clichés and at the same time so well-meaning. On the other hand there are those movies that are really quite inventive, dazzlingly so sometimes, that say that America is fine. How do you stand on that? Which would you rather be in, a critical banality or a piece of conformist invention?*

WALLACE SHAWN: Well, I tend to avoid almost all serious movies. I usually think, If it's really critical, how could it be using the banal clichés of American entertainment? If someone really has a critical view of the culture or of America, he's not going to be using those clichés. I tend to stick to the comedies because I really freak out when I get serious scripts—no matter what they supposedly are trying to say, I almost always feel there's something radically wrong with them. I much prefer to be in the funny ones.

MARK STRAND: *Aren't there any serious American films that are good?*

WALLACE SHAWN: There were scenes in Woody Allen's latest movie, *Another Woman,* that I thought were great. Usually I think intense emotion doesn't come off too well in movies. In theater it's great to see people sobbing and screaming and having very extreme feelings. But in movies I don't think it comes off well.

MARK STRAND: *What is the reason for that?*

WALLACE SHAWN: When I see people sobbing and going through agonies in films I tend to think that these aren't even real people. It's just a strip of plastic with light shining through it.

MARK STRAND: *But then you must fail to be involved in any movie, in anything in a movie.*

WALLACE SHAWN: For one thing, the sound of the sobbing is coming out of a box somewhere. The speakers are hanging in one place or another in the theater. The sobbing person is ten times life-size. You're cutting back and forth from the sobbing person to the person who is reacting to the sobbing.

MARK STRAND: *A lot of people get used to those conventions, and that's the way they see life. You bring up an issue that I never really considered—I mean the electronic aspect of going to a movie, which is an element of falsification. The sound is really so loud. You're so close to people when they're on the screen. You're never that close to people in real life. There's no such thing as a closeup in real life, because if you're that close to somebody you cease to see them.*

WALLACE SHAWN: Yeah, you certainly wouldn't be able to stare at them, anyway. A movie that had incredibly passionate scenes that I loved was *A Nos Amours* by Maurice Pialat.

MARK STRAND: *I've never seen it.*

WALLACE SHAWN: It's great.

MARK STRAND: *Let me go back to something you were saying. Are you going to continue being an actor even though you feel while acting you participate in something falsifying?*

WALLACE SHAWN: I would say that before becoming an actor the previous job that I had was as a Xerox-machine operator. I lived for ten years by borrowing money from friends, which is the sort of life that people traditionally find it very hard to return to. To give up acting would mean to give up the only way I've ever had of making a living. Of course, the thing about acting is that while I'm sitting around deciding whether I want to give it up, it could much more easily give *me* up. I started acting as a joke. It just seemed funny. It was not my idea. It was the idea of a man who died this year, Wilford Leach, a theater director who put me in a play. I translated *The Mandrake* of Machiavelli for him and Joe Papp, and then Will suggested that I appear in it. So it began very, very casually, as someone else's idea, and it's become a way of making a living. But the truth is, acting is very, very interesting. You could never be bored by being an actor; it's a fascinating intellectual exercise that has to be performed incredibly rapidly.

MARK STRAND: *Give me an example of what you mean by its being an intellectual exercise.*

WALLACE SHAWN: An example is I was in a scene where I was sitting at a desk and I was supposedly a businessman. The scene consisted of me talking on the telephone and I say, "Oh, hello, Dr. Jones. What were the results of the test? Oh! I only have six months to live? Oh, I see." These were my lines. Something like that. So there was one challenge before the scene was being shot, which was to figure out how in the world I could summon within myself [laughs] anything that might resemble being shocked by the news that I only have six months to live. And then, when I appeared to do the scene, naturally, the room was different from the one that I had pictured, and the desk was different. The director said, "Now, while you're making this phone call this lamp is going to be flickering on and off. I want you to try to be fixing it." So everything that I had previously been thinking was in a way not that relevant. I was set with a new assignment that incorporated the old assignment and made it more complicated, and I had to provide the answer to the dilemma immediately. If you're not challenged by that you must be insane. And every scene is sort of like that.

So of course I got interested in acting, because it is very interesting. It is sort of an intellectual challenge, but you cannot solve it intellectually. The intellectual element is only the beginning. You have to think of something that will bring out of you whatever is emotionally required by the scene. So it's challenging. Naturally I got quite interested in it. But I am always aware of the fact that I am, from the point of view of the people who hire me, just an odd color or an amusing little fragment of paint on the canvas. Tastes easily change. I happen to be on the list now of short, bald character actors, but I could easily fall off that list.

MARK STRAND: *What could possibly throw you off that list?*

WALLACE SHAWN: The only reason I'm on the list is one or two directors in a year think, I would like to have Wally in this movie. If there are not one or two in a year, then I'm not on the list. A lot of people do fall off the list. I'm not speaking insanely. Of course if you're Bob De Niro or Meryl Streep and you have the kind of incredible flair for acting they have, then as long as there's a demand for actors in the world, even if they are eighty years old, they would still be marvelously able to play the ancient servants in Chekhov. But for most actors it's not really like that. In movies, at any rate, it has a lot to do with how you look and the way your particular face and manner of speaking intersect with the taste of the culture at a particular moment. I've known a lot of actors who've been in movies for a while and somehow the tastes of the people who make movies changed.

MARK STRAND: *Do they live in hopes of going back?*

WALLACE SHAWN: No. Though some people do come back into fashion. I'm speaking of male character actors now.

MARK STRAND: *Are you satisfied with being a character actor?*

WALLACE SHAWN: In a way I'm quite embittered about it, because I sort of feel insulted that these people don't think that I could be the father of the family, the husband, the lover. Why, instead, do they see me as the bizarre priest who lurks on the edges of life, the peculiar, sexless psychiatrist who skulks in the corner of the lives of the real people? On the other hand there aren't that many roles of leading men that would be very appealing to me, because I think I would be too nauseated by those roles. But man's vanity is infinite. Man's capacity for being offended is infinite. The truth is that I enormously enjoy doing these things.

MARK STRAND: *This is the flip side of your anger with the culture.*

WALLACE SHAWN: It is. Maybe the whole idea that a person has to be only one person is a mistake. When I think a person should be one person, I become agitated. In practice I alternate between utterly different people. Something like *The Three Faces of Eve,* if you ever saw that movie.

MARK STRAND: *Yes.*

WALLACE SHAWN: And it's just fine. When I'm acting in a movie I throw myself 100 percent into it, I enjoy it totally, and I tend not to talk too much about the things that are preoccupying me during the other weeks of my life when I become Person B.

MARK STRAND: *Maybe when you're working you're busy working, and when you're not working you take a darker view of things partially because you are out of work, assuming you're not writing a play.*

WALLACE SHAWN: Person B has done all my writing. I've often been asked, "Why don't you write a movie for yourself? A movie that you could star in?" And the reason that I don't do it is because the only one of the two of us who can write is Person B, and he doesn't want Person A in his movie!

MARK STRAND: *Well, why not get a good friend of yours to write a movie for you?*

WALLACE SHAWN: To go back to what you said, if I worked twelve months a year as a character actor I could easily see that I would get a house in Beverly Hills and become entirely Person A. I can picture it very, very easily, but the thing is that since Person B in a way comes closer to being the real me, inevitably there would be some problems. I don't know quite how they would arise.

MARK STRAND: *So what are you going to do?*

WALLACE SHAWN: I do feel the world needs writers. Not necessarily me, of course, but, sure, one of the reasons that we do what we do is that we are a confused, terrible culture, which probably can be changed only because there are writers. But no one is ever going to give you a certificate for future writing, like a gift certificate that you know you can cash in. I mean, you can get a gift certificate at a store and you know that if you take it to the store, they will give you a certain amount of stuff, but nobody can give you a certificate that will guarantee that you'll keep on writing or keep on writing well.

Notes

INTRODUCTION

1. Quoted in Don Shewey, "The Secret Life of Wally Shawn," *Esquire* 100 (October 1983): 94.

2. W. D. King, telephone interview with Wallace Shawn (August 1993).

3. Wallace Shawn, statement in *Contemporary Dramatists,* 2nd ed., ed. James Vinson (New York: St. Martin's Press, 1977), 719.

4. *Contemporary Dramatists,* 4th ed., ed. D. L. Kirkpatrick (Chicago: St. James, 1988), 478–80.

5. Wallace Shawn, *Aunt Dan and Lemon* (New York: Dramatists Play Service, 1986), 83.

6. Mark Strand, "The Man behind the Voice," interview of Wallace Shawn, *Interview* 19 (March 1989): 72. In *My Dinner with André,* he encapsulates his biography as follows: "I grew up on the Upper East Side, and when I was ten years old I was rich, I was an aristocrat, riding around in taxis, surrounded by comfort, and all I thought about was art and music. Now I'm thirty-six, and all I think about is money" (Wallace Shawn and André Gregory, *My Dinner with André* [New York: Grove, 1981], 17).

7. David Savran, *In Their Own Words: Contemporary American Playwrights* (New York: Theatre Communications Group, 1988), 208.

8. Clive Barnes, "Sickest of Sick Jokes Undeniably a Joke," review of *Our Late Night, New York Times,* 10 January 1975, 20.

9. King, telephone interview (August 1993).

10. Savran, 211.

11. Shewey, "Secret Life," 94.

12. Savran, 212. On this subject, Lloyd Rose commented: "For the audiences who come to see his plays, he is always a conversationalist. He isn't interested in the conventional give and take of stage dialogue or, for that matter, in conventional plotting. His plays for the most part lack a beginning, middle, and end, and also scenes in which 'something happens.' What happens in Shawn's plays is that people talk, often wildly and shockingly—long

discourses on obsession, fear, and fantasy, or minute dissections of seemingly everyday events—while others listen with the minimal reaction common to the rigidly well bred and the mad" ("The Art of Conversation," *The Atlantic* 256 [November 1985]: 125).

13. Shawn and Gregory, *My Dinner*, 17.

14. Michael Billington, "A Play of Ideas Stirs Political Passions," *New York Times*, 27 October 1985, sec. 2, 1.

15. Strand, "Man behind the Voice," 75.

16. Shewey, "Secret Life," 96.

17. Strand, "Man behind the Voice," 126.

18. Shawn recalls: "Juliet Taylor [Allen's casting director] saw me in *The Mandrake*. She called me in to meet Woody Allen. It was a shock, but a totally pleasant one, like a dream, really. Not having been an actor, I didn't even know quite how amazing it was, to suddenly be called in to meet Woody Allen and to be called back the next day and then to be in this wonderful movie. I think *Manhattan* is one of the best movies ever made. I loved doing my scene with Diane Keaton and Woody Allen; I felt totally comfortable. I felt like I'd known them for years. Then when I saw the movie, I couldn't believe I was privileged to be in such a wonderful movie. I forgot that I was about to appear in it, because I don't show up until fairly late in the movie. I still find it fairly amazing that that happened" (Don Shewey, "Wallace Shawn," *Caught in the Act: New York Actors Face to Face* [New York: NAL, 1986], 223).

19. Savran, 211.

20. Rose, 126.

21. Erik MacDonald, *Theater at the Margins: Text and the Post-Structured Stage* (Ann Arbor: Univ. of Michigan Press, 1993), 3.

22. Shawn and Gregory, *My Dinner*, 87.

23. Gregory L. Ulmer, *Applied Grammatology: Post(e)-Pedagogy from Jacques Derrida to Joseph Beuys* (Baltimore: Johns Hopkins University Press, 1985).

24. Savran, 209. The fifth-grade play he wrote was about the death of Socrates, and Shawn played Socrates. Shawn told John Lahr: "It was a philosophical play, not that different from the plays I have written subsequently" (John Lahr, "The Dangling Man," *New Yorker* 72 [15 April 1996]: 49).

25. Shewey, "Secret Life," 94; Savran, 211.

26. Lucinda Franks, "The Shawns—A Fascinating Father-and-Son Riddle," *New York Times*, 3 August 1980, sec. II, 25.

27. Ibid.

28. King, telephone interview (August 1993).

29. King, telephone interview (August 1993). Brendan Gill wrote: "At times, one heard grumblings, in the corridors of the magazine and out in the world, that [William] Shawn was a masochist who took pleasure in wailing and beating his breast in exaggerated trepidation over the debased conduct of our national and international affairs, but as the facts slowly emerged, both in Southeast Asia and in Washington, Shawn's persistence was seen to be justified. Better than any other editor of our time, he has been able to measure the distance of our national fall from grace; better than any other, he measures today the difficulty of regaining that grace" (*Here at the New Yorker* [New York: Random House, 1975], 153–54).

30. Franks, 25. William Shawn's accepting of whatever his son wrote did not lead to an acceptance for publication in the *New Yorker*. Wallace Shawn's writing has never been published there.

31. Shewey, "Secret Life," 94.

32. Franks, 1.

33. David Gates, "A Lover of the Long Shot," obituary of William Shawn, *Newsweek*, 21 December 1992, 53. Wallace Shawn has said: "If you want to be a writer, it's dangerous to have a job. My own father was an example. He wanted to be a writer. He ended up getting a job, and his life followed the direction of the job" (Lahr, 50).

34. The literature on liberalism is vast, controversial, and finally, I think, tangential to this book. "Liberalism" means many different things to many different people, but the technicalities involved in defining the term are the concern mainly of intellectuals for whom there is something definite at stake in the discourse. Wallace Shawn is a writer who has evolved within a context that is functionally defined in part by liberalism as a political designation, but the term is one he rarely, if ever, uses in reference to himself. As I hope to make clear in this book, Shawn's relation to something loosely called liberalism is dialectical and ironical. Furthermore, his writings aim not at defining political ideas but at creating a many-layered experience in which political questions are opened and felt. Richard Rorty's idea of liberal ironism seems pertinent to Shawn, who is, in this view, the strong poet who by radical misprision revolutionizes the tradition of liberalism by dramatizing the very terms Rorty emphasizes—contingency, irony, and solidarity.

For assistance in reading Rorty, I turned to *Rorty's Humanistic Pragmatism: Philosophy Democratized* by Konstantin Kolenda (Tampa: Univ. of South Florida, 1990). Of the many books about liberalism, I found two collections of essays most useful: *Liberalism and the Moral Life,* edited by Nancy Rosenblum (Cambridge: Harvard Univ. Press, 1989), and *Liberalism Reconsidered,* edited by Douglas MacLean and Claudia Mills (Totowa,

N.J.: Rowman and Allanheld, 1983). For a discussion of American liberalism in the context of U.S. history in the 1960s, I used David Farber, *The Age of Great Dreams: America in the 1960s* (New York: Hill and Wang, 1994). Finally, I found especially evocative an essay by Julie Ellison, "A Short History of Liberal Guilt," *Critical Inquiry* 22 (winter 1996): 344–71.

35. Ross Wetzsteon, "The Holy Fool of the American Theater?" *Village Voice,* 2 April 1991, 37.

36. Savran, 220.

37. "Why Write for the Theater? A Roundtable Report," *New York Times,* 9 February 1986, sec. 2, 30.

38. Savran, 222.

39. Wetzsteon, 35–37. At the time of *Aunt Dan and Lemon* (around 1985), Shawn wrote: "Privacy is an illusion. What I do is public, and what I think is public. The fragility of my own thoughts becomes the fragility of the world. The ease with which I could become a swine is the ease with which the world could fall apart, like something rotten" (Wallace Shawn, "On the Context of the Play," *Aunt Dan and Lemon* [New York: Grove, 1985], 105).

40. Strand, "Man behind the Voice," 126.

41. "A Couple of Vanyas Sitting around Talking," *New York Times,* 19 February 1995, sec. H, 5.

42. Michael Sragow, "Two Women Stand Tall in *Vanya on 42nd Street:* In Yelena, a Faithful Wife and an Enchantress," *New York Times,* 4 December 1994, sec. H, 26.

43. Wallace Shawn, *The Designated Mourner* (London: Faber and Faber, 1996), 37–38.

44. William Wimsatt, *The Verbal Icon: Studies in the Meaning of Poetry* (Lexington: Univ. Press of Kentucky, 1954).

45. Shawn, "On the Context of the Play," in *Aunt Dan and Lemon,* 89–90.

46. Richard Rorty, *Contingency, Irony, Solidarity* (Cambridge, Mass.: Cambridge Univ. Press, 1989), xvi.

CHAPTER 1

1. Shewey, "Secret Life," 94.

2. Wallace Shawn, unpublished script of *Four Meals in May,* dated 1969, copyright 1973, 15. Subsequent page references to this play in this chapter are given in parentheses.

3. One might compare this to the speech in *Aunt Dan and Lemon* in which Dan declares that one should never shout at a waiter (24–25). Comparison might also be made to another Ruth Draper monologue, "The Diet," which

depicts a group of women at an elegant restaurant eating absurdly reduced meals.

4. Shawn, statement in *Contemporary Dramatists*, 719.

5. Savran, 212.

6. Michael Merschmeier, "Die Misere des Moralisten," *Theater Heute*, April 1994, 18.

7. Lahr, 48. Brackman added: "In many ways, Wally *was* like a little Mr. Shawn, who was the biggest fumbler in the world. Wally's fumbling was completely from his dad. He was very polite and very stylized: he was telling you that he's just a miserable little worm" (48).

8. My own transcription from *The King of Marvin Gardens,* directed by Bob Rafelson (1972).

9. Wallace Shawn, unpublished script of *The Old Man,* dated 1969, copyright 1973, 21. Subsequent page references to this play in this chapter are given in parentheses. This play was performed in the mid-1970s at the Lenox Art Center, with Timothy Mayer directing and Paul Schmidt in the role of the old man. Mayer introduced a second figure to the play, a nurse who sat silently by the bed.

10. Marcus Aurelius, *Thoughts of Emperor Marcus Aurelius Antoninus,* trans. George Long (Boston: Little, Brown, and Company, 1897), viii, 21; vii, 56.

CHAPTER 2

1. Shawn, statement in *Contemporary Dramatists,* 719.

2. Strand, 73.

3. Shawn, statement in *Contemporary Dramatists,* 719–20.

4. Wetzsteon, 35.

5. Don Shewey, "Wally Shawn's Grandstand Play," *Soho News* 18 (August 1981): 43.

6. Wallace Shawn, *The Hotel Play* (New York: Dramatists Play Service, 1982), 9. Subsequent page references to this play in this chapter are given in parentheses.

7. August Strindberg, *Strindberg: Five Plays,* trans. Harry G. Carlson (Berkeley: University of California Press, 1983), 205–6.

8. Shawn, *The Old Man,* 24.

9. Shewey, "Wally Shawn's Grandstand Play," 43.

10. Ibid.

11. Ibid.

12. Frank Rich, "A Misanthropic View," review of *The Hotel Play, New York Times,* 23 August 1981, sec. C, 3.

13. Shewey, "Wally Shawn's Grandstand Play," 43.

14. Wallace Shawn, unpublished script of *The Family Play*, dated 1970, copyright 1973, 13. Subsequent page references to this play in this chapter are given in parentheses.

15. Sigmund Freud, *The Interpretation of Dreams* in *The Basic Writings of Sigmund Freud*, trans. A. A. Brill (New York: Modern Library, 1938), 199.

16. Wallace Shawn, letter to the author, 2 December 1993.

17. King, telephone interview with Shawn (August 1993).

18. Wallace Shawn, unpublished script of *The Hospital Play*, dated 1971, copyright 1973, 3. Subsequent page references to this play in this chapter are given in parentheses.

19. Jonathan Schell, *The Time of Illusion* (New York: Vintage Books, 1975), 344–45.

20. King, telephone interview (August 1993).

CHAPTER 3

1. Powerhouse Repertory Company called the play "an edgy comedy" on a promotional flyer for their production, 27 August to 26 September 1993. This was the first of Shawn's plays to have a professional production, directed by André Gregory for his Manhattan Project. The company began working with the play in September 1972 and did not perform its final version until January 1975. ("I'd be very surprised if you were able to turn up a longer rehearsal period in the history of theatre," says Shawn (Savran, 210).) John Lahr reports that during those years Shawn was trying to write a modern version of *Peer Gynt* for the Manhattan Project (Lahr, "Dangling Man," 50).

2. Brendan Gill, "Dead Gull, Live Party," review of *Seagull* and *Our Late Night, New Yorker* 50 (20 January 1975), 62–63.

3. Shawn, letter to the author, 2 December 1993.

4. Gill, "Dead Gull," 62.

5. Ibid., 63.

6. Shewey, "Secret Life," 93. In the same interview, Shawn said: "I would like to know what the lives of other people are like in their quietest moments, what their relationships are like and what they feel about each other and what they feel about themselves when they're sitting alone in a room and what they do after the company has gone home and what suffering they experience in the middle of the night" (93).

7. Steven Mikulan, "Misery en Scène: Looking for Love in All the Wrong Places," review of *Our Late Night, Los Angeles Weekly*, 10–16 September 1993, 35.

8. Wallace Shawn, unpublished script of *Our Late Night,* dated 1972, copyright 1973, 1. Subsequent page references to this play in this chapter are given in parentheses.

9. Brendan Gill observed: "I have to confess that from time to time I was put vaguely in mind of *The Cocktail Party,* but I took care to remain vague. Like most writers with a bent for pornography, Mr. Shawn is on the side of the life-enhancers, while Eliot was on the side of the life-diminishers—the afterlife was what Old Possum smacked his dry lips over" (Gill, "Dead Gull," 63).

10. Franks, 25.

11. John Russell Brown, "Wallace Shawn," *Contemporary Dramatists,* 2nd ed., ed. James Vinson (New York: St. Martin's Press, 1977), 720.

12. Clive Barnes, "Sickest of Sick Jokes Undeniably a Joke," review of *Our Late Night, New York Times,* 10 January 1975, 20.

13. Shawn, letter to the author, 2 December 1993.

14. Brown, 720.

15. Shawn, letter to the author, 2 December 1993.

16. Ibid.

17. Wallace Shawn, unpublished libretto of *In the Dark,* dated 1976, 12–14.

18. Shawn, statement in *Contemporary Dramatists,* 719–20.

19. Shawn changed the title to encourage audiences to see the three parts as a unity (King, telephone interview, August 1993). In 1981, Max Stafford-Clark said: "One of the interesting American writers whose work has been done recently is Wallace Shawn, whose work, I think, is neglected in America. In fact, his plays were first done in Britain by Joint Stock. I directed three one-act plays, which were known as *A Thought in Three Parts.* In fact, a group of writers, David Hare and Howard Brenton and, I think, Barrie Keefe, said, 'Look, there are these plays we have read which have been turned down by the Court, turned down by Hampstead; they have been turned down by every theatre in London, and, therefore, there is good reason why Joint Stock should deviate from its policy of creating its own plays and perform them, because nobody else will.' It was the writers who brought my attention to the fact that Wallace Shawn was an original. I think his work has not really been appreciated yet, nor has it been as important as it should be, neither here nor in Britain. I think *My Dinner with André,* which was recently performed in the Theatre Upstairs, was a wonderful evening, and, in fact, is much better as a play than as a film. I think he is a major American writer. And because of that we feel a commitment to him. You get over the fact that he's American!" (Gresdna A. Doty and Billy J. Harbin, eds., *Inside the Royal Court, 1956–1981: Artists Talk* [Baton Rouge: Louisiana State University Press, 1990], 81).

20. "Experimental Work Yes, but Offensive, No—Says Peer," *The Stage and Television Today,* 31 March 1977, 1.

21. Barber's and Wardle's reviews are quoted in "What the Critics Said," published alongside Shawn's "Summer Evening," *Plays and Players* 24 (April 1977): 17.

22. The letter by Brenton, Churchill, Hare, and Keefe is reprinted in "What the Critics Said," published alongside Shawn, "Summer Evening," 17.

23. Ned Chaillet, "Joint Stock under Fire," *Plays and Players* 24 (April 1977): 21; Ned Chaillet, "Wallace Shawn," in *Contemporary Dramatists,* 4th ed., ed. D. L. Kirkpatrick (Chicago: St. James, 1988), 479; Chaillet, "Joint Stock Under Fire," 21.

24. Wallace Shawn, *A Thought in Three Parts,* in *Word Plays 2: An Anthology of New American Drama* (New York: Performing Arts Journal Publications, 1982), 41. Subsequent page references to this play in this chapter are from this edition and are cited in parentheses.

25. Robert Cushman, "The First Sex," *Observer,* 6 March 1977, 24.

26. Leonard Leff, "Warhol's *Pork,*" *Art in America* 60 (January–February 1972): 113. Shawn told me that he never saw *Pork,* but he did see *Chelsea Girls* in 1969 or 1970: "It did sort of evoke a big reaction of some kind in me. Probably I thought I was very 'opposed' to it, while actually being quite excited and fascinated by it" (letter to the author, 7 September 1995).

27. Franks, 25.

28. Shawn and Gregory, *My Dinner,* 112.

CHAPTER 4

1. Jack Kroll, "I Love You / I Hate You," *Newsweek,* 18 February 1980, 117.

2. Wallace Shawn, *Marie and Bruce* (New York: Grove, 1980), 1. Subsequent page references to this play in this chapter are to this edition and are given in parentheses.

3. Brendan Gill, "Out There and Down Here," *New Yorker* 55 (11 February 1980): 65.

4. Quoted in William Harris, "Off and On," *Soho Weekly News,* 24 January 1980, 48.

5. Quoted in John Corry, "Mary Hartman Is Now Marie Off-Broadway," *New York Times,* 3 January 1980, sec. C, 13.

6. Foster Hirsch, *Love, Sex, Death and the Meaning of Life: The Films of Woody Allen* (New York: Limelight Editions, 1990), 126, 124. Eric Lax quotes Allen describing Louise Lasser as "really and truly a wonderful, sensational person, but she was crazy as a loon. She was one of those persons

where you get two good weeks and two bad weeks a month, but the two weeks are so worth it. Then after a while you're down to two good *days* a month. Even the two days are almost worth it because two good days a month with Louise were better than a good year with most other people. It was like [Arthur Miller's] *After the Fall.* When I read some of the dialogue of that, I swear I thought to myself, 'God, I've heard Louise say these lines.' But she was extraordinary. All my friends and family remember her in the most affectionate way. I think I used some of this in Charlotte Rampling's character in *Stardust Memories*" (*Woody Allen: A Biography* [New York: Knopf, 1991], 170).

7. Brendan Gill, "And Now to Be Serious for a Moment," *New Yorker* 53 (12 December 1977): 92.

8. Wallace Shawn, trans., *The Mandrake* by Niccolò Machiavelli (New York: Dramatists Play Service, 1978), 6. Subsequent page references to this play in this chapter are given in parentheses.

9. Richard Eder described as "terribly funny" Shawn's performance of this "vehement and essentially meaningless prologue" ("Still Growing," *New York Times,* 18 November 1977, sec. C, 3).

10. Walter Kerr, "Among Its Virtues, Fine Acting Can Bare Weak Spots," *New York Times,* 3 January 1978, 37.

11. Shawn addresses parallel issues in his note on Leach's production in the Dramatists Play Service edition: "A few deliberately and outrageously anachronistic touches were used in the production, both to make it unmistakable that the play was about *us today,* however long ago it may have been written, and also in effect as tokens of the good faith of those presenting the performance. The spaghetti eaten by Ligurio, the travel folders he showed to Lord Nicia, the football appliqué on Callimaco's shirt, the Shriners' outfits used as disguises—all contributed to a feeling that Machiavelli's play was being performed precisely because it deals with human life as it still is today; it was not being presented in order to instruct the audience about history or offer it a chance to escape into a falsely harmless, pleasant world of the past" (65–66).

12. Savran, 212.

13. See Gerry Bamman et al., *"Alice in Wonderland": The Forming of a Company and the Making of a Play* (New York: Merlin House, 1973). In this book, Larry Pine is quoted as saying: "André says that one of the nice things about the group now is that all the actors are in a way directors, too. In *Alice,* each of us contributed different parts, scenic things. André would only choose" (62). Gregory himself spoke of his role in the power structure of this community in a somewhat different way: "I like to think I'm being so dem-

ocratic in allowing the actor to do whatever he wants, only very delicately and politely suggesting that this might be better than that. Refining things. But it may be the most egotistical way to be a director. I mean, everyone knows that directors like to play god. Well, there are small gods and big gods. The small gods have to show their power, so they move people around a lot and lay down the rules. But what could be more egotistical and closer to the image of god than to be completely absent? That to me is the cruelest and most interesting god of all" (44).

14. In *My Dinner with André,* Wally says, "I mean, I think maybe that's why actors are not given a great deal of respect: it's because actors spend most of their time actually playing, like children. I mean, each night when I was putting on my fake nose during the fourth act of *The Mandrake,* I would think about the fact that, when I was growing up, this wasn't what people had in mind for me. But I mean, there's always the excuse for an actor that, you know, you may be putting on a fake nose and running around acting like a jerk, but then after the performance you can hang up your nose and you can put on a suit and tie, and, you know, in England you can even be a lord and be quite a distinguished member of society, or Charlton Heston, you know, you can be a very important member of the National Endowment for the Arts and things like that—you can really act like a businessman" (Shawn and Gregory, 71–72).

15. Shawn and Gregory, *My Dinner,* 40.

16. Actually, Leach had already directed "Summer Evening," the first part of *Three Short Plays* (later called *A Thought in Three Parts*), in a workshop production in 1976, which, however, never opened to the general public. In the same workshop, "Youth Hostel" was directed by Leonard Shapiro, and "Mr. Frivolous" by Lee Breuer.

17. See Corry, "Mary Hartman," 13.

18. Howard Kissel, review of *Marie and Bruce, Women's Wear Daily,* 4 February 1980. The initial plan had been to have fifty extras play guests at the party. In a production note, Shawn wrote: "Marie, on the sofa, moved on the revolve through the party, at a speed that was scarcely visible. When the wall behind her moved in the opposite direction, the effect was uncanny" (*Marie and Bruce,* acting edition [New York: Dramatist Play Service, 1980], 30).

19. Walter Kerr, "Love-Hate Relationship," *New York Times,* 4 February 1980, sec. C, 13.

20. Robert Brustein, "Two Couples," *New Republic* 182 (5 April 1980): 29.

21. Gill, "Out There and Down Here," 65.

22. Tennessee Williams, *"27 Wagons Full of Cotton" and Other One-Act Plays* (Norfolk, Conn.: New Directions, 1953), 218.

23. Wallace Shawn, unpublished libretto of *The Music Teacher,* copyright 1983, 6. Subsequent page references to this opera in this chapter are given in parentheses.

24. Shawn and Gregory, *My Dinner,* 13.

CHAPTER 5

1. Wallace Shawn and André Gregory, *My Dinner with André* (New York: Grove, 1981), 17. Subsequent references to this screenplay in this chapter are from this edition and are given in parentheses.

2. Gregory's production of Shawn's *Our Late Night* opened early in 1975. The material for the film came from a series of conversations recorded over three or four months, beginning in December 1978. They met two or three times a week to talk "almost at random about everything and anything, including the subject of what sort of film ours might be and what sort of material might be included in it" (Wallace Shawn, "Some Notes on Louis Malle and *My Dinner with André,*" *Sight and Sound* [spring 1982], 119). A $7,000 grant from PBS enabled them to have the talks transcribed. It took about a year for Wally to shape some 2,200 pages of material into the version they performed at the Theatre Upstairs at the Royal Court in London, which opened for a limited run in November of 1980 (Marie Brenner, "My Conversation with André," *New York,* 19 October 1981, 40). That version was somewhat longer than the version published in 1981, which in turn was somewhat longer than the version used for the film.

Louis Malle had expressed an interest in directing the film based on the initial draft. Malle was the one who recommended that they perform the work on stage before filming to learn how the script would work with an audience: "From early on, Louis encouraged us to treat the script as if we'd received it in the mail, to forget the fact that we knew how the real André and Wally would say the lines. In other words, André and I instinctively started off trying to be just like ourselves, and Louis immediately realized that if we kept on doing that, it would be much better to hire two actors to play us, because any good actor would attempt to *interpret* his character, to show what was going on beneath his character's façade, while we were merely reproducing the façade" (Shawn, "Some Notes," 120). Malle helped Shawn and Gregory cut the script by about an hour and stage it.

The piece was initially performed for a very small audience at Upstate Films in Rhinebeck, New York (Michael Earley, interview of Wallace Shawn, in "Playwrights Making Movies," *Performing Arts Journal* 15 [1981]: 32). The Royal Court production was a *cause célèbre* — Gregory recalls how nervous he was looking out on an audience that included Sir Laurence Olivier,

Harold Pinter, and "at least one Redgrave," especially considering he had not acted on a stage since he was twenty-six (André Gregory, untitled speech at the University of California, Santa Barbara [UCSB], Campbell Hall, 10 January 1994). Julian Jebb recalled that the audience was "languorously aware that the play might be a weird occasion which it would be worth later boasting about having seen. I remember the early restlessness of the audience at the performance I attended. Then the gradual capitulation to the remarkable performances, followed by the sort of ovation which I associate more with Wagner than fringe plays. The trick, of course, was surprise" (Jebb, review of *My Dinner with André, Sight and Sound* [summer 1982], 208). The film was shot at the Jefferson Hotel in Richmond, Virginia, in about three weeks. It was shown at the New York Film Festival and then opened commercially on 11 October 1981.

3. The title seems to invoke *Ma nuit chez Maude,* a point implicitly made by Bruce Kawin, who believes that Malle's film goes beyond Eric Rohmer's in its "confronting of adult questions without resorting in difficult moments to the easy grace of an ironic pose" (Kawin, review of *My Dinner with André, Film Quarterly* [winter 1981–82], 62). The idea of telling the story to Debby is made interestingly complex by the fact that Debby refers to Deborah Eisenberg (at least, as much as Wally refers to Wallace Shawn). She was, in fact, working as a waitress during these years but was also writing short stories and even a play, *Pastorale,* commissioned by Joseph Papp for the Public Theatre but produced in 1982 at the Second Stage. Her stories have been collected in two widely respected volumes: *Transactions in a Foreign Currency* and *Under the 82nd Airborne.*

There are moments when reading these excellent stories when the student of Wallace Shawn is tempted to raise his hand and ask a personal question. In a profile of her, Mervyn Rothstein wrote: "In her stories, the narrators seem to have a sense of their own oddness." She responded to this idea: "There may be an element of first-hand experience about that. I do have a bit of feeling of myself as often being the stranger, often not understanding very well what's going on. It's very familiar to me, and it's a very vivid feeling to me, of being sort of displaced, dispossessed. It does seem to me to be true of people that you're just terribly lucky if you form an attachment with other people that makes you comfortable" ("An Ex-Waitress's Writing Success," *New York Times,* 22 April 1986, sec. III, 13). The feeling of displacement she describes might be seen as itself a displacement of André's feeling of displacement, but Wally, by his transit between the two, puts them both in place by recreating them as two people he is so terribly lucky to be comfortable with.

4. Gregory is perhaps as much the bearer of Chekhov's influence as Shawn. When André gives Wally an example of a typical theatrical improvisation (25), he uses a scene from *Seagull*. This play was the last one presented by Gregory's Manhattan Project (1977), and it was this play, he says, that broke his workaholic habit. At just this time, Gregory's mother, whom he describes as "sort of an Arkadina," was first diagnosed with cancer (Gregory, untitled UCSB speech, 1994).

5. In response to an interviewer who suggested that the film reveals "a new kind of intimacy" in Shawn's work, Shawn responded: "Of course this play has a script. Some of my earlier plays are in the unconscious half of the time. *My Dinner with André* is on the conscious level" (Earley, "Playwrights," 34–35).

6. Shawn, "Some Notes," 119.

7. Jack Kroll made the comparison to the *Symposium* in his review of the film (Kroll, "Conversation Piece," *Newsweek,* 26 October 1981, 78).

8. There are many interesting analyses of the dramatic qualities of Plato's dialogues. See Jacob Klein's *Commentary on Plato's "Meno"* (Chapel Hill: Univ. of North Carolina Press, 1975) for one of the seminal discussions. Nietzsche's discussion of the Socratic dialogue as the endpoint of the evolution of tragedy is in *The Birth of Tragedy*.

9. David Denby, review of *My Dinner with André, New York,* 26 October 1981, 96.

10. Joseph Gelmis reads disapproval into the facial twitches of the waiter ("Review of *My Dinner with André,*" *Newsday,* 8 October 1981, 46). Jack Kroll wrote: "As dinner ends, as Wally and André gaze into their coffee, a sense of the ludicrous and the heroic hovers over their table. Wally looks up and for the first time really sees the old waiter (Jean Lenauer) who's been serving them with shuffling deference. A faint shadow of wonder crosses Wally's cherub face: he's looking at mortal reality, beyond idea, beyond debate" ("Conversation Piece," 78). Gay Brewer also makes some interesting comments on the waiter and other employees of the restaurant, observing that Wally and André "seem unaware of a discrepancy increasingly obvious to viewers: the efficacy of the waiter's actions, his talent, grace, and simple, silent dignity in contrast to self-indulgent talk" (Gay Brewer, "Shawn's Problem of Morality," *American Drama* 2 [fall 1992]: 43). Brewer's article gives the most thorough overview of Shawn's career (*The Hotel Play* through *The Fever*) prior to this book.

11. Gelmis, 46.

12. Earley, 35.

13. Shawn, "Some Notes," 119. Shawn discusses in considerable detail the

challenge of acting himself as a character in this article, and also in Earley, passim.

14. Sartre, *Nausea,* trans. by Lloyd Alexander (New York: New Directions, 1964), 126.

15. I take it that the contrast between Wally's "pure being" and the state of "having any particular thing you were supposed to be doing" is essentially the contrast between Sartre's Being and Existence.

16. Still more powerful in its self-referential insistence is the moment just after Wally has postulated that "we" are all children, bored with playing with our plastic ducks and now wondering, "What can I do?" At that point, André says, "Okay. Yes. We're bored now. We're all bored" (91). This is a moment that, in my experience of watching this film with students and other audiences, always generates a strong, nervous laugh. That is a measure of how susceptible we are, still, to the Baudelairean *ennui.*

17. Sartre, 128

18. Gregory addresses these ideas more recently in terms of the writings of D. W. Winnicott, who asserts that the child is born authentic, but smart children conceal their authentic side and eventually lose track of it. Therapy is about dismissing all the wrong possibilities of who you might be (untitled UCSB speech, 1994).

19. Don Shewey, in his 1983 profile of Shawn, makes some pertinent, though painful, observations: "Approaching from afar, you just see the little weirdo with the mad cackle and the fringe of hair. The closer you get, the more he loses that strangeness, and you see him as warm and human and friendly and smart and wise. But Shawn carefully constructs the persona by which he wishes to be known, and if you try to slip past it, he starts throwing up the defenses, and strangeness sets in again. It's like looking back over your shoulder and catching the hostility behind the plastic smile. Why would anyone go to the effort of erecting such an elaborate masquerade? Perhaps it's the upper-class guilt of some millionaires who are quick to assure you that money isn't everything; or the celebrities who sniffle that it's lonely at the top. Perhaps it's animal instinct. 'If you want to attack me, attack me for my looks or my quirky eating habits, things I don't care about.' Shawn's oafish self-portrait in *My Dinner with André* seems to say, 'Anything that matters—my work, my family, my friends—I'm not going to show you.' Or perhaps it's the existential revenge of someone whom the world sees as a clown but who sees himself as a king. Just as camp, the extravagant style of mocking convention, expresses the homosexual's shock of self-discovery, Wally Shawn's through-the-looking-glass persona and his discomfiting, inside-out dramas reveal

the same truth over and over: You can't judge a person by what he looks like or where he came from; the real secret to someone's personality lies somewhere within, and it's so strange as to be practically unknowable" ("Secret Life," 97).

20. Sartre, 178.

21. Terry Keefe provides a very useful summary of the many conflicting interpretations of the ending of Sartre's novel, and in particular the question of whether the novel Roquentin intends to write is, in fact, *La Nausée* ("The Ending of Sartre's *La Nausée*," in *Critical Essays on Jean-Paul Sartre*, Robert Wilcocks, ed. [Boston: G. K. Hall and Co., 1988], 182–201). Nicholas Hewitt gives a valuable discussion of the admixture of philosophy and fiction in Sartre's book in the same Wilcocks volume cited ("'Looking for Annie': Sartre's *La Nausée* and the Inter-War Years," 209–24).

22. Gregory voiced these opinions at a public discussion of his life and work at the University of California, Santa Barbara, on January 10, 1994. Over the years, Gregory has become actively involved in the spiritual, political, and artistic movement that has come to be called New Age. The foundations of this movement lie in some of the ideas and organizations mentioned by Gregory in the film (e.g., Findhorn), and indeed *My Dinner with André* has operated as a focal point for discussion in this movement. Two years before his UCSB speech, he had addressed audiences at the Pacifica Graduate Institute, and in connection with that appearance was interviewed by Joan Crowder of the Santa Barbara *News-Press:* "The twentieth century has seen a disintegration of everything we believed in, Gregory said, capitalism, Communism, marriage and religion. But we have not replaced any of it yet. [Quoting Gregory:] 'We are waiting for a new age. We will have to recognize the importance of the feminine and the global. This is one world and the Earth is a woman. We had better take care of both.' People are very angry, Gregory said, and they can't connect with love while they are filled with rage" (Crowder, "My Breakfast with André," *News-Press* "Scene," 31 January 1992, 24).

23. Chaudhuri emphasizes that André's "critique of modern values, which he shares with the avant-garde, is shorn of the political explanations the avant-garde espoused" ("From the Sixties to the Seventies and Beyond: *My Dinner with André* and the American Avant-Garde," *Indian Journal of American Studies* 15 [summer 1985]: 20). Indeed, she asserts that in the film "the relativity and impermanence of the self is axiomatic, independent of all political systems" (20). Ironically, it is by way of Gregory's political reflections on the film that I have returned to this question. Ultimately, I believe, our readings are in agreement.

CHAPTER 6

1. Claude Lanzmann, *Shoah, an Oral History of the Holocaust: The Complete Text of the Film* (New York: Pantheon, 1985), 39.

2. In a *Time* magazine interview, Shawn said: "At the risk of sounding self-pitying, the project taxed my resources to the limit and sometimes beyond. It took more brains than I had, and to figure out how to write it, I had to borrow some of next year's brains and the next year's brains as well." He also said: "I'm a rather amiable person, but I believe that our society is not just a little bit sick, but very, very, very sick. That's why I write the things I do about these diseased minds. There's something dangerous about the play in that it shows brutality made intellectually respectable" (Gerald Clarke, "Now Comes the Just Dessert," *Time,* 18 November 1985, 105).

3. Wallace Shawn, *Aunt Dan and Lemon* (New York: Grove, 1985), 1. Subsequent references to this play in this chapter are from this edition, except as noted, and are given in parentheses.

4. Ironically, the role of the father, which was initially going to be played in London by John Heard, was taken over at the last minute by Shawn himself. Shawn later played the role in the New York production, as well as the roles of Freddie and Jasper. Frank Rich described Shawn's performance: "The most ferocious comic turn, however, comes from Mr. Shawn himself, who appears in three roles. The first and best of them is that of Lemon's American-born father, a proper auto-parts executive who suddenly flies into a digressionary rage about the dog-eat-dog Darwinism of the business world. Described by his daughter as 'kind of a caged animal,' the character is typical of those proper-looking monsters who have exploded before us from a safe distance in past Shawn plays" ("Turn to the Right," review of *Aunt Dan and Lemon, New York Times,* 30 October 1985, sec. C, 13).

5. Ironically, Frank Rich observed that at times Linda Hunt, who played Aunt Dan, seemed "to be impersonating Dr. Jeane Kirkpatrick" ("Turn to the Right," 13). *New York* published a report saying that Shawn was seen at lunch with Kissinger and Renata Adler at the Four Seasons Grill Room in March of 1986. Kissinger indicated to the reporter that he had read but not seen the play and had invited Shawn to lunch after Shawn had written to him; "Shawn, after debating whether anyone had the right to inquire about the origins of the lunch, said finally, 'Quite frankly, I wish you would just forget about it'" (*New York,* 24 March 1986).

6. See Harold Bloom, *The Anxiety of Influence: A Theory of Poetry* (New York: Oxford University Press, 1973). See also Harold Bloom, *A Map of Misreading* (New York: Oxford University Press, 1975).

7. Wallace Shawn, *Aunt Dan and Lemon,* acting edition (New York: Dramatists Play Service, 1986), 60.

8. Shawn, *Aunt Dan and Lemon,* acting edition, 6.

9. Michael Billington, "A Play of Ideas Stirs Political Passions," *New York Times,* 27 October 1985, sec. II, 30.

10. Laurie Winer asked Shawn if he wrote "On the Context of the Play" specifically to correct those who grossly misinterpreted the play as a neo-Nazi statement: "Is that why you felt a need to write the essay? Do you think a play is for raising issues and an essay for answering them?" Shawn replied: "Yes, the play is meant to be a provocation and to leave the audience unsatisfied. If there had been an uplifting ending to the play in which the evil views had been roundly trounced and defeated, then the audience would leave satisfied and the play wouldn't have much impact. So I leave the play unsatisfying and leave it up to the audience to deal with it. But these questions have been raised, and I, as a private citizen, like anyone else, I have my views on these issues, and I began to think, 'Well, I had no desire to put my own responses into the play, but why shouldn't I put them down in a little essay?' . . . I saw no reason to keep my personal position mysterious. Why shouldn't I reveal it? And, of course, I had a strong impulse to reveal it because I want everyone in the world to know that I'm a nice fellow" ("My Breakfast with Wally," *Wall Street Journal,* 20 November 1985, 30). Note: this interview was published on the same page as the Sylviane Gold review discussed below.

11. Savran, 218.

12. Frank Rich, "Once Again, Theater Was a Place for Wonder," *New York Times,* 29 December 1985, sec. II, 5.

13. John Peter, "Observing the Perilous Lessons of Life," *Sunday Times* (London), 8 September 1985, 43.

14. Sylviane Gold, "Unopposed Neo-Nazism Is Irresponsible," *Wall Street Journal,* 20 November 1985, 30. Gold was not alone in objecting to this play on the basis of its perceived use of the theater for political purposes. Robert Brustein wrote: "Liberalism, however discredited, and for all its admitted hypocrisy and frequent silliness, remains committed to the life principle, and to the quest for peace in an aggressive world. And so does conservatism, for all its confrontational 'realism' and paranoid style. But this is not true of the ideological extremism expressed in *Aunt Dan and Lemon,* with its effort to elevate a strain in human nature into a general all-embracing dark principle. Which tempts one to say to Wally Shawn, 'Don't hang back with the brutes'" ("Addressing a Hostile Audience," *New Republic* 193 [9 December 1985]: 27). Shawn commented on Brustein and other critics in

Savran, 215–19. Another interesting debate on the play, attacking Shawn's play from the left as ultimately liberal humanist, is in Bonnie Marranca, Johannes Birringer, and Gerald Rabkin, "The Controversial 1985–86 Theatre Season: A Politics of Reception," *Performing Arts Journal 28* vol. 10, no. 1 (1986): 7–33. Further discussion of the play, comparing it to *The Fever,* is in Bonnie Marranca, Elinor Fuchs, and Gerald Rabkin, "The Politics of Representation: New York Theatre Season 1990–91," *Performing Arts Journal 39* vol. 13, no. 3 (1991): 1–19.

15. Savran, 216. See also Savran's interview of Maria Irene Fornes, in the same volume, in which she argues that the play promotes fascism among those who do not know, independently, Shawn's political attitudes. She says, "That girl was a little too convincing for me" (62–63). Fortunately, Fornes was not, in fact, converted to fascism by the monologue.

16. Frank Rich, "Birth of the Big Lie," review of *Aunt Dan and Lemon, New York Times,* 28 March 1986, sec. C, 3.

CHAPTER 7

1. Shawn and Gregory, *My Dinner,* 84–85.

2. Ibid., 87–88.

3. Wallace Shawn, *The Fever* (New York: Farrar, Straus, and Giroux, 1991), 69. Subsequent page references to this piece in this chapter are from this edition, except as noted, and are given in parentheses. At the time it was awarded an Obie, Shawn was quoted as saying, "I didn't think this was actually a play and I was trying to get out of the theater" (Amy Virshup, "Sticking It Out: The 1990–91 Obie Awards," *Village Voice,* 21 May 1991, 99). The first truly public presentation of the work was at the Public Theatre in January 1991. Shawn then toured the work in England, later performing it in New York at Second Stage, La Mama, and Lincoln Center. He has also performed the work in Los Angeles and San Francisco. Several other actors, male and female, young and old, have performed the work since then. It has been performed many times in Europe, including a production with the Berliner Ensemble in 1995, directed by Shawn. A review of a recent production of the piece (performed by a woman) at Cleveland Public Theatre observed that it "is so filled with [Shawn's] idiosyncratic phrases and inflections that even when well-performed by another actor he seems to inhabit it like a shade" (Linda Eisenstein, "Playwright's Voice Permeates Monologue Play," *Plain Dealer* [Cleveland], 11 April 1996, sec. E, 9).

4. Wallace Shawn, *The Fever,* acting edition (New York: Dramatist Play Service, 1992), 40–41.

5. Ibid., 41.

6. Mervyn Rothstein, "A Monologue Takes On a Life of Its Own," *New York Times,* 9 March 1991, 12.

7. Savran, 220.

8. At just about the time when he was writing this piece, Shawn made two trips to Central America. He was also interviewed by Jerry Tallmer in connection with his performance as the critic L'Oiseau in the Alan Rudolph film, *The Moderns:* "[M]y interest in going to Central America is because it's a very good place to find out our own real nature. . . . You learn a lot by going to a country like El Salvador. That's where I was two days ago. Before that, Guatemala, Honduras, Nicaragua." When asked what it was he learned, Shawn answered: "Well . . . I would say . . . I met a lot of people who were risking their lives to try to struggle for a better life for their people . . . and the greatest enemy they face in that struggle . . . is . . . us." He added: "I'm not going to necessarily sit down this afternoon and write a play that's set in Tegucigalpa." (Tallmer: "Six beats. The straight face.") "But I don't promise not to" (Tallmer: "Okay, and we'll send funny little Mr. L'Oiseau to review it") ("Comic Actor Gets Serious," *New York Post,* 20 April 1988, 28).

9. Billington, "Play of Ideas," 30.

10. Critical response from the liberal press was especially harsh toward this work. Thomas M. Disch, for example, wrote in *The Nation* that the work "fascinated" him in the way that one is fascinated by the spectacle of "an intelligent, cultivated, well-spoken and genial person" suddenly deciding to vote for Jesse Helms or join the Klan. Calling *The Fever* "a sonata version of his *Aunt Dan and Lemon*" and Shawn a "diminutive Machiavelli" and (paradoxically) "a rhapsodist of liberal guilt," Disch condemned the work as "fraught, overwrought, unearned." Disch has the solution to the speaker's fever, which he exactly equates with Shawn's, and offers it in two words: "Practical Charity." He wants Shawn to get out more and extend a hand to others and does not hear the irony implicit in his attack on Shawn's breast-beating: "The soul he bares is not his own but one as merely theoretical as Ralph Waldo Emerson's, pure intellect nattering in a social void" (*The Nation* 252 [7 January 1991]: 24–25). Robert Brustein dismissed the work as Shawn's mid-life crisis or, worse, the outcry of "an incipient fanatic." What Brustein heard was the sort of political expression a man of settled opinions crosses the street to avoid: "Shawn's exhortations to the audience ('We can't escape our connection to the poor') may be politically correct, but they seem to be manufactured by a guilt machine running on self-hatred" ("Tripping into the Abyss," *New Republic* 204 [21 January 1991]: 29).

Ross Posnock brings an important perspective to this sort of attack: "To dismiss *The Fever* (as Frank Rich and others have done) as transparent, an embarrassingly intimate autobiographical confession of a particularly intractable case of liberal guilt, is to ignore the complexity of tone and intention which colors with facetiousness all the efforts at self-flagellation in Shawn's play. . . . His humor is not only black but corrosive as it dissolves any easy moral sympathy or identification one might be tempted to make with him, and arouses doubts about the transparent sincerity of his project. The cruel wit of the play's juxtapositions is not only disorienting but baffles any effort to fix its meaning, until *The Fever* becomes, like *My Dinner with André,* an immanent critique of contemporary liberal consciousness that works by a homeopathic logic: It seeks to break the fever of liberal masochism by infecting itself with the illness." His discussion of Shawn is interestingly coupled with a review of Richard Sennett's *The Conscience of the Eye: The Design and Social Life of Cities* (New York: Alfred A. Knopf, 1991) — a juxtaposition worthy of further examination ("New York Phantasmagoria," *Raritan* 11 [fall 1991]: 157–58).

Shawn gives his own reply to these critiques in an interview by Ross Wetzsteon. In particular, he responds to the assertion that *The Fever* is an autobiographical work: " 'To me the work is so transparently a work of artifice,' he bristles, 'that I can only say that I was absolutely *flabbergasted* when some critics dealt with it as some kind of autobiographical narrative. It seems to me so obviously a fable or fairy tale, yet at least two critics not only took it absolutely for granted that it was literally me talking, but had the nerve to complain that I didn't include more details about aspects of my personal life that they might have found more interesting! My goodness,' he exclaims, his exasperation turning plaintive, *'I made most of it up!'* " ("The Holy Fool of the American Theater?" *Village Voice*, 2 April 1991, 36).

11. Mervyn Rothstein inaccurately reported that Shawn was donating all proceeds to the theaters (Rothstein, "Monologue," 12); Shawn made a special point of denying this rumor (Wetzsteon, 35).

12. Sylvie Drake, "*The Fever* Cooled by Self-Flagellation," *Los Angeles Times*, 23 May 1991, sec. F, 4.

13. Ibid.

EPILOGUE I

1. Anton Chekhov, *Uncle Vanya: A Play,* adapted by David Mamet from a literal translation by Vlada Chernomordik (New York: Grove Press, 1989), 5. Gregory has said that he was the one who had Mamet do the adaptation (Gerald Carpenter, "André Gregory: Love in the Ruins," *Santa Barbara Independent*, 23 November 1994, 67), but this version was initially produced at the American Repertory Theatre in 1988, directed by David Wheeler.

2. Shawn and Gregory, *My Dinner,* 22–23.

3. "A Couple of Vanyas Sitting around Talking," interview of Wallace Shawn and Tom Courtenay, *New York Times,* 19 February 1995, sec. H, 5.

4. Florence A. Falk, "Dangling Conversation," *American Theatre* 8 (December 1991): 20.

5. Ibid.

6. Gregory, unpublished UCSB speech.

7. Gregory, unpublished UCSB speech; Falk, 21.

8. Amy Taubin, "The Discreet Charm of Vanya," *Village Voice,* 21 June 1994, 25.

9. Janet Maslin, "Spare Chekhov Begins Sneakily," *New York Times,* 19 October 1994, sec. C, 13.

10. Taubin, 25.

11. Shawn, *The Fever,* 27.

12. Taubin, 25.

13. Jack Kroll, "Saying Uncle in New York," *Newsweek,* 31 October 1994, 67.

14. Terrence Rafferty, "Plays on Film," *New Yorker* 70 (31 October 1994): 106.

15. Gregory, unpublished UCSB speech.

16. Falk, 21.

17. Gerald Carpenter, "André Gregory: Love in the Ruins," *Santa Barbara Independent,* 23 November 1994, 67.

EPILOGUE II

1. The similarities to Jones's *The Slave* are sufficiently close to lead one to wonder if some sort of direct influence is at work. Or was Shawn perhaps recalling the play from having seen it performed in its original production at the Cherry Lane Theatre in 1964? Both plays take place in a future time of armed uprising. Both have three characters, and in each play one of the characters is an older man associated with English literature, one is a younger man who is antagonistic to the older, and the third is woman who has been married to the younger man but who later turns her loyalty to the older. The older man and the woman suffer violent deaths by the end of both plays, and the younger man lives on. In Jones's play, the younger man is black and the other two characters white. This is what gives rise to the conflict in the drama and, at large, to the armed revolution taking place in the street. In Shawn's play, the contrast that gives rise to conflict is a bit more difficult to define, having to do with political attitudes, and the association between the younger man's beliefs and the uprising in the streets is much more uncertain.

Jones's play begins with the younger man, now costumed as a sort of Uncle Tom figure, a slave, speaking a convoluted prologue directly to the audience, with a strong undercurrent of self-mockery. There are also many points of contrast between the two plays, of course, such that I am reluctant even to venture a theory about how the plays might reflect each other. Walker Percy's novel also offers several strong points of similarity with *The Designated Mourner* and invites a comparative interpretation.

2. Wallace Shawn, *The Designated Mourner* (London: Faber and Faber, 1996), 1. Subsequent page references to this play in this epilogue are given in parentheses.

3. I cannot resist citing here the words of Lloyd Bentsen to Dan Quayle during the vice-presidential debates of the 1988 election campaign: "Senator, I served with Jack Kennedy. I knew Jack Kennedy. Jack Kennedy was a friend of mine. Senator, you are no Jack Kennedy" (Jack W. Germond and Jules Witcover, *Whose Broad Stripes and Bright Stars? The Trivial Pursuit of the Presidency, 1988* [New York: Warner Books, 1989], 440). Kennedy was, arguably, the exception, not the generic aspirant, but somehow royal, or, as it was said, Arthurian. In employing that name for his character Jack, Shawn would, of course, be ironizing it, as Quayle unintentionally was.

4. In a typescript of the play, dated 17 June 1995, which is what I worked from, this passage begins somewhat differently. In place of the first sentence I quoted, Judy says simply, "I love beautiful things" (7). I associate that sentence with images in *The Fever*.

5. The first production of *The Designated Mourner* opened in London at the National Theatre, in the Cottesloe Theatre, on 24 April 1996. Shawn told Jack Kroll that he had worked on the play for five years, with Mike Nichols in mind for Jack: "For some uncanny reason, I'd lie in bed at night and read it to myself in his voice" ("Why Mike Nichols Is Working without a Net," *Newsweek*, 6 May 1996, 84). Nichols had not acted in a play since 1980, but he agreed to take this part because "there's nothing more fun than scaring the shit out of an audience. And I think *The Designated Mourner* really scares the shit out of an audience" (Lahr, 46). David de Keyser played Howard, and Miranda Richardson took the role of Judy. David Hare, whom Shawn had known since the 1970s, directed the production. Shawn said: "I decidedly lose my underdog status with this production. It's being done in a way that anyone in the world would envy" (46). Hare staged the play with the actors seated behind a long table covered with books. Physical action was limited to the actors rising once to change position and, finally, leaving the stage. The performances, especially Nichols's, were strongly praised. Alastair Macaulay wrote: "[Nichols's] is a superbly conceived and most unusual per-

formance—perfectly judging the endless callowness and irony of the character" ("Cast into Mysterious Irony," *Financial Times* [London], 26 April 1996, 13).

Many critics found the play too difficult to offer an interpretation, but even those who found the play too coded were often caught by its strange rhythms and its thematic excursions. John Peter wrote: "This is a bitter, difficult and brilliant play. Wallace Shawn's world is a purgatorial no man's land where men and women, living and partly living, breathe the heady, poisonous air of culture and its discontents. . . . The text is a triple sonata of oppression and incomprehension. Why all this literature, all these opinions? . . . Shawn is writing about the tyrannies and moral posturings of intellectual life and how it can politicize you into anger and a bleak escape" (Review of *The Designated Mourner, London Times,* 28 April 1996, *Culture,* sec. 10, 14). John Lahr interprets the character of Jack as "a projection of Shawn's fears—what he has no wish to be but what he sees our distracted society becoming." Lahr reads this character in terms of the playwright he has known since the early 1970s when Shawn showed up at his front door with his early plays, at the suggestion of André Gregory. In a way, the play represents the culmination of a progress from the peculiar selfless egotism of that early Shawn, who said to Lahr, "I want you to read these. But I don't want to know what you think," to a writer who now connects his private alienation with a public discourse: "The play brings together in one metaphor the fear of envious attack and the appeasing defensive maneuvers around which Shawn's whole social persona is organized: it is Shawn's 'A Modest Proposal.' Through Jack, he is demonstrating the systematic devaluation of the self in modern life as an adaptation to envy, which finally leads to the dumbing of society" (Lahr, 48, 51). Benedict Nightingale wrote: "This is a playwright who does not just tell you what it is like to be arrested at night by goons or to fall morally apart and become an aimless yet weirdly contented ghost of yourself. He has the originality to make you feel it" ("Inspector of the Thought Police," *London Times,* 26 April 1996, 36).

6. Zeami, *On the Art of the Nō Drama: The Major Treatises of Zeami,* trans. J. Thomas Rimer and Yamazaki Masakazu (Princeton, N.J.: Princeton Univ. Press, 1984), 28.

7. Ibid., 3.

8. John Donne, *Complete Poetry and Selected Prose,* ed. John Hayward (New York: Random House, 1946), 195.

9. Ibid., 203.

10. Ibid., 202.

Bibliography

PRIMARY SOURCES

Shawn, Wallace. *Aunt Dan and Lemon*. New York: Grove, 1985.

———. *Aunt Dan and Lemon*. New York: Dramatists Play Service, 1986.

———. *The Designated Mourner*. Unpublished typescript, dated 17 June 1995.

———. *The Designated Mourner*. London: Faber and Faber, 1996.

———. *The Family Play*. Unpublished typescript, dated 1970, copyright 1973.

———. *The Fever*. New York: Farrar, Straus, and Giroux, 1991.

———. *The Fever*. New York: Dramatists Play Service, 1992.

———. *The Fever* (excerpt). *Harper's* 282 (April 1991): 42.

———. *Four Meals in May: A Play in Four Scenes*. Unpublished typescript, dated 1969, copyright 1973.

———. "Good Night Sweet Prince." Memoir of Joseph Papp. *Village Voice,* 12 November 1991, 34.

———. "Guatemala Noché: A Conversation with Francisco Goldman." *Village Voice,* 21 July 1992, 90–93.

———. *The Hospital Play*. Unpublished typescript, dated 1971, copyright 1973.

———. *The Hotel Play*. Written in 1970, copyright 1973. New York: Dramatists Play Service, 1982.

———. *In the Dark*. Unpublished libretto, dated 1976.

———. *Marie and Bruce*. New York: Dramatists Play Service, 1980.

———. *Marie and Bruce*. New York: Grove, 1980.

———. *The Music Teacher*. Unpublished libretto, dated 1982, copyright 1983.

———. *The Old Man*. Unpublished typescript, dated 1969, copyright 1973.

———. *Our Late Night*. Unpublished typescript, dated 1972, copyright 1973.

———. *Our Late Night*. New York: Targ Edition, 1984.

———. "Some Notes on Louis Malle and *My Dinner with André*." *Sight and Sound,* spring 1982, 118–20.

———. Statement in *Contemporary Dramatists*. 2nd ed. Ed. James Vinson. New York: St. Martin's Press, 1977, 718–20.

———. "Summer Evening." *Plays and Players* 24 (April 1977): 16–19.

———. "Tall, Dark, and Obsessed." Interview of Bruce Wagner. *Interview* 19 (March 1989): 76, 126.

———. *A Thought in Three Parts*. In *Word Plays 2: An Anthology of New American Drama*. New York: Performing Arts Journal Publications, 1982.

———, trans. *The Mandrake* by Niccolò Machiavelli. New York: Dramatists Play Service, 1978.

Shawn, Wallace, and André Gregory. *My Dinner with André*. New York: Grove, 1981.

Wallace Shawn has answered my questions by letter, in telephone conversations, and in person on several occasions, beginning in the summer of 1992, but the particular opinions and facts I have cited all come from one lengthy telephone conversation in August of 1993 and two letters, dated 2 December 1993 and 7 September 1995.

FILM APPEARANCES

Manhattan, dir. Woody Allen, 1979
Starting Over, dir. Alan J. Pakula, 1979
All That Jazz, dir. Bob Fosse, 1979
Cheaper to Keep Her, dir. Ken Annakin, 1980
Simon, dir. Marshall Brickman, 1980
Atlantic City, dir. Louis Malle, 1981
My Dinner with André, dir. Louis Malle, 1981
A Little Sex, dir. Bruce Paltrow, 1982
Deal of the Century, dir. William Friedkin, 1983
The First Time, dir. Charlie Loventhal, 1983
Lovesick, dir. Marshall Brickman, 1983
Strange Invaders, dir. Michael Laughlin, 1983
Saigon—The Year of the Cat, dir. Stephen Frears, 1983
Crackers, dir. Louis Malle, 1984
The Bostonians, dir. James Ivory, 1984
The Hotel New Hampshire, dir. Tony Richardson, 1984
Micki and Maude, dir. Blake Edwards, 1984
Heaven Help Us (also known as *Catholic Boys*), dir. Michael Dinner, 1985
Head Office, dir. Ken Finkleman, 1986

The Bedroom Window, dir. Curtis Hanson, 1987

Nice Girls Don't Explode, dir. Chuck Martinez, 1987

Prick Up Your Ears, dir. Stephen Frears, 1987

The Princess Bride, dir. Rob Reiner, 1987

Radio Days, dir. Woody Allen, 1987

The Moderns, dir. Alan Rudolph, 1988

Scenes from the Class Struggle in Beverly Hills, dir. Paul Bartel, 1989

She's Out of Control, dir. Stan Dragoti, 1989

We're No Angels, dir. Neil Jordan, 1989

Mom and Dad Save the World, dir. Greg Beeman, 1992

Nickel and Dime, dir. Ben Moses, 1992

Shadows and Fog, dir. Woody Allen, 1992

The Double-O Kid, dir. Duncan McLachlan, 1992

The Cemetery Club, dir. Bill Duke, 1993

Unbecoming Age, dirs. Alfredo and Deborah Ringel, 1993

The Meteor Man, dir. Robert Townsend, 1993

Diary of the Hurdy-Gurdy Man, dir. Gabe von Dettre, 1994

Mrs. Parker and the Vicious Circle, dir. Alan Rudolph, 1994

Vanya on 42nd Street, dir. Louis Malle, 1995

A Goofy Movie, dir. Kevin Lima, 1995

Clueless, dir. Amy Heckerling, 1995

The Wife, dir. Tom Noonan, 1995

Toy Story, dir. John Lasseter, 1995

House Arrest, dir. Harry Winer, 1996

TELEVISION APPEARANCES

Civil Wars

Clueless

The Cosby Show

Davis Rules

Deep Space Nine

How to Be a Perfect Person in Just Three Days, dir. Joan Micklin Silver

Murphy Brown

One Life to Live

Taxi

SECONDARY SOURCES

Atlas, James. "The Artistic Recipe for *My Dinner with André.*" *New York Times,* 28 February 1982, sec. D, 1.

"*Aunt Dan* and Uncle Henry." *New York,* 24 March 1986.

Aurelius, Marcus. *The Thoughts of Marcus Aurelius Antoninus*. Trans. George Long. Boston: Little, Brown, and Company, 1897.

Bamman, Gerry, Tom Costello, Saskia Noordhoek Hegt, Jerry Mayer, Angela Pietropinto, Larry Pine, and André Gregory. *"Alice in Wonderland": The Forming of a Company and the Making of a Play*. New York: Merlin House, 1973.

Barnes, Clive. *"Aunt Dan and Lemon* Raise Many Questions." Review of *Aunt Dan and Lemon. New York Post,* 30 October 1985.

———. "Mary Hartman? Louise Lasser! 'Marie and Bruce,' Bleep, Bleep!" Review of *Marie and Bruce. New York Post,* 4 February 1980.

———. "Our Late Night at the Public Theater." *New York Times,* 10 January 1975, sec. L, 20.

———. "Sickest of Sick Jokes Undeniably a Joke." Review of *Our Late Night. New York Times,* 10 January 1975, 20.

Beaufort, John. "What 'Nice' People Talk about in the Family Garden." *Christian Science Monitor,* 11 November 1985.

Billington, Michael. "Fascism Echoes Patrician Culture." *Manchester Guardian,* 25 April 1996, 2.

———. "A Play of Ideas Stirs Political Passions." Review of *Aunt Dan and Lemon. New York Times,* 27 October 1985, sec. II, 1, 30.

Bloom, Harold. *The Anxiety of Influence*. New York: Oxford Univ. Press, 1973.

———. *A Map of Misreading*. New York: Oxford Univ. Press, 1975.

Bosworth, Patricia. "Why 'Vanya,' and Why Now?" *New York Times,* 16 October 1994, sec. H, 13, 20.

Brenner, Marie. "My Conversation with André." *New York,* 19 October 1981, 36–39.

Breslauer, Jan. "Wallace Shawn Skewers Yuppie Angst." Review of *Our Late Night. Los Angeles Times,* 3 September 1993, sec. F, 10.

Brewer, Gay. "He's Still Falling: Wallace Shawn's Problem of Morality." *American Drama* 2 (fall 1992): 26–58.

Brown, John Russell. "Wallace Shawn." *Contemporary Dramatists,* 2nd ed. Ed. James Vinson. New York: St. Martin's Press, 1977, 720.

Brustein, Robert. "Addressing a Hostile Audience." Review of *Aunt Dan and Lemon. New Republic,* 9 December 1985, 26–28.

———. "Tripping into the Abyss." Review of *The Fever. New Republic,* 21 January 1991, 29.

———. "Two Couples." Review of *Marie and Bruce. New Republic,* 5 April 1980, 28–29.

Burgin, Richard. "Sick at Heart." Review of *The Fever. New York Times,* 24 March 1991, sec. VII, 17.

Campbell, James. "Conversation and Its Discontents." Review of *The Designated Mourner*. *Times Literary Supplement,* 10 May 1996, 19.

Canby, Vincent. ". . . And So Does the Screen." *New York Times,* 1 July 1979, sec. II, 1, 17.

Carpenter, Gerald. "André Gregory: Love in the Ruins." *Santa Barbara Independent,* 23 November 1994, 67.

Chaillet, Ned. "Joint Stock under Fire." Review of *A Thought in Three Parts*. *Plays and Players,* April 1977, 20–21.

————. Review of *My Dinner with André*. *London Times,* 7 November 1980, 12.

————. "Wallace Shawn." *Contemporary Dramatists,* 4th ed. Ed. D. L. Kirkpatrick. Chicago: St. James, 1988, 478–80.

Chaudhuri, Una. "From the Sixties to the Seventies and Beyond: *My Dinner with André* and the American Avant-Garde." *Indian Journal of American Studies* 15 (summer 1985): 15–23.

Chekhov, Anton. *Uncle Vanya: A Play*. Adapted by David Mamet from a literal translation by Vlada Chernomordik. New York: Grove, 1989.

Christon, Lawrence. "A Clue to 'Marie and Bruce.'" *Los Angeles Times, Calendar,* 31 July 1983, 41.

Clarke, Gerald. "Now Comes the Just Dessert." Review of *Aunt Dan and Lemon*. *Time,* 18 November 1985, 105.

Coleman, John. Review of *My Dinner with André*. *New Statesman,* 14 May 1982, 30.

Corry, John. "Mary Hartman Is Now Off Broadway." *New York Times,* 3 January 1980, sec. III, 13.

"A Couple of Vanyas Sitting around Talking." Interview of Wallace Shawn and Tom Courtenay. *New York Times,* 19 February 1995, sec. H, 5.

Crowder, Joan. "My Breakfast with André." *News-Press* (Santa Barbara), "Scene," 31 January 1992, 23–24.

Cushman, Robert. "Committing High Treason." Review of *My Dinner with André*. *London Observer,* 9 November 1980, 31.

————. "The First Sex." Review of *A Thought in Three Parts*. *Observer* (London), 6 March 1977, 24.

Denby, David. Review of *My Dinner with André*. *New York,* 26 October 1981, 96.

Disch, Thomas M. Review of *The Fever*. *Nation,* 7–14 January 1991, 24–26.

Dixon, Wheeler Winston. Review of *The Fever*. *Prairie Schooner* 66 (fall 1992): 126–29.

Doty, Gresdna A., and Billy J. Harbin, eds. *Inside the Royal Court, 1956–1981: Artists Talk*. Baton Rouge: Louisiana State Univ. Press, 1990.

Drake, Sylvie. " 'The Fever' Cooled by Self-Flagellation." *Los Angeles Times,* 23 May 1991, sec. F, 4.

Earley, Michael. Interview of Wallace Shawn. In "Playwrights Making Movies." *Performing Arts Journal 15* vol. 5 (1981): 29–35.

Eder, Richard. "The Devil in Moscow." Review of *The Master and Margarita. New York Times,* 21 November 1978, sec. C, 13.

———. "Of Ballet and Stars." Review of *Chinchilla* by Robert David MacDonald. *New York Times,* 5 June 1979, sec. C, 8.

———. "Still Growing." Review of *The Mandrake* by Niccolò Machiavelli, trans. Wallace Shawn. *New York Times,* 18 November 1979, sec. C, 3.

Eisenstein, Linda. "Playwright's Voice Permeates Monologue Play." Review of *The Fever. Plain Dealer* (Cleveland), 11 April 1996, sec. E, 9.

Ellison, Julie. "A Short History of Liberal Guilt." *Critical Inquiry* 22 (winter 1996): 344–71.

"Experimental Work, Yes, But Offensive, No—Says Peer." *The Stage and Television Today,* 31 March 1977.

Falk, Florence A. "Dangling Conversation." *American Theatre* 8 (December 1991): 20–21.

Farber, David. *The Age of Great Dreams: America in the 1960s.* New York: Hill and Wang, 1994.

Fields, Sidney. "Only Human: Shawn Is Beginning to Shine." *Daily News* (New York), 13 December 1977.

Franks, Lucinda. "The Shawns—A Fascinating Father-and-Son Riddle." *New York Times,* 3 August 1980, sec. II, 1, 25.

Freud, Sigmund. *The Interpretation of Dreams,* in *The Basic Writings of Sigmund Freud.* Trans. by A. A. Brill. New York: Modern Library, 1938.

Gates, David. "A Lover of the Long Shot." Obituary of William Shawn. *Newsweek,* 21 December 1992, 53.

Gelmis, Joseph. Review of *My Dinner with André. Newsday,* 8 October 1981, 46.

Germond, Jack W., and Jules Witcover. *Whose Broad Stripes and Bright Stars?: The Trivial Pursuit of the Presidency, 1988.* New York: Warner Books, 1989.

Gill, Brendan. "And Now to Be Serious for a Moment." *New Yorker* 53 (12 December 1977): 92.

———. "Dead Gull, Live Party." Review of *The Seagull* and *Our Late Night. New Yorker* 50 (20 January 1975): 62–63.

———. *Here at the New Yorker.* New York: Random House, 1975.

———. "Out There and Down Here." Review of *Marie and Bruce. New Yorker* 55 (11 February 1980): 64–65.

————. Review of *Aunt Dan and Lemon*. *New Yorker* 61 (4 November 1985): 128.

Gold, Sylviane. "Unopposed Neo-Nazism Is Irresponsible." Review of *Aunt Dan and Lemon*. *Wall Street Journal*, 20 November 1985.

Gregory, André. "Ruth Nelson: 1905–1992." *American Theatre* 9 (December 1992): 34–35.

————. Untitled speech at the University of California, Santa Barbara, Campbell Hall, 10 January 1994.

Gussow, Mel. "Close to the Marrow." Review of *Aunt Dan and Lemon*. *New York Times*, 10 November 1985, sec. II, 5.

Harris, William. "Off and On." *Soho Weekly News*, 24 January 1980, 48.

Hatch, Robert. Review of *My Dinner with André*. *Nation*, 7 November 1981, 483–84.

Hentoff, Nat. "Mr. Shawn's *New Yorker*." *Village Voice*, 29 December 1992, 22–23.

Hewitt, Nicholas. " 'Looking for Annie': Sartre's *La Nausée* and the Inter-War Years." In *Critical Essays on Jean-Paul Sartre*, ed. Robert Wilcocks. Boston: G. K. Hall and Co., 1988, 209–24.

Hirsch, Foster. *Love, Sex, Death and the Meaning of Life: The Films of Woody Allen*. New York: Limelight Editions, 1990.

Hoberman, J. Review of *My Dinner with André*. *Village Voice*, 14–20 October 1981, 52.

Jebb, Julian. Review of *My Dinner with André*. *Sight and Sound*, summer 1982, 208.

Kael, Pauline. *Taking It All In*. New York: Holt, Rinehart Winston, 1987.

Kaplan, James. Review of *Vanya on 42nd Street*. *New York*, 12 September 1994, 62.

Kauffmann, Stanley. "From Russia with Love." Review of *Vanya on 42nd Street*. *New Republic*, 7 November 1994, 34–36.

Kaufman, David. "Bitter Food for Thought." Review of *Aunt Dan and Lemon*. *Soho Arts Weekly*, 27 November 1985, sec. B, 20.

Kawin, Bruce. Review of *My Dinner with André*. *Film Quarterly*, winter 1981–82, 62.

Keefe, Terry. "The Ending of Sartre's *La Nausée*." In *Critical Essays on Jean-Paul Sartre*, ed. Robert Wilcocks. Boston: G. K. Hall and Co., 1988, 182–201.

Kelly, Kevin. " 'Marie and Bruce': Two Bruisers in a Relentlessly Bad Relationship." Review of *Marie and Bruce*. *Boston Globe*, 14 July 1990.

Kerr, Walter. "Among Its Virtues, Fine Acting Can Bare Weak Spots."

Review of *The Mandrake* by Niccolò Machiavelli, trans. Wallace Shawn. *New York Times,* 3 January 1978, 37.

———. "Love-Hate Relationship." Review of *Marie and Bruce. New York Times,* 4 February 1980, sec. C, 13.

King, W. D. "Beyond 'A Certain Chain of Reasoning': Wallace Shawn's *Aunt Dan and Lemon.*" *Journal of American Drama and Theatre* 6 (spring 1994): 61–78.

———. "Dionysus in Santa Barbara: Wallace Shawn's Euripidean Fever." *Theater* 22 (winter 1992): 83–87.

Kissel, Howard. Review of *Aunt Dan and Lemon. Women's Wear Daily,* 30 October 1985.

———. Review of *Marie and Bruce, Women's Wear Daily,* 4 February 1980.

———. Review of *My Dinner with André. Women's Wear Daily,* 12 October 1981, 20.

Klein, Jacob. *Commentary on Plato's "Meno."* Chapel Hill: Univ. of North Carolina Press, 1975.

Knight, Frances. Review of *Marie and Bruce. Plays and Players* 27 (October 1979): 28–29.

Kolenda, Konstantin. *Rorty's Humanistic Pragmatism: Philosophy Democratized.* Tampa: Univ. of South Florida Press, 1990.

Kornbluth, Josh. "My Phone Call with Wally." *San Francisco Examiner,* 5 September 1993, "Image," 12–17.

Kroll, Jack. "Cast of Thousands." Review of *The Hotel Play. Newsweek,* 7 September 1981, 81.

———. "Conversation Piece." Review of *My Dinner with André. Newsweek,* 26 October 1981, 78.

———. "I Love You/I Hate You." Review of *Marie and Bruce. Newsweek,* 18 February 1980, 117.

———. "Saying Uncle in New York." Review of *Vanya on 42nd Street. Newsweek,* 31 October 1994, 67.

———. "That Nice Mr. Hitler." Review of *Aunt Dan and Lemon. Newsweek,* 18 November 1985, 90.

———. "Why Mike Nichols Is Working without a Net," *Newsweek,* 6 May 1996, 84–85.

Lahr, John. "The Dangling Man." *New Yorker* 72 (15 April 1996): 45–51.

Lanzmann, Claude. *Shoah, an Oral History of the Holocaust: The Complete Text of the Film.* New York: Pantheon, 1985.

Lawson, Carol. "Broadway." Note on *The Hotel Play. New York Times,* 10 July 1981, sec. III, 2.

Lax, Eric. *Woody Allen: A Biography.* New York: Knopf, 1991.

Leff, Leonard. "Warhol's 'Pork.'" *Art in America* 60 (January–February 1972): 113.

Macaulay, Alastair. "Cast into Mysterious Irony." Review of *The Designated Mourner*. *Financial Times* (London), 26 April 1996, 13.

MacDonald, Erik. *Theater at the Margins: Text and the Post-Structured Stage*. Ann Arbor: Univ. of Michigan Press, 1993.

MacLean, Douglas, and Claudia Mills, eds. *Liberalism Reconsidered*. Totowa, N.J.: Rowman and Allanheld, 1983.

Marranca, Bonnie, Johannes Birringer, and Gerald Rabkin. "The Controversial 1985–86 Theatre Season: A Politics of Reception," *Performing Arts Journal 28* vol. 10 (1986): 7–33.

Marranca, Bonnie, Elinor Fuchs, and Gerald Rabkin. "The Politics of Representation: New York Theatre Season 1990–91," *Performing Arts Journal 39* vol. 13 (September 1991): 1–19.

Maslin, Janet. "Spare Chekhov Begins Sneakily." Review of *Vanya on 42nd Street*. *New York Times*, 19 October 1994, sec. C, 13.

Merschmeier, Michael. "Die Misere des Moralisten." Interview of Wallace Shawn. *Theater Heute,* April 1994, 17–19.

Mikulan, Steven. "Misery en Scène: Looking for Love in All the Wrong Places." Review of *Our Late Night*. *Los Angeles Weekly,* 10–16 September 1993, 35.

Morley-Priestman, Anne. Review of *A Thought in Three Parts*. *The Stage and Television Today,* 10 March 1977, 13.

Nightingale, Benedict. "Inspector of the Thought-Police." Review of *The Designated Mourner*. *London Times*, 26 April 1996, 36.

Pall, Ellen. "Two Women Stand Tall in *Vanya on 42nd Street:* In Sonya, a Portrayal of Almost Unbearable Vulnerability." *New York Times,* 4 December 1994, sec. H, 13, 27.

Pekar, Harvey. "Grubstreet, U.S.A." Comic book story with Wallace Shawn as a character. *American Splendor* 13 (1984).

Peter, John. "Observing the Perilous Lessons of Life." Review of *Aunt Dan and Lemon*. *Sunday Times* (London), 8 September 1985, 43.

———. Review of *The Designated Mourner*. *London Times,* 28 April 1996, "Culture," sec. 10, 14.

Posnock, Ross. "New York Phantasmagoria." *Raritan: A Quarterly Review* 11 (fall 1991): 142–59.

Pym, John. Review of *My Dinner with André*. *Monthly Film Bulletin,* June 1982, 109.

Radin, Victoria. "Citric Acid." Review of *Aunt Dan and Lemon*. *New Statesman* 110 (6 September 1985): 31–32.

———. "Life with Marie." Review of *Marie and Bruce*. *Observer* (London), 22 July 1979, 14.

Rafferty, Terrence. "Plays on Film." Review of *Vanya on 42nd Street*. *New Yorker* 70 (31 October 1994): 105–6.

Ratcliffe, Michael. "Devil's Advocate." Review of *Aunt Dan and Lemon*. *Observer* (London), 8 September 1985, 17.

Reed, Rex. " 'Mary'? 'Marie'? . . . What a Relief to Meet Louise!" *Sunday News* (New York), 10 February 1980, 3, 18.

Rich, Frank, "Birth of the Big Lie." Review of *Aunt Dan and Lemon*. *New York Times*, 28 March 1876, sec. C., 3.

———. "Cast of 70 at La Mama." Review of *The Hotel Play*. *New York Times*, 28 August 1981, sec. C, 3.

———. "A Misanthropic View." Review of *The Hotel Play*. *New York Times*, 23 August 1981, sec. C, 3.

———. "Once Again, Theater Was a Place for Wonder." *New York Times*, 29 December 1985, sec. II, 5.

———. Review of *The Fever*. *New York Times*, 29 November 1990, sec. C, 17.

———. "A Turn to the Right." Review of *Aunt Dan and Lemon*. *New York Times*, 29 October 1985, sec. C, 13.

Robinson, Marc. "Four Writers." *Theater* 24 (spring 1993): 31–42.

Rorty, Richard. *Contingency, Irony, Solidarity*. Cambridge, Mass.: Cambridge Univ. Press, 1989.

Rose, Lloyd. "The Art of Conversation." *Atlantic* 256 (November 1985): 125–27.

Rosenblum, Nancy L., ed. *Liberalism and the Moral Life*. Cambridge, Mass.: Harvard Univ. Press, 1989.

Rothstein, Mervyn. "An Ex-Waitress's Writing Success." *New York Times*, 22 April 1986, sec. III, 13.

———. "A Monologue Takes On a Life of Its Own." *New York Times*, 9 March 1991, sec. I, 12.

Sartre, Jean-Paul. *Nausea*, trans. Lloyd Alexander. New York: New Directions, 1964.

Savran, David. Interview of Wallace Shawn. In *In Their Own Words: Contemporary American Playwrights*. New York: Theatre Communications Group, 1988.

Schell, Jonathan. *The Time of Illusion*. New York: Vintage Books, 1975.

Schickel, Richard. "Small Bore." Review of *My Dinner with André*. *Time*, 26 October 1981, 94.

Shewey, Don. "The Secret Life of Wally Shawn." *Esquire* 100 (October 1983): 90–97.

————. "Wallace Shawn." In *Caught in the Act: New York Actors Face to Face.* Photographs by Susan Shacter. New York: NAL, 1986.

————. "Wally Shawn's Grandstand Play." *Soho News,* 18 August 1981, 23, 43.

Smith, Michael. "George Gaynes: Commuting to *Vanya.*" *Independent* (Santa Barbara), 1 December 1994, 55.

Smith, Sid. "Appendix Rescue." Review of *Aunt Dan and Lemon. Chicago Tribune,* 2 November 1986, 8–9.

Sragow, Michael. "Two Women Stand Tall in *Vanya on 42nd Street:* In Yelena, A Faithful Wife and an Enchantress." *New York Times,* 4 December 1994, sec. H, 13, 26.

Sterritt, David. Review of *My Dinner with André. Christian Science Monitor,* 22 October 1981, 18.

Strand, Mark. "The Man behind the Voice." Interview of Wallace Shawn. *Interview* 19 (March 1989): 72–75, 124, 126.

Strick, Philip. Review of *Vanya on 42nd Street. Sight and Sound* 5 (January 1995): 61.

Strindberg, August. *Strindberg: Five Plays,* trans. Harry G. Carlson. Berkeley: Univ. of California Press, 1983.

Sullivan, Dan. "The Ideas Outpoint the Play in Shawn's *Aunt Dan and Lemon.*" Review of *Aunt Dan and Lemon. Los Angeles Times,* 5 March 1988, sec. VI, 12.

————. "Taming of a Shrewed-Up Marriage at Odyssey." Review of *Marie and Bruce. Los Angeles Times,* 11 August 1983, sec. VI, 1.

————. "Throwing the Audience Out of the Boat." Review of *Aunt Dan and Lemon. Los Angeles Times,* 29 March 1987, "Calendar," 44.

Tallmer, Jerry. "Comic Actor Gets Serious." *New York Post,* 20 April 1988, 28.

Taubin, Amy. "The Discreet Charm of Vanya." *Village Voice,* 21 June 1994, 25.

Thomas, Kevin. Review of *My Dinner with André. Los Angeles Times,* 1 November 1981, "Calendar," 28.

Turan, Kenneth. "In Street Clothes, *Vanya* Invites You In." *Los Angeles Times,* 4 November 1994, sec. F, 10.

Ulmer, Gregory L. *Applied Grammatology: Post(e)-Pedagogy from Jacques Derrida to Joseph Beuys.* Baltimore: Johns Hopkins Univ. Press, 1985.

Virshup, Amy. "Sticking It Out: The 1990–91 Obie Awards." *Village Voice,* 21 May 1991, 98–99.

"Wally and André Dissect the Theater." *New York Times,* 17 January 1982, sec. II, 1, 26.

Wardle, Irving. "Grounds for Atrocity." Review of *Aunt Dan and Lemon*. *London Times*, 3 September 1985, 9.

Watt, Douglas. "The Latitudes of Lasser." Review of *Marie and Bruce*. *New York Daily News*, 4 February 1980.

———. "Making Lemonade from a Real Lemon." Review of *Aunt Dan and Lemon*. *New York Daily News*, 30 October 1985.

Weales, Gerald. "American Theater Watch, 1985–1986." *Georgia Review* 40 (spring 1986): 520–31.

———. "Bobbing and Invading." Review of *Aunt Dan and Lemon*. *Commonweal*, 28 March 1986, 179–80.

———. "Degrees of Difference." Review of *The Fever*. *Commonweal*, 11 January 1991, 18.

Wetzsteon, Ross. "The Holy Fool of the American Theater?" *Village Voice*, 2 April 1991, 35–37.

"What the Critics Said." Quotations published alongside "Summer Evening." *Plays and Players* 24 (April 1977): 16–17.

"Why Write for the Theater? A Roundtable Report." Interview of Wallace Shawn, Athol Fugard, David Mamet, and Arthur Miller. *New York Times*, 9 February 1986, sec. II, 1, 30.

Williams, Tennessee. *"Twenty-Seven Wagons Full of Cotton" and Other One-Act Plays*. Norfolk, Conn.: New Directions, 1953.

Wimsatt, William. *The Verbal Icon: Studies in the Meaning of Poetry*. Lexington: Univ. Press of Kentucky, 1954.

Winer, Laurie. "Anton Chekhov, Our Contemporary." *Los Angeles Times*, 6 August 1995, *Calendar*, 46.

———. "My Breakfast with Wally." *Wall Street Journal*, 20 November 1985, 30.

Winer, Linda. "Brutal and Brilliant." Review of *Aunt Dan and Lemon*. *USA Today*, 30 October 1985.

Winston, Archer. Review of *My Dinner with André*. *New York Post*, 9 October 1981, 49.

Wolf, Matt. Review of *Aunt Dan and Lemon*. *Plays and Players*, October 1985, 27–28.

Zeami. *On the Art of the Nō Drama: The Major Treatises of Zeami*, trans. J. Thomas Rimer and Yamazaki Masakazu. Princeton, N.J.: Princeton Univ. Press, 1984.

Index